JavaScript™ For Dummies®

COMPUTER BOOK SERIES FROM IDG

Cheat Sheet

S0-ADG-199

Helpful Hints

To Do This...	Do This...
Load a JavaScript-enabled Web page	
In Navigator:	Double-click on the Navigator icon (local); **OR** File⇨Open File (local); **OR** File⇨Open Location (remote)
In Internet Explorer:	File⇨Open
Look at someone else's JavaScript code	
In Navigator:	View⇨Document Source
In Internet Explorer:	View⇨Source
Copy and paste someone else's JavaScript code	Ctrl+C to copy; Ctrl+V to paste
Find a news group in Navigator	Window⇨Netscape News; Options⇨Show All Newsgroups
Create a link	<A>...</A>
Submit a form to a CGI program	<FORM>...</FORM>

Why Doesn't Anything Work?!

Stuck? Clueless? *Nothing* works and no idea where to start? Not to worry; take a look at the following suggestions (scanning them in order will work best).

- ✔ Is your Web browser installed and configured correctly, including your communications stuff? (See Chapter 2.)

- ✔ Is JavaScript enabled?

  - Navigator

    Check Options⇨Network Preferences⇨Languages⇨Enable JavaScript

  - Internet Explorer

    Check View⇨Options⇨Security⇨Run ActiveX scripts

- ✔ Are all of your JavaScript statements between <SCRIPT>...</SCRIPT> tags (except for event handlers such as onClick, which don't have to be)?

- ✔ Does your HTML file work as it should by itself if you delete your JavaScript statements?

- ✔ Do the names of your JavaScript variables all start with an alphabetic character (or an underscore)?

Object Terms

JavaScript is an object-based language, so to get the most out of it, you need to understand some basic object-related terms. Below are the ones you're likely to find most useful.

Term	JavaScript example
An object is a thing (noun).	*A button is an object.*
You can describe an object with adjectives (properties).	*A button object has a name and a type.*
An object can do things (methods).	*A button object can* click().
An object can respond to events (event handlers).	*A button can recognize when it's been clicked (*onClick*).*

...For Dummies: #1 Computer Book Series for Beginners

JavaScript™ For Dummies®

Cheat Sheet

JavaScript Object Model

This JavaScript object hierarchy lists all of the built-in objects you can work with in JavaScript, along with their relationships to each other.

Object	JavaScript syntax
window	**window** (optional)
parent, frame, self, top	**frame, parent, self, top**
location	**location**
history	**history**
document	**document**
form	document.***someForm***
applet	document.***applets[0]***
area	document.***SomeArea***
button	document.*someForm*.***someButton***
checkbox	document.*someForm*.***myCheckbox***
fileUpload	document.*someForm*.***myFileUpload***
hidden	document.*someForm*.***someHidden***
image	document.*someForm*.***someImage***
password	document.*someForm*.***somePassword***
radio	document.*someForm*.***someRadio***
reset	document.*someForm*.***someReset***
select	document.*someForm*.***someSelect***
submit	document.*someForm*.***someSubmit***
text	document.*someForm*.***someText***
textarea	document.*someForm*.***someTextarea***
link	document.***someLink***
anchor	document.***someAnchor***
plugin	document.***embeds[0]***

This table lists all of the stand-alone objects you can work with in JavaScript.

Stand-alone object	JavaScript syntax
Date	**Date**
Math	**Math**
navigator	**navigator**
string	**"some string"**

...For Dummies: #1 Computer Book Series for Beginners

®

References for the Rest of Us!®

COMPUTER BOOK SERIES FROM IDG

Are you intimidated and confused by computers? Do you find that traditional manuals are overloaded with technical details you'll never use? Do your friends and family always call you to fix simple problems on their PCs? Then the *...For Dummies*® computer book series from IDG Books Worldwide is for you.

...For Dummies books are written for those frustrated computer users who know they aren't really dumb but find that PC hardware, software, and indeed the unique vocabulary of computing make them feel helpless. *...For Dummies* books use a lighthearted approach, a down-to-earth style, and even cartoons and humorous icons to diffuse computer novices' fears and build their confidence. Lighthearted but not lightweight, these books are a perfect survival guide for anyone forced to use a computer.

> *"I like my copy so much I told friends; now they bought copies."*
>
> **Irene C., Orwell, Ohio**

> *"Quick, concise, nontechnical, and humorous."*
>
> **Jay A., Elburn, Illinois**

> *"Thanks, I needed this book. Now I can sleep at night."*
>
> **Robin F., British Columbia, Canada**

Already, hundreds of thousands of satisfied readers agree. They have made *...For Dummies* books the #1 introductory level computer book series and have written asking for more. So, if you're looking for the most fun and easy way to learn about computers, look to *...For Dummies* books to give you a helping hand.

7/96r

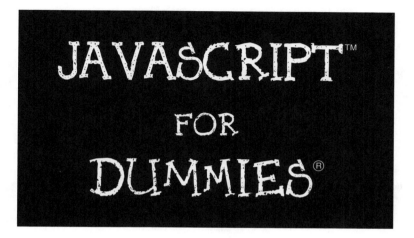

JAVASCRIPT™ FOR DUMMIES®

by Emily A. Vander Veer

IDG BOOKS™ WORLDWIDE

IDG Books Worldwide, Inc.
An International Data Group Company

Foster City, CA ♦ Chicago, IL ♦ Indianapolis, IN ♦ Southlake, TX

JavaScript™ For Dummies®

Published by
IDG Books Worldwide, Inc.
An International Data Group Company
919 E. Hillsdale Blvd.
Suite 400
Foster City, CA 94404
www.idgbooks.com (IDG Books Worldwide Web Site)
http://www.dummies.com (Dummies Press Web Site)

Copyright © 1996 IDG Books Worldwide, Inc. All rights reserved. No part of this book, including interior design, cover design, and icons, may be reproduced or transmitted in any form, by any means (electronic, photocopying, recording, or otherwise) without the prior written permission of the publisher.

Library of Congress Catalog Card No.: 96-77948

ISBN: 0-7645-0071-6

Printed in the United States of America

10 9 8 7 6 5 4 3 2 1

1E/RV/RQ/ZW/IN

Distributed in the United States by IDG Books Worldwide, Inc.

Distributed by Macmillan Canada for Canada; by Contemporanea de Ediciones for Venezuela; by Distribuidora Cuspide for Argentina; by CITEC for Brazil; by Ediciones ZETA S.C.R. Ltda. for Peru; by Editorial Limusa SA for Mexico; by Transworld Publishers Limited in the United Kingdom and Europe; by Academic Bookshop for Egypt; by Levant Distributors S.A.R.L. for Lebanon; by Al Jassim for Saudi Arabia; by Simron Pty. Ltd. for South Africa; by Pustak Mahal for India; by The Computer Bookshop for India; by Toppan Company Ltd. for Japan; by Addison Wesley Publishing Company for Korea; by Longman Singapore Publishers Ltd. for Singapore, Malaysia, Thailand, and Indonesia; by Unalis Corporation for Taiwan; by WS Computer Publishing Company, Inc. for the Philippines; by WoodsLane Pty. Ltd. for Australia; by WoodsLane Enterprises Ltd. for New Zealand. Authorized Sales Agent: Anthony Rudkin Associates for the Middle East and North Africa.

For general information on IDG Books Worldwide's books in the U.S., please call our Consumer Customer Service department at 800-762-2974. For reseller information, including discounts and premium sales, please call our Reseller Customer Service department at 800-434-3422.

For information on where to purchase IDG Books Worldwide's books outside the U.S., please contact our International Sales department at 415-655-3172 or fax 415-655-3295.

For information on foreign language translations, please contact our Foreign & Subsidiary Rights department at 415-655-3021 or fax 415-655-3281.

For sales inquiries and special prices for bulk quantities, please contact our Sales department at 415-655-3200 or write to the address above.

For information on using IDG Books Worldwide's books in the classroom or for ordering examination copies, please contact our Educational Sales department at 800-434-2086 or fax 817-251-8174.

For authorization to photocopy items for corporate, personal, or educational use, please contact Copyright Clearance Center, 222 Rosewood Drive, Danvers, MA 01923, or fax 508-750-4470.

 is a trademark under exclusive license to IDG Books Worldwide, Inc., from International Data Group, Inc.

About the Author

Emily A. Vander Veer was a (somewhat reluctant) computer geek for several years. A part-time college-tuition-paying job in word processing hooked her on desktop computing and the seductive power of information management, and the rest, as they say, is history. She changed her major to Computer Information Systems, landed a plum job on a three-tier client-server, object-oriented development project (try saying *that* three times fast), and never looked back. Since then she has spent her days working as a software consultant and marketer, most recently at IBM, where she is currently having more fun pursuing her newest challenge — writing computer-related books and magazine articles — than humans should be allowed to have.

Dedication

To my husband, Clay, without whom this book (and so very much more) would never have been possible; and to Rusty, wherever and whenever you are.

Author's Acknowledgments

Many, many thanks to Gareth Hancock, for giving me the opportunity to write this book, and to the rest of IDG Books' wonderfully competent and professional staff: Jennifer Ehrlich, my project editor, whose insight and suggestions were invaluable; Diana Conover, lead copy editor, who kept me on the grammatical straight and narrow; Greg Guntle, who lent his eagle eye to the arduous task of editing this book for technical content; and Joyce Pepple, who put in a lot of time making sure that all the right goodies were included on the accompanying CD.

I'd also like to thank my colleagues at IBM, for whose generosity and support during the writing of this book I am humbly grateful.

Publisher's Acknowledgments

We're proud of this book; please send us your comments about it by using the Reader Response Card at the back of the book or by e-mailing us at feedback/dummies@idgbooks.com. Some of the people who helped bring this book to market include the following:

Acquisitions, Development, and Editorial

Project Editor: Jennifer Ehrlich

Assistant Acquisitions Editor: Gareth Hancock

Product Development Manager: Mary Bednarek

Permissions Editor: Joyce Pepple

Lead Copy Editor: Diana R. Conover

Technical Reviewer: Greg Guntle

Editorial Manager: Mary C. Corder

Editorial Assistant: Chris H. Collins

Production

Associate Project Coordinator: Regina Snyder

Layout and Graphics: E. Shawn Aylsworth, Brett Black, Cameron Booker, Linda Boyer, Elizabeth Cárdenas-Nelson, Dominique DeFelice, Maridee V. Ennis, Todd Klemme, Drew R. Moore, Anna Rohrer, Theresa Sanchez-Baker, Brent Savage, Gina Scott, Kate Snell, Michael Sullivan

Proofreaders: Joel Draper, Rachel Garvey, Nancy Price, Dwight Ramsey, Rob Springer, Carrie Voorhis

Indexer: Nancy Anderman Guenther

Special Help

Kevin Spencer, Associate Technical Editor; Stephanie Koutek, Proof Editor; Access Technology, CD Developer

General & Administrative

IDG Books Worldwide, Inc.: John Kilcullen, President and CEO; Steven Berkowitz, COO and Publisher

Dummies, Inc.: Milissa Koloski, Executive Vice President and Publisher

Dummies Technology Press and Dummies Editorial: Diane Graves Steele, Associate Publisher; Judith A. Taylor, Brand Manager

Dummies Trade Press: Kathleen A. Welton, Vice President and Publisher; Stacy S. Collins, Brand Manager

IDG Books Production for Dummies Press: Beth Jenkins, Production Director; Cindy L. Phipps, Supervisor of Project Coordination; Kathie S. Schutte, Supervisor of Page Layout; Shelley Lea, Supervisor of Graphics and Design; Debbie J. Gates, Production Systems Specialist

Dummies Packaging and Book Design: Patti Sandez, Packaging Assistant; Kavish+Kavish, Cover Design

♦

The publisher would like to give special thanks to Patrick J. McGovern, without whom this book would not have been possible.

♦

Contents at a Glance

Cartoons at a Glance

By Rich Tennant • Fax: 508-546-7747 • E-mail: the5wave@tiac.net

Page 91

Page 329

Page 157

Page 293

Page 7

Table of Contents

Introduction

●●

*W*elcome to the wonderful world of World Wide Web programming with JavaScript. If you've worked with HTML before but want to add more flexibility and punch to your pages, or even if you've never written a stick of code in your life but are eager to hop on the Infobahn-wagon, this book's for you.

I've done my best to describe how JavaScript works by using real-world examples — and not a foo(bar) in sight. When explaining things in formal notation makes sense, I do it — but not without a recap in plain English. Most important, I've included tons of sample programs that illustrate the kinds of things you're actually going to want to do in your own pages.

Along with this book comes a companion CD-ROM. This CD-ROM contains all of the sample code listings covered in the text along with many other interesting widgets and example programs. If you want, you can play around with the files as you read the book in order to reinforce your understanding of the concepts. For more information, see the About the CD appendix in the back of this book.

System Requirements

Here's what you need to get the most out of this book and the enclosed CD-ROM:

- ✔ A computer with a CD-ROM drive and a modem
- ✔ A sound card (okay, this is strictly optional, but it's a lot of fun!)
- ✔ Windows 3.1, Windows 95, Windows NT, or Macintosh already installed, with the following:
    - 386sx or faster processor, at least 8MB of RAM, and at least 3MB of free disk space if you're running Windows 3.1;
    - 386sx or faster processor, at least 8MB of RAM, and at least 9MB of free disk space for those running Windows 95/NT;
    - 68020 or faster processor, at least 9MB or RAM, and at least 6MB of free disk space for Macintosh users;
    - A copy of either Netscape Navigator 3.0 or Microsoft Internet Explorer 3.0 (Chapter 2 tells you how to get a copy and install it, if you haven't already).

About This Book

Think of this book as a good friend who started at the beginning, learned the ropes the hard way, and now wants to help you get up to speed. In this book, you can find everything from JavaScript basics and common pitfalls to answers to embarrassingly silly questions (and some really cool tricks, too), all explained from a first-time JavaScript programmer's-eye-view.

Some sample topics you can find in this book include the following:

- ✔ Creating interactive Web pages
- ✔ Verifying user input with JavaScript
- ✔ Using object-oriented techniques to get the most out of your scripts
- ✔ Testing and debugging your JavaScript scripts
- ✔ Integrating JavaScript with other technologies

Building intelligent Web pages with JavaScript can be overwhelming — if you let it. You can do so *much* with JavaScript! In order to keep the deluge to a minimum, this book concentrates on the practical considerations that you need in order to get your interactive pages up and running in the least amount of time possible.

How to Use This Book

The rules are pretty simple. All code appears in monospaced font, like this:

```
<TITLE>JavaScript For Dummies</TITLE>
```

Make sure that you follow the examples' syntax exactly; sometimes your scripts work if you add or delete spaces or type your keywords in a different case, but sometimes they don't — and you want to spend your time on more interesting bugs than those caused by spacing errors.

Type anything you see in code font letter for letter. These items are generally JavaScript keywords, and they need to be exact. Directives in italics are placeholders, and you can substitute other values for them. For example, in the following line of code you can replace state and "confusion" and leave the equal sign out entirely, but you need to type var the way that it's shown.

```
var state="confusion"
```

Due to the margins of this book, sometimes code examples are wrapped from one line to another. You can copy the code exactly the way it appears; JavaScript doesn't have a line continuation character. There's only one place where you can't break a line and still have the code work, and that's between two quotes. For example, the following line is invalid:

```
var state="confu                    // wrong!
sion"
```

All of the URLs listed in this book are accurate at the time of this writing; however, because the Internet is such a dynamic medium (there's that word again!) a few may be inaccessible by the time you get around to trying them. If so, try using a search engine, such as Yahoo! or Webcrawler, to help you find the slippery Web site.

Foolish Assumptions

Everybody's got to start somewhere, right? I'm starting out with the following assumptions about you, the reader:

- ✔ You know how to navigate through an application with a mouse and a keyboard.
- ✔ You want to build interactive Web pages for fun, for profit, or because building them is part of your job.
- ✔ You have, or can get, a working connection to the Internet.
- ✔ You have, or can get, a copy of Netscape Navigator 3.0 or Microsoft Internet Explorer 3.0.

How This Book Is Organized

This book contains five major parts. Each part contains several chapters, and each chapter contains several sections. You can read the book start-to-finish if you like, or you can dive in whenever you need help on a particular topic (although if you're brand-new to JavaScript, skimming through Part I first sure couldn't hurt). Here's a breakdown of what you can find in each of the five parts:

Part I: Building Killer Web Pages for Fun and Profit

This part explains how to turn JavaScript from an abstract concept to something happening on the screen in front of you. It takes you step-by-step through installing your choice of Netscape Navigator or Microsoft Internet Explorer, learning object-oriented basics, and getting comfortable with HTML. Part I finishes up with an overview of the JavaScript language itself.

Part II: JavaScript in Action

By the time that you finish Part II, you'll have seen sample code for all of the basic uses that you're likely to have for JavaScript: displaying forms with features (such as push buttons and scroll boxes), gathering and verifying user input, and integrating color and graphics into your page. You'll also have gotten a crash course in alternative application design with tips on when and how to plug Java, Netscape plug-ins, and CGI programs into your scripts.

Part III: JavaScript Language Reference

Every useful JavaScript construct, including objects, properties, methods, functions, event handlers, keywords, and color values, is arranged in this part, both alphabetically and grouped by utility. More than just a comprehensive list, Part III contains full explanations of each element along with usage tips and examples.

Part IV: Teaming Up JavaScript with Other Cool Stuff

JavaScript is one player in a crowded field. Part IV shows you how to integrate your scripts with other powerful languages and tools to create full-blown Internet applications.

Part V: The Part of Tens

The concluding part pulls together tidbits from the rest of the book, organized in lists of ten. The categories include great JavaScript-related Web sites, JavaScript-related user groups, common mistakes, and debugging tips.

Icons Used in This Book

Ever get in one of those moods where you're reading along, and you get really excited, and you just wish there was a way to cut to the chase and absorb an entire chapter all at once? Well, if so, you're in luck! Not only is this book organized in nice, easily digestible chunks, with real-life figures and code examples, but there's an extra added value, too: eye-catching icons to give you a heads-up on the most useful tidbits, categorized so that you can tell at a glance what's coming up.

Take just a second to get familiar with the kind of information you can expect from each icon:

This icon flags some of the cool stuff that you can find on the CD-ROM included in the back of this book. Because all of the JavaScript source code listings are on the CD (plus lots more besides), you can load up the scripts for each section and follow along while you read if you want.

This icon lets you know that some really nerdy technical information is coming your way. You can skip it if you want; reading through all of these isn't absolutely necessary if you're after the bare-bones basics (but they do give you a little show-off material!).

Next to the tip icon you'll find handy little tricks and techniques for getting the most bang out of your JavaScript buck.

When you see this icon, a really cool Web site URL is coming up that you just don't want to miss.

Before you jump in and start applying the information in any given section, check out the text next to these babies — chances are they'll save you a lot of time and hassle!

Where to Go from Here

So, what are you waiting for? Pick a topic, any topic, and dive in. Or, if you're like me, begin at the beginning and read until you get so excited that you have to put the book down and try stuff out for yourself. And remember: From now on, your life will be divided into two major time periods — *before* you mastered JavaScript and *after* you mastered JavaScript. Enjoy!

Part I
Building Killer Web Pages for Fun and Profit

IF BOB DYLAN HAD PURSUED A CAREER IN COMPUTERS.

"PUT HIM IN FRONT OF A TERMINAL AND HE'S A GENIUS, BUT OTHER-WISE THE GUY IS SUCH A BROODING, GLOOMY GUS HE'LL NEVER BREAK INTO MANAGEMENT."

In this part . . .

*J*avaScript is one of the coolest new Web tools around — and its use is spreading like wildfire. An extension to Hyper Text Markup Language (HTML), JavaScript enables you to get at the data that is stored in Web page forms. With JavaScript, you can make what's known as *intelligent* Web pages: pages that verify user input, calculate it, and make presentation decisions based on it. All this, all on the client, without having to learn an industrial-strength language, such as C or C++!

Part I gives you a quick peek at the highlights of JavaScript and shows you how JavaScript fits into HTML. Then Part I tells you the *least* that you need to know in order begin scripting. Finally, this part dives (from the edge, not the diving board!) into object-oriented concepts and the JavaScript object model.

Chapter 1

Hitting the Highlights: JavaScript Basics

. . . .

In This Chapter

▶ Finding out about the basics: JavaScript, HTML, Navigator, and Internet Explorer

▶ Making sure that you have everything you need to get started

▶ Getting up-to-the-minute online information

. . . .

*E*verybody, but everybody, is talking about JavaScript these days. For quite some time, JavaScript was the exclusive buzzword for netheads (*netheads* are folks with a penchant for staying up late at night to cruise the Internet, either in a professional capacity or just to get out of feeding the dog). Now that the Internet, in all its wonderful permutations, has invaded the lives of Mr. and Ms. Average, JavaScript has actually become the stuff of which happy-hour banter is made. This chapter tells you all that you need to know in order to impress the other celebrants the next time *you* indulge in a little post-work socialization.

What Is JavaScript? (Hint: It's Not the Same Thing as Java!)

JavaScript is the brand-spanking-new brainchild of Netscape Communications. Based on Netscape's association with Sun Microsystems and Sun's Java implementation, JavaScript is a *scripting* language that lets you create interactive Web pages quickly and easily. Now, if truth be known, the difference between a *scripting* language and a *programming* language isn't all that huge—after all, they're both languages humans use to communicate with computers. Usually, though, scripting languages are easier to use because they're smaller in scope than programming languages (you can do less, so there's less to learn). There are a couple more differences between the two, but that's the biggie.

It's easy!

JavaScript was specifically designed to work closely with the "language of the Web," HTML to augment the most useful Web page-building functions — which means you can do things like create and manipulate forms, buttons, text elements, and data — using a simple, easy-to-use language. Those who want more advanced features than JavaScript can handle simply need to hook their scripts up to programs written in other, more complicated programming languages such as Java, C, and C++ (Part IV is devoted to just that). This capability to connect to other programming languages gives JavaScript a great deal of the same flexibility and power that you'd find in a really complex language while allowing JavaScript to remain easy to use.

It's speedy!

Besides being easy, JavaScript is also pretty speedy. Like most scripting languages, it's *interpreted,* as opposed to *compiled,* so when you make changes to your script, the entire Web page that contains your script doesn't have to be reprocessed before you can bring it up and interact with it. This factor saves a great deal of time during the debugging and enhancing stages of Web page development.

The beauty of an interpreted language is that if you've made a mistake halfway through your script, the first part still runs; creating a script is not an all-or-nothing proposition, the way it is with a compiled language. Unfortunately, using an interpreted language also means that if you don't test your script thoroughly, it may look fine when it loads, and the script may even run fine — until a user does something that you didn't test!

Testing an interpreted language like JavaScript is "on the honor system." There's no compiler to nag you, so you can leave your testing until the last minute (or — gasp! — skip it altogether). Of course, if you do neglect to test your work, you'll have no one to blame but yourself when the folks who try to view your JavaScript-enabled Web page run into problems and e-mail you nasty notes (or, even worse, ignore your page altogether)! Chapters 22 and 23 are chock-full of helpful debugging tips to help make testing your JavaScript code as painless as possible.

Everybody's doing it! (Okay, almost everybody!)

Currently, Netscape's Web browser, called *Navigator,* is the only generally available product on the market that supports JavaScript.

Join the club!

So far, more than 25 companies have publicly announced their endorsement of JavaScript as an open standard for object-scripting languages and have announced their intent to provide support for it in the future. You may recognize some of the names: America Online, Inc., Apple Computer, Inc., AT&T, Digital Equipment Corporation, Hewlett-Packard Company, Intuit, Inc., Oracle Corporation, Toshiba Corporation, and Vermeer Technologies, Inc.

This book focuses on client-side JavaScript, which is where the big bang for the buck lies. Server-side JavaScript, though, which you explore in Chapter 9, has tremendous potential.

Navigator is currently available for the Macintosh, Windows 3.1, Windows 95, and several flavors of UNIX. Netscape and Sun have made the JavaScript language itself, however, available for other companies to license and implement in their own products. Because to date over two dozen industry-leading companies have publicly expressed their intent to provide JavaScript-enabled tools in the future (see the nearby sidebar "Join the club!" for details), Navigator won't be the only Web browser to support JavaScript for long! (As a matter of fact, the 3.0 version of Microsoft's Internet Explorer, due out very soon, supports JavaScript. See the "Internet Explorer" section later in this chapter for details.)

The support of all these companies is good for another reason besides just providing you more JavaScript-enabled product choices. Their participation is a good sign that JavaScript can become (Attention: buzzword alert!) an open standard. An open standard is a Good Thing. An *open standard* means that one company won't have a lock on the way JavaScript works. Of course, each company's product will have its own bells and whistles and proprietary value, but a JavaScript script produced by one company will be compatible with a JavaScript script produced by any other company, regardless of platform. So don't worry that all your nice new Web pages won't be viewable by anyone in another year or two. If present trends continue, those Web pages will be accessible to *everyone* in a year or two!

JavaScript and the World Wide Web

So what's all the fuss? Just this: The number of computers hooked up to the Internet is rising about 10 percent each month. A recent Consumer Online Services report estimates that online industry revenues, which reached $2.2 billion in 1995, will top $14 billion by the year 2000. Yes, folks, there's a great deal of money to be made. And for some unspecified length of time (because we all know that the tax man will find a way to take all the fun out of it before long), it's there for the taking — and you don't have to have a degree in computer science in order to take advantage of it, either.

Professional marketing and sales types especially love the Web because

- It's cheap.
- It's in color.
- It's dynamic. (Unlike with other electronic media or print media, lead times for making changes to a Web page are pretty short.)
- The potential market is staggeringly enormous. (The market now has an estimated 30 million Internet users worldwide — most of whom have access to a Web browser — and the number is increasing by the minute.)

Non-business folks love the Web because

- It's cheap.
- It's fun.
- It's dynamic.
- There's nothing quite like the feeling of sharing your opinions, knowledge, and interests with millions of people all over the world — instantly!

So, how can you join in the fun and construct a Web page that doesn't scream "I know nothing about computers, and this is obviously my first attempt" if you're not a programming geek? With JavaScript, of course!

JavaScript and HTML

JavaScript is an *extension* to HTML; an add-on, if you will. This is how it works: HTML is a standard language that everyone agrees on (okay, everyone in the committee responsible for producing the standard, anyway), and when a Web browser (like Navigator) claims to "support HTML," that means it supports, at the very least, standard HTML. (The version of HTML that most browsers currently support is 2.0.)

In addition to supporting the standard HTML language, however, some vendors — like Netscape — support certain proprietary HTML *extensions,* like the one that lets you insert JavaScript statements into an HTML file (the <SCRIPT>... </SCRIPT> tag, which you become intimate with in Chapter 3). The reason for extensions is simple: Tool providers like Netscape didn't want to wait while a standards body hammered out the next version of standard HTML — they wanted to use JavaScript (and other features) *now.*

Brave new world

You are likely to concentrate on creating really cool Web pages with JavaScript — at first. But consider this: A fine line exists between a Web page and an application. You've got a way to implement user interfaces (with HTML), data verification (JavaScript), and storage (for now, via a CGI program on a server). Think of the possibilities! (Of course, if you don't feel much like thinking right now, no sweat. This topic is discussed tons o' times throughout the book.)

Of course, it's to everyone's advantage if extensions become part of the standard (or at the very least are adopted by lots of vendors and so become a de facto standard), so folks who come up with HTML extensions typically submit their extensions to the WWW Consortium (the committee responsible for the HTML standard) for approval as soon as possible.

JavaScript and Your Web Browser

At the time of this writing, you need to use Netscape's Navigator 2.0 (or higher) Web browser (or Microsoft's Internet Explorer 3.0 or higher) in order to use JavaScript. Navigator is the Internet's most popular graphical Web browser. In fact, of all the browser users surveyed, about 70 percent say that they use Navigator (and would rather fight than switch). Internet Explorer, on the other hand, is fairly new — and very promising!

You can use another browser (or even another Internet protocol, such as ftp) to download either Navigator 2.0 (or higher) or Internet Explorer 3.0 and try them for free. Chapter 2 is devoted to the ins and outs of obtaining and installing a JavaScript-enabled browser. For now, suffice it to say that

- ✔ You need Navigator or Internet Explorer in order to work with JavaScript, which means that you have to be running one of the client platforms they support (Macintosh or Windows).

- ✔ You need to be aware that people may use other, non-JavaScript-enabled browsers to view your Web pages in the short term, which means not everyone will be able to see your JavaScript handiwork.

What Can I Do with JavaScript That I Can't Do with HTML?

"So," you're probably saying to yourself, "this JavaScript stuff sounds all well and good, but my cousin Arnold put up a really great-looking Web page last month — I saw it and it had pictures and everything — and he doesn't know anything about JavaScript. So why do I need to learn JavaScript, anyway? Why can't I just use HTML, like Arnold?"

Excellent question. You have, no doubt, noticed quite a few mighty fine-looking Web pages out there that predate JavaScript. How did they do it? Does JavaScript do something special, or easier, or what? In other words, what *value-add* does JavaScript have? (See, Mom, that money spent on a business degree wasn't wasted!)

The answer, I'm happy to say, is a mixture of both: JavaScript does more than HTML alone (that's why JavaScript is called an *HTML extension*), and JavaScript is much easier to use than the alternatives.

Keep client-side processing where it belongs—on the client!

The key to understanding JavaScript's purpose in life begins with the concept of the difference between a *client* and a *server*. Understanding the difference is pretty easy, actually. A *client* is somebody who makes a request, or asks somebody for something. A *server* is somebody who answers the request, or "serves." Of course, I'm anthropomorphizing here; the "somebodies" in these cases are computers. A rule of thumb for our purposes is that a *client computer* is a PC that a person uses to get something done (like surf the Web!). A *server computer* is a beefed-up machine (often a UNIX workstation) that may not even have a user interface because its job is to answer other computers' questions, not mere mortals' direct inquiries.

If Web clients and servers are different machines (and they typically are), some indeterminate amount of phone line is connected between them. Thus, every time a client asks a server for a favor (usually to check a database or run some complicated program that the client doesn't want to bother cluttering up its disk space with), the client has to wait for the message to travel to the server and for the answer to make the return trip home. Obviously, the potential for some slowed-down processing is found here, to say nothing of the expense (*somebody's* paying the phone bill for all this chitchatting).

"Wouldn't it be great if some services could be moved to the client instead of having to live on some server clear over in Greenland?" you may be asking. Yes, it would! That's where JavaScript runs (on the client, not in Greenland).

Actually, we're going to discuss server-side JavaScript in Chapter 9, but why strain our brains until we have to?

Here's how this arrangement works: Netscape Navigator and Internet Explorer, the two Web browsers that currently support JavaScript, are installed on client machines. Web pages are physically stored on a Web server. When you run Navigator or Internet Explorer and open a URL so you can see a particular Web page, the browser (the client) makes a request to the appropriate Web server. (The browser knows which server to ask because the name of the Web server is part of the requested page's URL.) The server then returns all the Web page information it has, and the client browser formats the Web page information as best it can and displays it in living color.

 Some browsers are "more equal" than other browsers when it comes to being able to interpret and display Web pages. If somebody creates a really cool JavaScript-enabled Web page and somebody else tries to look at it by using an old-fashioned character-based browser, the display definitely suffers. The character-based browser has to leave out fancy details, such as animation and graphics, that it doesn't understand how to display.

Interact with users

One of the neatest things you can do with JavaScript and HTML that you can't do with HTML alone is to enable the person viewing your Web page to type in some information and then display something appropriate based on that input.

"Well," I hear some of you saying, "that's going on right now, and I know for a fact that it's going on in Web pages that aren't JavaScript-enabled!" As a matter of fact, you *can* have user interaction in your Web pages without JavaScript (gasp!). But if you don't use JavaScript, you have to use HTML in conjunction with something called a *CGI program* — a "real" program that can only live on a Web server — in order to work with the values that your users type in. You can get into the ring with CGI later (in Chapter 19, for those who feel compelled to find out immediately). At this point, suffice it to say that when you enter CGI-land, you must pause, say a prayer, and don a seriously large pocket protector. A pocket protector the size of, oh, say, Cleveland.

Besides, CGI programs run on the server, not the client; so even if you bribe the nearest code jockey by shoving a really juicy piece of meat under his door and succeed in obtaining a CGI program, that CGI program can potentially slow down the response that your Web page viewers experience each time it (the CGI program) is invoked. Maybe this delayed response isn't a problem for the Web pages you're going to write — and maybe it is. Remember, we live in a culture that would rather squeeze a processed cheese-like substance from a tube than take five minutes to microwave real cheddar.

Keyboard interaction

A *keyboard event* occurs when someone types some information into a form you have provided them. (See, this isn't so tough now, is it?) If you've used a search engine (such as Yahoo! or Magellan) on the Web, you've had firsthand experience with initiating keyboard events, because in all likelihood you've typed the name of a subject into an entry field to search for related Web pages. Each keystroke that you type represented a keyboard event.

If, after you type **armadillo**, you press the Enter key to begin the search process, you initiate another keyboard event. On the other hand, if you put your mouse pointer (also called a *cursor,* but this is a family-values kind of book, so I say *pointer* instead) over a button marked Search and click the mouse button, you initiate a *mouse event,* which is described in more detail in the following section.

Mouse interaction

A *mouse event* occurs when someone uses the mouse in order to interact with a Web page. You can probably capture mouse events in as many ways as you can originate mouse events (and a good thing, too!). Often, the place on the screen where a user is expected to click is called a *control.* Controls, as shown in Figure 1-1, include such things as text fields, push buttons, checkboxes, and radio buttons (so called because they resemble buttons on an old-style radio, the type of radio where, when you pushed down one button, all the other buttons popped up).

A user doesn't have to click on something in order to initiate a mouse event, though. (If that were the case, mouse events would probably have to be renamed *mouse click events.*) Just dragging the mouse pointer across the screen generates mouse events — dozens of them — because the pointer being at a single point on the screen is one event; having it move a fraction of an inch (in geek-speak, a *pixel*) is another mouse event, and so on. Tracking this kind of mouse event is useful if you want people to see the name of each URL that your page links to: They just move their mouse pointers from one item to another and the URL displays in the status line.

Page navigation

In addition to keyboard and mouse events, you (as a JavaScript author) should be aware of *page navigation events.* As you may expect, a page navigation event occurs whenever a Web page does something — namely, whenever a Web page is loaded (opened) or unloaded (closed). (The `onLoad` and `onUnload` event handlers, which is how you implement page navigation events, are discussed in detail in Chapter 14.)

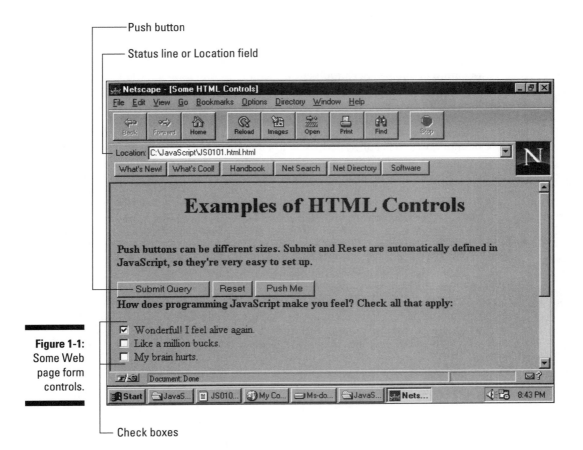

Push button

Status line or Location field

Check boxes

Figure 1-1:
Some Web
page form
controls.

For example, when a user clicks on File⇨Open Location
http://www.idgbooks.com, the instant that the page comes up on the user's
screen marks a *page open event*. You can write a JavaScript script that plays a
little welcoming tune every time that your page is loaded if you want. Or you
can time how long a user takes between loading your page and unloading it.

What Do I Need to Get Started?

I'm sure that you're champing at the bit to get started on your first JavaScript-
enabled Web page. First things first, though. You've got an idea of what
JavaScript can do for you, and by now you've probably already got something
specific in mind for your very first attempt. Now's the time to dive into the
preliminaries: what you need to get started and how to get what you need if you
don't already have it. After you've dispensed with the setup, you can go on to
the *really* fun stuff!

Hardware

This book assumes that you're running JavaScript on a client and that you're beginning your JavaScript adventure with either an IBM-compatible computer or a Macintosh computer. Your machine (or *box,* to use the vernacular) should be a 386 or better (unless it's a Mac) computer, which should have at least 8MB of RAM and at least 11MB free disk space (6MB to install a browser, and another 5MB to have ready in case the browser needs to recruit disk space for stand-in memory, which is called *disk caching*). If none of this makes sense, you may try asking your local hardware guru (every organization seems to have at least one). I've found, through trial and error, that most gurus are fairly responsive to sugar-based snack foods.

You also need hardware installed that lets you connect to the Internet. This hardware usually consists of a modem and a phone line. Depending on your computer, you may have an internal model installed (IBM Thinkpads, for example, come complete with a built-in modem). If not, you can buy a modem at your local computer discount store. Something to look for is the modem line speed: the faster, the better. Netscape suggests a modem speed of 14.4 Kbps or faster. If you don't already have a modem and need to purchase one, consider buying the fastest modem in your price range; you'll be very glad that you did when you try to look at really spiffy Web pages with many graphics, each of which (because graphics files are typically so large) takes a loooong time to load.

Software

This book assumes that you're beginning your JavaScript adventure with a computer that's already loaded with Windows 3.1 or Windows 95, or, alternatively, a Macintosh. It also assumes that you have some way to create text files. (Most operating systems come packaged with a variety of text editors and word processors, any of which will work just fine.)

If you're already connected to the Internet, disregard this section

First off, you need software that enables you to connect to the Internet. I won't even begin to pretend that I have the magical powers to spell out what is necessary to accomplish this. In plain English, you need

- A way to talk to other computers. The type of software that provides this is called a *communications protocol;* the most common is *TCP/IP* (transmission control protocol/internet protocol).

- Some kind of dialing mechanism installed on your machine so your computer can talk on the phone to all the other computers, who probably all have their own phone lines and get to stay up late, too.

> ✔ Access to an *Internet service provider* (those nice folks who cheerfully charge you for providing you access to software that enables you to prowl around the 'Net).

Unfortunately, instructions for installing communications software rarely involve plain English. So if you get stuck, you may want to take a look at *The Internet For Dummies,* 2nd Edition by John Levine and Carol Baroudi for a really great detailed explanation of how to get set up.

JavaScript-specific software

Basically, you need two items to work with JavaScript: a web browser that can display your document's results, and a program to create and edit HTML documents that use JavaScript.

Netscape Navigator (Netscape Communication's commercial Web browser) is the only generally available browser that supports Javascript at the time of ths writing — but Microsoft Internet Explorer is close on its heels. So, the first thing to do is to get a copy of Navigator or the JavaScript-capable version of Internet Explorer.

Netscape Navigator

Three choices for Navigator client browsers are currently available: Netscape Navigator, Netscape Navigator Gold, and Netscape Navigator Personal Edition. Whichever product you choose, make sure the version number is 3.0 or higher.

The differences among these packages are minimal for our purposes. Navigator is the basic model. Navigator Gold adds a JavaScript-enabled *WYSIWYG* (what you see is what you get) editor along with some templates and wizards to make your life easier. And Navigator Personal Edition adds an Internet access kit to the rest of Navigator's features.

You can download a copy of Navigator for a free trial period if you'd like by visiting `http://home.netscape.com/`; unfortunately, that assumes that you already have a Web browser installed or that you have access to *ftp* (short for *file transfer protocol,* which is an Internet application that enables you to nab files from other people's machines). Of course, you can also run right out and buy a copy of Navigator at pretty much any store that sells software.

Internet Explorer

On the Microsoft side, you need to get Version 3.0 of Internet Explorer or higher (the earlier versions don't include JavaScript support). Internet Explorer Version 3.0 is a Web browser that's tightly integrated with Windows 95 and boasts integration with a lot of really cool technologies, including Java applets and something called ActiveX (more about ActiveX in Chapter 2). At the time I'm writing this, it's only available for Windows 95/NT; if you're interested, it's available for free via download.

Chapter 2 is devoted to helping you get the correct version of Navigator or Internet Explorer, installing it, and using it. Skip ahead and check this chapter out right now if you want. I'll wait for you.

On the CD included with this book are some utilities for Windows and Macintosh that you'll find very useful in creating and editing your HTML and JavaScript documents. In the strictest sense, you only need some kind of text editor (like Notepad and SimpleText, included with Windows and Macintosh software, respectively.) But text editors aren't loaded with features that help you design HTML without forgetting the necessities. So, I know you'll find the goodies on the CD to be very useful and tie-saving.

Documentation

For Netscape Navigator and Microsoft Internet Explorer documentation, respectively, check out the following URLs:

```
http://home.netscape.com/comprod/products/navigator
http://www.microsoft.com/ie/
```

To get a copy of the *JavaScript Authoring Guide,* the must-have tome that explains JavaScript basics and language concepts (and includes an extensive reference section), visit the following Web page:

```
http://home.netscape.com/eng/mozilla/2.01/handbook/
          javascript/index.html
```

For HTML, the first of the following two URLs points to a user-friendly version of the *HTML DTD Reference, Level 2* (*DTD* stands for *Document Type Definition,* and it represents a formal specification); the second URL points to an HTML design guide you may find useful.

```
http://www.w3.org/pub/WWW/MarkUp/html-spec/html-spec_toc.html
http://www.narpes.fi/design/html_design.html
```

Chapter 2

First Things First: Firing Up A JavaScript Enabled Browser and Getting Started with JavaScript

• •

In This Chapter

▶ Choosing a browser

▶ Installing Navigator

▶ Installing Internet Explorer

▶ Surfing the Web for JavaScript examples

▶ Loading JavaScript scripts

▶ Viewing JavaScript source

▶ Identifying the JavaScript hierarchy

• •

*I*f you want to learn JavaScript, Netscape Navigator and Microsoft's Internet Explorer are currently the only games in town. Sure, that situation may change, but you want to start using JavaScript now — so taking the time to choose between Navigator or Internet Explorer, install one of them, and get comfortable with your choice are the first tasks at hand. Later, of course, you'll want to know how to load and display your very own JavaScript-enabled Web pages.

Well, you're in luck, because this chapter explains everything you need to know to get either Navigator or Internet Explorer to run like a champ on the machine in front of you. Not only that, but you also discover how to execute and display the source of a real, live JavaScript program. Whoopee!

Navigator or Internet Explorer: Which One Is Best?

Both Navigator and Internet Explorer are fine Web browsers with unique strengths and features. Both support standard HTML, and both support JavaScript.

To help you decide which one to use for your JavaScript adventures, this section offers some comparative facts on each. Keep in mind that although this information is complete and accurate as I write, it could change in the blink of an eye (everybody knows how volatile the software industry is—that's why it's so exciting!).

For up-to-the-minute information on Navigator and Internet Explorer, visit the following sites:

```
http://home.netscape.com/comprod/products/navigator/
index.html
http://www.microsoft.com/ie/default.htm
```

Hardware + software = platform

The first thing to consider is the platform availability of each browser. If you're running Macintosh, for example, you won't be able to use Internet Explorer (unless you run out and buy an IBM-compatible running Windows 95). Take a look at the following table and see if it doesn't narrow down your choice a little bit.

Table 2-1	Web Browser Platform Availability (JavaScript-Enabled Versions Only)	
	Netscape Navigator	*Microsoft Internet Explorer*
Windows 3.1	Yes	No
Windows 95/NT	Yes	Yes
Macintosh	Yes	No
UNIX	Yes (8 flavors)	No

You mean there's more than one version?!

Because some versions of both Navigator and Internet Explorer support JavaScript and some don't, selecting the correct version number of a Web browser is almost as important as selecting the product itself. Following is a list of all of the versions of Navigator and Internet Explorer that support JavaScript at the time of this writing. A good rule of thumb to follow: the higher the version number, the more JavaScript support is likely to be included. (For example, Netscape Navigator Version 3.0 supports more JavaScript features than Navigator Version 2.02 does.)

- ✔ Netscape Navigator 2.*x* or higher
- ✔ Netscape Navigator Personal Edition 2.*x* or higher
- ✔ Netscape Navigator Gold 2.*x* or higher
- ✔ Microsoft Internet Explorer 3.0

Installing and Using The Chosen One

Once you've decided on a particular version of a particular Web browser, you're ready to hit the trail. Depending on your choice, you'll want to read either the section devoted to Navigator and then skip ahead, or read the one on Internet Explorer and ignore the Navigator section. Of course, there's no law against installing and using them both, but if you're like me, you'll pick one and stick with it until you're good and comfortable. (Hey, why make things more confusing than they have to be, that's my motto!)

Netscape Navigator

Because Navigator was the first browser to support JavaScript, they've had some time to tinker around with it. While all Versions 2.*x* or higher support JavaScript to some degree, the latest (3.0 at the time of this writing) provides the most bang for the buck. That's because with Version 3.0 you can interact with Java applets and Netscape plug-ins directly with JavaScript statements (tons more on this in Part IV). You can't do that with any of the 2.*x* versions.

How do I get it? How do I install it?

You can get a copy of Navigator in two different ways: either get Navigator electronically (via another Web browser or ftp) or go the old-fashioned route and buy Navigator in a shrink-wrapped box at your local computer software store.

The old-fashioned way: over the counter

If you're going to buy a copy of Netscape Navigator, you'll be glad to know that it comes complete with easy-to-follow, step-by-step installation instructions. All you have to do is invoke the setup file (the instructions tell you exactly how to do this for whatever operating system you're running), and the Install Wizard takes it from there!

TIP

If at first you don't succeed . . .

If you run into errors installing Navigator, try installing it again. And again. Yours truly made the attempt a grand total of six times before the final, fulfilling moment when the `You have successfully completed installation` prompt appeared on my screen. Mind you, I changed absolutely nothing in between the attempts. Some things you're just better off not knowing.

Plus, because you've plunked down cold, hard cash, you're entitled to phone and e-mail support if you have any problems installing Navigator. Oh, and make sure that the copy you purchase is compatible with your operating system (this caution should go without saying, but they make those little Windows 95 icons on the box so small . . . at least that's *my* excuse).

The newfangled way: hot off the press from "We Be Navigators"

If it's raining really hard and you don't want to run down to the store, and if you have another Web browser, such as Mosaic, or some other communications protocol like ftp already installed on your computer, you can visit the Netscape Navigator Download page and follow the instructions you see on the screen. Because there's a separate version of Navigator for each platform, make sure you select the correct version for your setup (Windows 3.1, Windows 95, Macintosh, etc.). The installation process is refreshingly simple, by the way; all you need to do is run the self-extracting file after you download it, just like the instructions say. The installation process asks you where you want Navigator to live on your hard drive, and that's all there is to it!

```
http://www.netscape.com/comprod/mirror/client_download.html
```

Make sure you check that the size of the file you transferred is equal to the size of the original file. Some communications software pretends that it has successfully transferred the entire file when it really hasn't (ha, ha!). If an incomplete transfer happens, you may be very surprised when you try to decompress and install the file. (Want to know how I know?!)

Be aware that your free trial copy doesn't come with technical support from Netscape. Hey, you get what you pay for.

Okay, now how do I use it?

After you install Navigator and configure it properly, all you need to do to bring it up and automatically load the Netscape home page is to double-click on the Navigator icon on your desktop. Figure 2-1 shows you what you should see when Navigator launches.

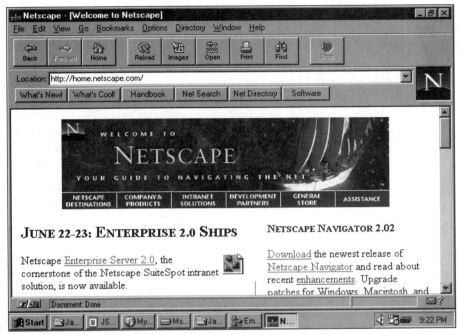

Figure 2-1:
Netscape
Navigator
Web
browser.

At this point, you're ready to surf. I suggest familiarizing yourself with Netscape's menu by the old-fashioned trial-and-error method. Go ahead: Click on something and see what happens!

Navigator all by its lonesome

If you're having trouble deciding where to begin, you may want to try the buttons marked What's New!, What's Cool!, and Net Search. The first two buttons take you to lists of randomly selected, sometimes bizarre, and usually interesting Web sites. (You can use the left-arrow button on the Navigator toolbar to go back and revisit pages and the right-arrow button to go forward.) The Net Search button takes you to a search engine where you can type in a keyword and pull up Web pages from all over the world — Web pages that contain the keyword you specified. Try typing **JavaScript** and see how many Web pages come up!

Free-form Web surfing can be highly addictive and is becoming a sport in its own right (look for it at the 2000 Olympics). However, if you feel the need to justify the inordinate amount of time you spend doing this when you first get hold of Navigator, look at it this way — free-form Web surfing is a learning experience. In the back of your mind, keep an eye out for compelling graphics and captivating animations. Be alert for pages that are fascinating and easy to navigate (as well as those that are painfully confusing) and try to figure out exactly what causes each reaction. Think of this Web surfing as the pre-production phase of your own design efforts. (Okay, your family may be annoyed at you for cutting out on dinner for four days running, but your boss may go for it!)

The main event: JavaScript

Alert readers may have noticed that there's not a big JavaScript button anywhere on the Navigator toolbar or menu (although there is a way to turn JavaScript support on or off, JavaScript support is turned on by default). What's the deal? How do you load JavaScript-enabled Web pages and run them, anyway?

Here's how it works: to run JavaScript scripts, you load a Web page that contains embedded JavaScript statements. When you interact with the loaded page (click a button, type in some text — that kind of thing), Navigator's interpreter recognizes the JavaScript statements and performs them for you without your having to do anything special at all.

In addition to viewing JavaScript-enabled Web pages, you can also view the behind-the-scenes, uninterpreted JavaScript statements that are responsible for the display you see. An important distinction exists here: there's the *runtime* (what you see when you interact with the page) and the *source* (the JavaScript statements that Navigator interprets and displays). You do quite a bit of this in Chapters 4 and 6, but if you'd like to see what JavaScript source looks like right now, select File⇨Open Location from the Navigator menu to open the following URL (or type the following URL directly into the Location text field at the top of the Navigator window to open the URL):

```
http://www.gis.net/~carter/madlibs/hillbill.html
```

Figure 2-2 shows you the display you should see.

To see the JavaScript source, select View⇨Document Source from the Navigator menu.

In Windows 95, after you've installed Navigator, every text file that you create with an .html ending displays as a little Navigator icon. If you've got an HTML file with a Navigator icon visible, you can start a Navigator session and load that HTML file automatically by double-clicking on the HTML's Navigator icon. So much easier than starting Navigator first and then loading the HTML file through the menu options!

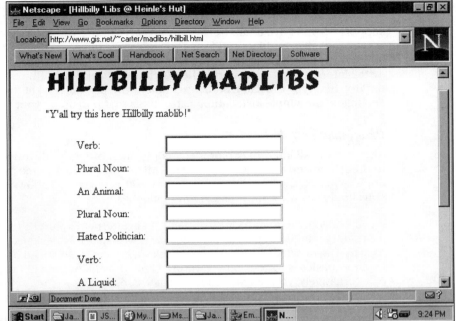

Figure 2-2:
Viewing a
JavaScript-
enabled
Web page
with
Navigator.

JavaScript and Microsoft Internet Explorer: Coming Soon to a Server Near You

As of this writing, Netscape Communication's Navigator is the only generally available Web browser that supports JavaScript. By the time you read this, though, Version 3.0 of Microsoft Internet Explorer may very well have hit the streets, which bumps the count up to two. It's currently in beta, and it looks so promising I figured you'd want to know all about it!

Because the version of Internet Explorer that boasts JavaScript support — Version 3.0 — is still in beta as this book goes to press, there's a chance that the descriptions and URLs you see listed here in this section may be a little out of date by the time you give 'em a try.

How do I get it? How do I install it?

If you've got any Web browser at all installed on your machine, you can visit the URL below and follow the instructions you find there to download your very own free copy of Internet Explorer:

```
http://www.microsoft.com/ie/download/
```

You'll be guided through a series of pages that ask you things like what platform you want (remember, you need the Version 3.0 or higher to get JavaScript support, so you have to answer Windows 95/NT to this question) and what server you'd like to download from (try the location nearest you first). The file you download will be a self-extracting executable, so all you need to do to install Internet Explorer is to run the executable (click Start⇨Run from the desktop and type the name of the executable you downloaded at the prompt) and follow the simple installation instructions that pop up on your screen.

Okay, now how do I use it?

After you install Internet Explorer and configure it properly, all you need to do to bring it up and automatically load the Microsoft Network home page is to double-click on the Internet icon on your desktop. Figure 2-3 shows you what you should see when Internet Explorer launches.

If you've used Windows 95 for very long at all, Internet Explorer's toolbar will look pretty familiar to you. That's because it was specially designed to be easy to use for Windows 95 users! A quick way to get up to speed on Internet Explorer basics is to click on the Tutorial link near the bottom of the page — or, alternatively, you can load the tutorial URL directly:

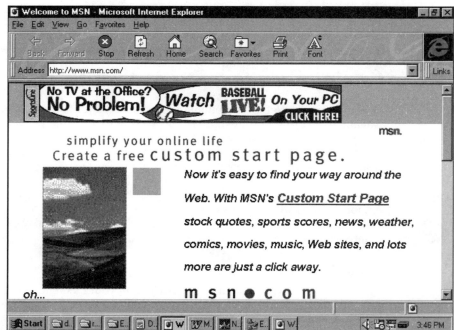

Figure 2-3:
Microsoft
Internet
Explorer
Web
browser.

http://www.msn.com/tutorial/default.html

Internet Explorer all by its lonesome

If you're having trouble deciding where to begin, you may want to try clicking on the links marked Links and Search. The first one takes you to lists of randomly selected, sometimes bizarre, and usually interesting Web sites. (You can use the left-arrow button on the Internet Explorer toolbar to go back and revisit pages and the right-arrow button to go forward.) The Search link takes you to a list of popular search engines where you can type in a keyword and pull up Web pages from all over the world — Web pages that contain the keyword you specified. Try typing **JavaScript** and see how many Web pages come up!

JavaScript, Jscript . . . Whatever!

Technically, Internet Explorer supports a scripting language called JScript, which is JavaScript-compatible. (Whew, try saying that three times fast!)

As you'd expect, Internet Explorer's scripting object model is compatible with Navigator's object model (meaning you can use the same form elements in Internet Explorer as you can in Navigator), and the way that JavaScript is invoked is the same (using the <SCRIPT>...</SCRIPT> tags or by assigning JavaScript statements directly to an event handler like onClick). What's more, Microsoft claims that Internet Explorer's implementation of JavaScript will be able to interact directly with ActiveX controls. (For those of you who like to keep up on these things, ActiveX controls used to be called *OCXes,* or *OLE controls.* Like Java applets, they're live programs that can be embedded inside your Web pages—in fact, they can be implemented in Java.)

Check out the following URLs for an overview of Internet Explorer's JavaScript implementation, including ActiveX integration and plans for Java support:

http://www.microsoft.com/ie/most/howto/script.htm
http://www.microsoft.com/ie/ie3/activex.htm

Alert readers may have noticed that there's not a big JavaScript button anywhere on the Internet Explorer toolbar or menu (although there is a way to turn JavaScript support on or off, JavaScript support is turned on by default). What's the deal? How do you load JavaScript-enabled Web pages and run them, anyway?

Here's how it works: to run JavaScript scripts, you open an HTML file that contains embedded JavaScript statements. When you interact with the loaded page (click a button, type in some text—that kind of thing), Internet Explorer's interpreter recognizes the JavaScript statements and performs them for you without your having to do anything special at all.

In addition to viewing JavaScript-enabled Web pages, you can also view the behind-the-scenes, uninterpreted JavaScript statements that are responsible for the display you see. An important distinction exists here: there's the *runtime* (what you see when you interact with the page) and the *source* (the JavaScript statements that Internet Explorer interprets and displays). You do quite a bit of this in Chapters 4 and 6, but if you'd like to see what JavaScript source looks like right now, select File⇨Open from the Internet Explorer menu to open the following URL (or type the following URL directly into the Address text field at the top of the Internet Explorer window to open the URL):

```
http://www.gis.net/~carter/madlibs/hillbill.html
```

Figure 2-4 shows you the display you should see.

To see the JavaScript source for this Web page, select View⇨Source from the Internet Explorer menu while the page is loaded.

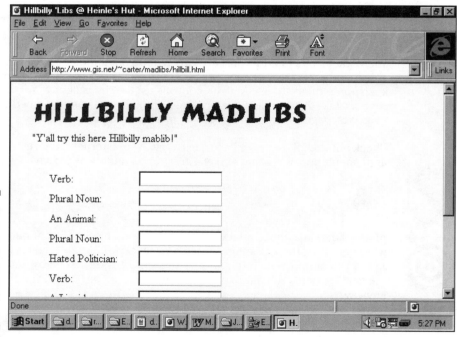

Figure 2-4:
Viewing a
JavaScript-
enabled
Web page
with
Internet
Explorer.

Some browsers are more equal than others

Now, I'm a glass-half-empty kind o'gal, I admit; but if you're planning on creating JavaScript-enabled Web pages that can be seen and enjoyed by all (and who isn't?) you might want to keep on top of the "JavaScript compatibility" issue.

For example: the <SCRIPT>...</SCRIPT> tag is an extension to HTML, and not all browsers support it in fact, the only ones that do at present are Navigator and Internet Explorer. Well, my guess — and this is just a guess, but it's a fairly educated one, if I may flatter myself to say so —

is that extensions to JavaScript will appear on the scene in the very near future. That means that someday soon you may need to be aware of the difference between standard JavaScript and JScript, which is JavaScript-compatible (but that might add some non-standard goodies).

The rule, as always, is to go ahead and exploit all the extensions that tickle your fancy; just be sensitive to the fact that you can't predict what percentage of your target audience will be using any given browser, and plan accordingly.

Down With Monarchy! We Want Hierarchy!

JavaScript is an object-based language, and that means that the majority of the JavaScript statements you write will reference objects. To be more specific, they reference JavaScript objects. That's right, the same objects that you defined with HTML statements, you can look at, change, and display with JavaScript statements. The first thing to do, then, is to get a feel for the objects you'll deal with. The next section describes all the objects in detail; this section explains how they're organized — called a *hierarchy* — and why that is.

Your JavaScript-enabled Web browser creates an *object hierarchy* (a bunch of related objects) for you each time you load a page. Whatever is defined in that page with HTML tags — a window, a form, a radio button, a text field — becomes an object that you can access with JavaScript statements. You can examine a group of radio buttons to see which one was clicked, for instance, or verify that a user actually typed something into a text field.

As you may expect, the object hierarchy parallels the HTML hierarchy exactly. Because input text elements must be placed inside a form, for example (that is, you have to put the <INPUT> tag for a text element inside bounding <FORM>...</FORM> tags), the form object is said to be the *containing* object, and the input element is said to be the *contained* object.

Why do you need to know about the hierarchy? Because when it comes time for you to write JavaScript code, you need to refer to the *entire* hierarchy when you describe an object (computers are *so* literal-minded). Fortunately, it's easy: just separate each element, from the most general to the most specific, with a period. For example, following is a hierarchical representation (not code exactly, just a representation to help you understand how objects in a hierarchy can be accessed) that explains where I live:

```
Earth.NorthAmerica.UnitedStates.Texas.Austin.myHouse
```

The point is to start with a frame of reference that everyone understands (in my example, it's *Earth;* in your Web browser, it's *Window*) and then zero in on the specific element you're trying to describe.

The following sections show what the JavaScript object hierarchy looks like.

Navigator instance hierarchy

When you want to reference one of the following objects, you must precede its name with the name of all of its predecessors, if any, separated by a period (as shown). The `window` object is the only exception to this rule; since there's only one at the top — and the `window` is it — it's a given.

Object	*Syntax*
window	`window` (optional)
frame, parent, self, top	`frame, parent, self, top`
location	`location`
history	`history`
document	`document`
applet	`document.applets[0]`
area	`document.someArea`
form	`document.someForm`
button	`document.someForm.someButton`
checkbox	`document.someForm.myCheckbox`

fileUpload	`document.someForm.myFileUpload`
hidden	`document.someForm.someHidden`
image	`document.someForm.someImage`
password	`document.someForm.somePassword`
radio	`document.someForm.someRadio`
reset	`document.someForm.someReset`
select	`document.someForm.someSelect`
submit	`document.someForm.someSubmit`
text	`document.someForm.someText`
textarea	`document.someForm.someTextarea`
link	`document.someLink`
anchor	`document.someAnchor`
plugin	`document.imbeds[0]`

Navigator stand-alone objects

The objects below don't fit anywhere in the hierarchy; they're freewheeling and responsible to no one! Since they aren't considered "part of" any other object, you specify them all by themselves when you want to use them, like so:

Stand-Alone Object	*JavaScript Syntax*
array	`Array`
Date	`myBirthday = new Date()`
Math	`randomNumber = Math.random()`
navigator	`alert("Version is " + navigator.appVersion)`
option	`Option`
string	`var myString = "strings are surrounded by quotes"`

All of the objects in the JavaScript object hierarchy represent real-world graphical *objects* — objects such as buttons, list boxes, text fields, and titles. Together, these objects make up a Web page. Each object, in turn, may contain other objects (just like North America contains Canada and the United States, and the United States contains individual states).

In addition, each of the objects contains one or more associated *properties* (one-word descriptions) that, together, describe it fully. In the example `Earth.NorthAmerica.UnitedStates,Texas.Austin.myHouse`, the term `myHouse` would include properties such as `color` (*yellow*), `numberOfBedrooms` (*three*), `yard` (*yes*) and `stateOfCleanliness` (*dreadful*). Part III details each and every object available to you as a JavaScript author, along with each object's properties and the ways you can interact with them programmatically.

Chapter 3

Low Budget HTML Primer (Or, The Least You Have to Know about HTML to Use JavaScript Effectively)

● ●

● ●

*H*ere's the ten-cent definition of *HTML*: HTML (Hypertext Markup Language) is a character-based method for describing and displaying Web page content. It can't really be considered a programming language in the traditional sense of the word; it's really more of a mini-language. In an HTML file you specify the text that you want to display on your Web page, and then you surround the text with keywords called *tags* to tell the HTML interpreter how you want each section of text displayed: what size, font, color, position, and so on.

Those of you who want a full-fledged description of HTML should check out *HTML For Dummies,* 2nd Edition, by Ed Tittel and Steve James. It covers everything from the basics to advanced HTML-related topics like finding a home for your Web page — and best of all, it comes complete with an example-packed disk.

"So what," I can hear you saying. "My word processor does pretty much the same thing." Well, okay, I'll give you that. But HTML has a few characteristics that no word processor alone can match, and they're the reason that everyone is so excited about it:

  ✔ HTML is a standard that's available on multiple platforms.

  ✔ HTML isn't limited to textual display; it also handles the inclusion of multimedia elements such as pictures, movies, sounds, and third-party software applications.

> ✔ HTML supports linking documents together to form hypertext compound documents.
>
> ✔ Some implementations of HTML, including Netscape Navigator and Internet Explorer, support JavaScript.

In a nutshell, HTML is what enables folks with different computers to browse the Web. Heck, I'll go so far as to say that HTML is what *makes* the Web! Many of the objects (see Chapter 4 for more on objects) that you use as a budding JavaScript author are actually HTML objects, such as forms and form elements. You create them with HTML statements, and you inspect and manipulate them (their contents, actually) with JavaScript statements.

From the preceding description, you may deduce that HTML is a good place to start learning the specific syntax that you need to know in order to create JavaScript scripts — and you'd be right. *Syntax* means the rules that apply to a language: the specific words you can use, what they mean, and how they can be combined to form complete statements. In this chapter, you take a whirlwind tour through the basics of HTML syntax, paying particular attention to how JavaScript fits in. After you're comfortable with the material in this chapter, you're halfway home!

The extension for an HTML file is always either *.html* (for operating systems like Windows 95 and the Macintosh OS that support long filename extensions) or *.htm* (for those that don't).

Tag, You're It!

An *HTML tag* is a special word, usually surrounded by angle brackets (<>), that tells the Navigator HTML interpreter (and the HTML interpreters of other Web browsers, of course) how to display text, colors, controls, and sounds on your Web page. Many (but not all) tags come in pairs: one that turns on a *display mode* (such as centering, bolding, or italicizing) and one that turns the display mode off again. Coming up is the official ultra-generic description of tag syntax; this description is followed by some real-life examples, which will probably make more sense.

HTML 101: tag syntax

The basic HTML tag syntax can be used to describe any HTML tag. Seriously, all you have to do is know how to decode it, and you will after you read this section (I promise!).

```
<TAG-NAME [ATTRIBUTE[="VALUE"]...]>[some text][</TAG-NAME>]
```

Whew! Kind of makes IRS forms seem well-written by comparison, doesn't it? The statement is actually pretty clear, though, when you know what each of the symbols means. (By the way, the preceding example is standard notation for expressing just about any computer language syntax, so learning this standard notation now means that the next time that you run into it, it will seem like a dear old friend.)

Here's how it works: The words in italics (*TAG-NAME*, *ATTTRIBUTE*, *VALUE*, and *some text*) are placeholders. In real, live JavaScript statements, each of these would be replaced with a real tag name (one example is "INPUT"), one or more attributes ("NAME" is an attribute associated with the "INPUT" element), a real value ("button", perhaps) and some meaningful text (like "Push Me"), respectively. The ellipses (...) and square brackets ([]) mean something special, too.

It's probably easier to take things one at a time, so I'll break this puppy up into little chunks and take a look at each one separately, okay? All together, from left to right, there are six different components that make up HTML tag syntax: angle brackets, tag name, square brackets, attribute-value, ellipses, and text.

You call them less-than/greater-than; we call them angle brackets

Every HTML tag needs to be surrounded both by an opening angle bracket (<) and a closing angle bracket (>). Attribute-value pairs, which are used to customize certain HTML tags (see the upcoming section called "Attribute-value pair"), are considered part of the overall HTML tag definition; so depending on the tag you're defining, the angle brackets may enclose the tag name alone or the tag name plus some attribute-value pairs. Either way, though, leave off one of the brackets and you're bound to receive a not-so-gentle reminder from the HTML interpreter when you load your page!

Some tags, like the <INPUT> tag, are one-part tags; others, like <TITLE>... </TITLE>, are two-part tags. Angle brackets need to surround both.

Most HTML tags are two-part tags. Like English rules, though, there doesn't seem to be a lot of rhyme or reason to which is which — you just have to look 'em up and remember 'em.

Angle bracket syntax:

```
<TAG-NAME [ATTRIBUTE[="VALUE"]...]>[some text][</TAG-NAME>]
```

Angle bracket example:

```
<HR>
```

HR has no associated attributes, so the opening and closing angle brackets surround it directly.

```
<INPUT TYPE="button" NAME="calculateButton"
          VALUE="Calculate">
```

The `<INPUT>` tag has a few attributes that need to be defined for it, so in the preceding example the closing angle bracket follows the attribute definitions.

```
<A HREF="http://www.idgbooks.com"> IDG Books </A>
```

`<A>`, the HTML tag that lets you define a hypertext link, is a two-part tag. Notice that angle brackets surround both parts.

A tag by any other name...

There are tons of tags in HTML. Some tags let you format text; others let you define form elements, like push buttons and text input fields; still others let you incorporate images and hypertext links into your Web pages. Although the basic tag syntax is always the same, each tag is unique (some have associated attributes that you get to customize, for example, and some don't; some are two-part tags, and some aren't). That means your HTML statements, like those in the example below, will look slightly different depending on the tag you're defining.

Table 3-1, later in this chapter, contains a partial list of the most commonly used tags with a short description of what each does. For a complete listing, though, you'll want to consult an HTML guide such as *HTML For Dummies,* 2nd Edition, by Ed Tittel and Steve James.

The word `TAG-NAME` in the syntax below is in italics, and that means it's a placeholder. As you can see in the example that follows it, actual JavaScript statements don't contain the *word* `TAG-NAME` — instead, a real, live tag name follows the opening angle bracket.

Tag name syntax:

```
<TAG-NAME [ATTRIBUTE[="VALUE"]...]>[some text][</TAG-NAME>]
```

Tag name example:

```
<HR>

<IMG SRC="images/clown.gif" ALT="Our CEO and founder"
          ALIGN="TOP">

<TITLE>Bartholomew's Grizzly Bear Web Page</TITLE>
```

Notice that the closing half of a two-part tag always contains a forward slash (located within the ending `</TITLE>` tag above).

In order to interpret your HTML source correctly, the interpreter needs to know that you've finished the tag name — and the only way it can tell this is if it sees both angle brackets around a valid tag. If you leave off one of the brackets (easy to do, especially when you're in a hurry!), you get some interesting results when you test your page.

Brackets are for squares

You'll never see square brackets ([and]) in an actual HTML statement. Square brackets *are* used in the HTML tag syntax, though, to let you know that some things are optional. Take a look at the syntax below, and then the examples, and you'll see what I mean.

Square bracket syntax:

```
<TAG-NAME [ATTRIBUTE[="VALUE"]...]>[some text][</TAG-NAME>]
```

Square bracket example:

```
<HR>
```

Talk about your minimalist tags! Nothing optional in the preceding.

```
<INPUT TYPE="radio" NAME="petChoice" CHECKED>
```

The preceding shows an example of a couple of attribute-value pairs along with one attribute (CHECKED) that has no corresponding value (not only attribute-value pairs but also values alone are optional according to the syntax, remember?).

```
<TITLE>The Many Moods of Moe</TITLE>
```

The syntax says a closing tag is optional, depending on the specific tag; the <TITLE> tag needs one, so it goes at the end of the title text.

Customizing HTML tags with attribute-value pairs (no extra charge!)

You've seen examples of attributes and values, and you probably have a good idea of what they are, but to make absolutely sure, let's run through some definitions.

Attribute

An attribute is a general characteristic (name, type, size, color — that type of thing) that can be associated with a given object. Attributes let you customize your HTML objects (there's that *word* again!).

Value

If an attribute is a general characteristic of an object, a *value* is a specific characteristic (belonging to a specific instance) of an object. For example, all kitty-cat objects have an associated name attribute, but the *values* for each individual cat's name will vary (Scooter, Fluffy, Zeke, Boots…). It's the same way with HTML objects: all INPUT objects have an associated NAME attribute, but the *values* for each instance of an INPUT object will all be different ("firstName", "lastName", "calculateButton", etc.)

Attribute-value assignment

In computer language terms, *assignment* means setting one thing equal to another thing. In HTML and JavaScript, you set one thing equal to another thing with an equal sign (=), like this:

```
SIZE=15
TYPE="text"
NAME="firstNameInputField"
```

Can you find the attributes in this picture? I thought you could! They're SIZE, TYPE, and NAME. (Extra bonus points for identifying the values being assigned to the attributes, which are 15, "text", and "firstNameInputField".)

Attribute-value pair

Attributes and values have a tendency to hang out together, and it's a good thing, too, because values only make sense in the context of their attributes. Can you imagine having a value like 15 floating around by its lonesome? What sense could you possibly make out of "15," unless you knew that it was an age, or a number of dollars, or a street number — in short, unless you knew its associated attribute? And it's not just us humans, either. When data from a Web page is submitted to a program on a server for processing, it's always passed in attribute-value pairs so that the server program can make sense of it.

Attribute-value syntax:

```
<TAG-NAME [ATTRIBUTE[="VALUE"]...]>[some text][</TAG-NAME>]
```

Attribute-value example:

```
<INPUT TYPE="radio" NAME="languageChoice"
          onClick="displayChoice()">
<IMG SRC="http://home.netscape.com">
```

Ellipses, a little-known Greek philosopher

When you see ellipses (…), you know that something's been left out. In the following HTML tag below, the ellipses indicate that multiple attribute-value pairs may be required. For example, the <INPUT> tag defines several attributes:

TYPE, NAME, VALUE, and SIZE. The <B> tag, however, doesn't define any. The ellipses shows you where to put a string of attribute-value pairs if they're necessary, and if they aren't necessary for the HTML tag you're defining, you can just skip them altogether.

As you've seen in many of the previous examples, you don't actually type the ellipses when you're constructing an HTML statement. Instead, you replace them (if necessary) with an attribute-value pair assignment (or two, or three, or however many attribute-value pair assignments are called for).

Ellipses syntax:

```
<TAG-NAME [ATTRIBUTE[="VALUE"]...]>[some text][</TAG-NAME>]
```

Ellipses example:

```
<B>This text will boldly display where no text has displayed
        before.</B>
```

The preceding little piggy had none — no attributes, that is.

```
<INPUT TYPE="text", NAME="petName", VALUE="Your pet\'s name
        here", SIZE=25>
```

You can define quite a few attributes for the <INPUT> tag, as you can see in the preceding.

Express yourself with text

For some HTML form elements you define, you'll want to specify some text to display on the page — usually right next to the element. Specifying text is optional, but in some cases (links, radio buttons, multiple selection fields) it's a darn good idea. How else will your users know what they're in for when they select a link or click on a radio button?

Text syntax:

```
<TAG-NAME [ATTRIBUTE[="VALUE"]...]>[some text][</TAG-NAME>]
```

Text example:

```
<A HREF="www.idgbooks.com"> IDG Books Worldwide, Inc.
```

```
<INPUT TYPE="radio" NAME="partyChoice" VALUE="dem"> Democrat
```

```
<SELECT NAME="party" MULTIPLE>
<OPTION> Democrat
<OPTION> Republican
<OPTION> Independent
</SELECT>
```

What they don't tell you in school: HTML tag gotchas

Okay, so you've got HTML syntax down cold. You understand how it works, and once you've seen a couple dozen examples (like the ones later in this chapter) your understanding will be reinforced and your confidence level will soar with the eagles.

There are just a few more tips I'd like to pass on to you before you leave HTML-land (okay, you never actually leave HTML-land, but you will start to take it for granted a chapter or two from now when you start to concentrate on JavaScript proper). This section lets you in on how the HTML interpreter views life, and reading it should make your life much easier when you begin building your own Web pages.

Spaced out

Make sure not to insert spaces between the characters that make up HTML tag names (or, for that matter, to run HTML keywords together by deleting spaces). The HTML interpreter is a very literal creature, and unexpected spacing throws it right off the old track, which means that you get stuck trying to decipher a goofy-looking page display. With practice, you'll soon be able to tell at a glance where spaces should and shouldn't go.

Right	*Wrong!*
`<HTML>`	`<  HTML   >`
`</TITLE>`	`</ TITLE>`
`<BODY>`	`<BODY  >`
`<INPUT TYPE="text">`	`<INPUTTYPE="text">`
`<FORM NAME="myForm">`	`<FORMNAME="myForm">`

Case in point

Although tag names and attributes can be uppercase or lowercase, writing them all in uppercase is a good idea. When tag names and attributes are all uppercased, they're easier to pick out when you're eyeballing a page of HTML source, and if all-uppercase ever becomes a requirement instead of just a standard (and it may), you're covered.

Right	*Wrong!*
`<HTML>`	`<Html>`
`</TITLE>`	`</title>`
`<INPUT TYPE="text">`	`<INPUT type="text">`
`<INPUT TYPE="text">`	`<INPUT Type="text">`

Double trouble

Make sure that you check not only that your angle brackets match (that is, a closing bracket for every opening bracket), but also that your beginning and ending tags (if appropriate) both exist. These errors are some of the most common ones that folks make when they begin writing HTML code. Count on getting bitten in the butt by these mistakes on a regular basis until your eye becomes accustomed to the way HTML statements are supposed to look. (It won't take too long, I promise!)

Always go forward; never go straight!

Every closing HTML tag contains a forward slash. Notice I didn't say "slash," I said "forward slash." There's a big difference, at least as far as the HTML interpreter is concerned. That means `</SCRIPT>` is acceptable, while `<\SCRIPT>` will earn you the electronic equivalent of a scolding every time.

Q: What do birds, squirrels, and HTML have in common? A: Nesting!

In HTML terms, the verb *to nest* refers to the ability of some HTML tags to enclose others. Here's an example:

```
<FORM>
<INPUT TYPE="text" NAME="age" SIZE=3>
</FORM>
```

In the code snippet above, you can see that the `<INPUT>` tag is nested inside the `<FORM>`...`</FORM>` tag. There are two things to be aware of regarding tag nesting in HTML:

- Some tags *can't* be nested.

  Tags like `<TITLE>`...`</TITLE>` can't surround other HTML tags. No way, no how. It just doesn't make sense, when you think about it — and when you know what the `<TITLE>`...`</TITLE>` tag's purpose in life is, which is to display a piece of text on the title bar of a window.

- Some tags *must* be nested.

  Any form element tag (`<INPUT>`, `<TEXTAREA>`...`</TEXTAREA>`, `<SELECT>` `</SELECT>`) must be nested inside an opening and closing `<FORM>`... `</FORM>` tag (where else would a form element go, if not inside a form definition?). If it's not, the HTML interpreter will completely ignore it, or otherwise behave in an unruly fashion (depending on where you ended up sticking it).

How do you sort it all out? How do you know how and where you can use what tags? Simple: by studying examples (this includes stealing code that you know works perfectly, which is covered in Chapter 20, and by looking up tags in HTML reference works (may I recommend *HTML for Dummies,* 2nd Edition?). For now, though, just be aware that some HTML tags need to be used in conjunction with others.

Seeing is believing: a real-life tag example

Examples are the best way to learn just about anything, so if you read the last section and it left you scratching your head, don't worry — the light bulb will click on in five or ten minutes, tops. First, take a look at the source code statements and then take a look at the top of Figure 3-1 to see how the source is interpreted.

```
<HTML>
<TITLE>JavaScript For Dummies Home Page</TITLE>
</HTML>
```

The following minitable explains what's going through the HTML interpreter's brain as it deciphers the three HTML statements in the preceding example:

When the HTML interpreter sees this...	It thinks this...
`<HTML>`	Time to go to work...
`<TITLE>`	Hmm, a title's coming; the next line should be text.
`JavaScript For Dummies Home Page`	Okay, I'll stick this text in the window's title area.
`</TITLE>`	Guess that's it for the title. What's next?
`</HTML>`	Cool! That was quick. Now I'll display the page.

The most popular HTML tags according to recent polls

Table 3-1 doesn't represent an exhaustive list of HTML tags; for that, I suggest one of the reference works listed in Chapter 1. This list *can* give you an idea of the kinds of things that you can do with HTML tags, though. Note that an ellipses (...) appears between tags that come in pairs, so you can tell at a glance that you need to specify both. Also note that some of these tags have additional elements that need to be defined before they can be used.

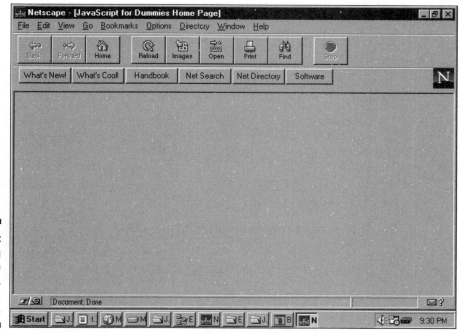

Figure 3-1:
Displaying
the
<TITLE>...
</TITLE>
HTML tag.

Table 3-1	Some HTML Tags
HTML Tag	*Description*
<!-...->	Surrounds a comment
<HTML>...</HTML>	Surrounds the entire HTML document (required)
<HEAD>...</HEAD>	Surrounds a document's header section
<BODY>...</BODY>	Surrounds a document's body section
<TITLE>...</TITLE>	Specifies a title label for the whole page
<H1>...</H1>	Specifies first-level heading
<H2>...</H2>	Specifies second-level heading
<A>...</A>	Specifies an anchor (a link)
 	Forces a line break
<IMG>	Inserts the referenced image into the page
<FORM>...</FORM>	Surrounds user input form area
<INPUT>	Defines type and appearance of input controls
<B>...</B>	Produces boldfaced text
<I>...</I>	Produces italicized text

Shoehorning JavaScript into HTML with the <SCRIPT> tag

Here's the moment you've been waiting for (drum roll, please!). The way you JavaScript-enable an HTML file is to use the `<SCRIPT>...</SCRIPT>` tag pair, as follows:

```
<SCRIPT LANGUAGE="JavaScript"> </SCRIPT>
```

The HTML file containing the code in Listing 3-1 is called list0301.htm.

Listing 3-1 shows a more complete example with an actual statement sandwiched between the `<SCRIPT>...</SCRIPT>` tags:

Listing 3-1:   My First JavaScript Script (first.htm)

```
<HTML>

<SCRIPT LANGUAGE="JavaScript">
alert("In JavaScript, wish you were here!")
</SCRIPT>

This text has nothing to do with JavaScript<BR>
whatsoever; it's plain old HTML text.

</HTML>
```

Is this exciting, or what? The line between the opening `<SCRIPT>` tag and the closing `</SCRIPT>` tag constitutes, all by itself, a JavaScript script. Granted, it's a small one; but hey, like the saying goes, a journey of 10,000 miles begins with a single step, and all that jazz. Once again, here's a sneak peek at what's going on in the HTML interpreter's mind when it encounters the HTML file first.htm (which is, of course, on your companion CD, so you can load it up and play around with it as you read along, if you like).

Heads or tails?

An HTML document is composed of a header (`<HEAD>...</HEAD>`) and a body (`<BODY>...</BODY>`). You can access the document's title and its base URL in the header section; everything else (all the other HTML elements for the document) must be placed, and can only be accessed, in the body section.

When the HTML interpreter sees this...	It thinks this...
`<HTML>`	Time to go to work...
`<SCRIPT LANGUAGE="JavaScript">`	Whoa! Not my job! Over to you, JavaScript! (JavaScript interpreter takes over, pops up a message.)
`alert("In JavaScript, wish you were here!")`	
`</SCRIPT>`	JavaScript interpreter: That's it for me — back to you, Chet.
`This text has nothing to do with JavaScript`	HTML interpreter: Hmm. Text. Okay, I'll display it...
` `	Followed by a line break.
`whatsoever; it's plain old HTML text.`	Followed by some more text.
`</HTML>`	Here's the page — I'm going back to my mah-jongg.

Form-Fitting

Forms are special HTML constructs that are destined to become near and dear to your heart. Bounded by the `<FORM>...</FORM>` tags, forms enable viewers of your Web pages to interact with you. Form elements (or form objects), as you find out in Chapter 2, include such things as checkboxes, text fields, push buttons, radio buttons, and so on. Of course, to make your form comprehensible to your viewer, you'll also want to add such things as a heading and some explanatory text to clue the viewer of your page in to what you expect, as shown in Figure 3-2.

Just in case you'd like to load the form pictured in Figure 3-2 and check out how it works, here's the URL:

```
http://203.17.138.90:80/./product/BUILD.HTM
```

It's a nice one, isn't it?

In the old days, if you had a Web page, the only way to do something useful with all the feedback that users were giving you was to bundle it up and pass it to something called a *CGI program* on a Web server. The CGI program — a full-blown computer program capable of validating input, computing values, accessing databases, and handling any other processing tasks necessary — would cogitate on the data for awhile and then, more than likely, pass back a

Figure 3-2:
Example
HTML form.

new and improved Web page to display to your user. With JavaScript, a great deal of the processing that you're likely to do can take place right on the user's machine. That means you may be able to escape learning CGI altogether (whew!) and in any case, you save

- ✔ Up-front time, because you don't have to go through the request process to get your CGI program installed on a Web server

- ✔ Execution (ouch!) time, because you don't have to send a message to the Web server each time you want to do your processing

Listing 3-2 shows the source code of an example that hooks a popular event (the user pressing a push button) to custom JavaScript code. You may want to load this up and try it out yourself (if so, the filename is list0302.htm), or perhaps just take a peek at Figure 3-3 in order to get a better understanding of what each of these statements is doing.

Listing 3-2: Accessing HTML Form Elements with JavaScript: Event Handlers

```
<HTML>
<HEAD>
<TITLE>Form object example</TITLE>
</HEAD>
<SCRIPT LANGUAGE="JavaScript">
```

```
function setCase (caseSelection) {
    if (caseSelection == "upper") {
        document.form1.firstName.value =
            document.form1.firstName.value.toUpperCase()
        document.form1.lastName.value =
            document.form1.lastName.value.toUpperCase()
    }
    else {
        document.form1.firstName.value =
            document.form1.firstName.value.toLowerCase()
        document.form1.lastName.value =
            document.form1.lastName.value.toLowerCase()
    }
}
</SCRIPT>
<BODY>
<FORM NAME="form1">
<B>First name:</B>
<INPUT TYPE="text" NAME="firstName" SIZE=20>
<BR><B>Last name:</B>
<INPUT TYPE="text" NAME="lastName" SIZE=20>
<P><INPUT TYPE="button" VALUE="Names to uppercase"
            NAME="upperButton"
    onClick="setCase('upper')">
<INPUT TYPE="button" VALUE="Names to lowercase"
            NAME="lowerButton"
    onClick="setCase('lower')">
</FORM>
</BODY>
</HTML>
```

Whooee! Nothing like trial by fire, is there? This probably looks really strange (and hard!) now, but trust me — it won't for long. For right now, just get familiar with the way a JavaScript script looks. You can read over it and see if it makes any sense to you intuitively, if you like, or you can load it up (it's on the companion CD) and play around with it. Or not — your choice! Like I said, though, don't sweat it if it doesn't make much sense to you now. In Chapters 4 and 5, each one of the statements you see in Listing 3-2 is pulled apart, examined, and explained.

Figure 3-3 shows you what the finished product looks like and is identical to what you'll see if you load list0302.htm, the HTML file for Listing 3-2, from the companion CD.

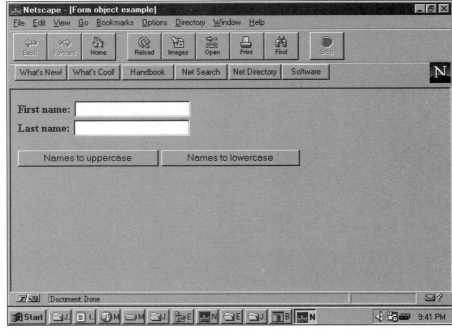

First Come, First Served

As you may expect, Navigator interprets and displays HTML statements sequentially, from left to right and top to bottom. Because in JavaScript you can't refer to something until it exists (oddly enough), defining any JavaScript functions that you may want to work with at the top of your file, in the header section, is important, so that those functions are available to the statements that come later in the file. You'll notice, for example, that in Listing 3-2 the custom function setCase() is defined near the top of the code, and it's called near the bottom. Chapter 4 contains a whole section on functions if you're a little fuzzy on what they're used for and how (and why) they're called. (Hint: it's *not* "Soooeee! Here, function! Come here, girl!")

In Hiding

Not only is Netscape Navigator the only generally available JavaScript-enabled browser on the market at the time of this writing, but it also boasts the lion's share of the total browser market (hmmm, think there might be a connection?). Other browsers, Microsoft's Internet Explorer in particular, are due out with JavaScript-enabled versions very soon (in the case of Internet Explorer, it may already be available by the time you read this). Quite a few browsers that aren't

JavaScript-enabled are out there, though, and will be for some time. This situation poses an interesting problem: What if you create a really great, gee-whiz JavaScript-enabled Web page — and somebody looks at it with a (gasp) character-oriented browser that can't even display *images*? Just what is this person going to see?

Hiding from non-JavaScript-enabled browsers: Sneaky 1

Unfortunately, a good chance exists that the viewer can see your JavaScript statements, just hanging out there in the breeze in the middle of the page. Oops! How tacky. A way to get around this dilemma exists, though, and it's pretty simple, too. If you surround *all* of your JavaScript statements with a beginning and ending HTML comment tag (Table 3-1, right at the top, contains an example of the comment tag), browsers that can't make heads or tails of them ignore them. JavaScript-enabled browsers, however, *should* pick them out and interpret them — business as usual. An example of the proper placement for these comments can be found in Listing 3-3. Notice that comment tags are inside the <SCRIPT>...</SCRIPT> tags and that each occupies its very own line. (That makes them easy to spot.)

Listing 3-3:   Hiding JavaScript Script from Non-JavaScript-Enabled Browsers

```
<HTML>

<SCRIPT LANGUAGE="JavaScript">
<!-- In hiding!
alert("In JavaScript, wish you were here!")
// -->
</SCRIPT>

This text has nothing to do with JavaScript<BR>
whatsoever; it's plain old HTML text.

</HTML>
```

The ultra-alert among you may be wondering if the lines that start with comment tags in the code above contain typos. After all, you clearly remember that in Table 3-1, the HTML comment tag looked like this: <!-...-> (only one hyphen on each side), not like this: <!--...//--> (two hyphens on each side and a couple of slashes to boot).

Well, there's nothing wrong with your memory, but the code snippet in Listing 3-3 is perfectly legit. Why? Because the comment tags aren't HTML comment tags at all — they're JavaScript comment tags. You know this because they're inside <SCRIPT>...</SCRIPT> tags, and anything inside a <SCRIPT>...</SCRIPT> tag must be a scripting statement. I know, I know, it's a stupid coincidence that they're so similar—it's easy to make a mistake and type one where you really meant to type the other. That's where the template on the companion CD (templ1.htm) comes in handy; it already contains the special "hiding" comment lines, so you never have to type them in yourself!

Keep in mind that even though folks with other browsers may not be able to see your gunky source if you surround it with HTML comment tags, they *still* won't be seeing what folks with JavaScript-enabled browsers are getting to see. If it's important to you that everyone have equal access to your splendid Web page with its highly original layout and thought-provoking content, consider investing some time perusing *Creating Web Pages For Dummies* by Bud Smith and Arthur Bebak (published by IDG Books Worldwide, Inc.). (You may be glad that you did!)

Hiding from JavaScript-enabled browsers: Sneaky II

Unfortunately (or fortunately, depending on how you look at it), even if your source doesn't splash on the screen, folks can still get access to it. How? The same way that *you* get access to *their* source code — by selecting View⇨Document Source from the Navigator menu (or, if you're running Internet Explorer, by selecting View⇨Source). If you want to nip this kind of information-sharing, tree-hugging free-for-all in the bud, separate your JavaScript statements from the rest of your HTML statements and put them in a separate file with a js extension. Then, in the <SCRIPT>...</SCRIPT> tag, specify the name of the source file, like this:

```
<SCRIPT LANGUAGE="JavaScript" SRC="http://www.mydomain.com/
          myscript.js">
</SCRIPT>
```

Consider, however, that just because you *can* do this doesn't mean you *have* to do it. Unless there's some million-dollar, patent-pending secret in your source, why not let others who are interested take a look?

Chapter 4

Object-Oriented Concepts

● ●

In This Chapter

▶ Exploring object-oriented analysis and design

▶ Defining object-oriented terms

▶ Accessing object properties

▶ Executing methods, functions, and event handlers

● ●

*J*avaScript is an *object-based language.* Even if you don't have much computer programming experience under your belt, I think that you'll find that this approach is pretty intuitive — even more so than the traditional *procedural approach,* where everything happens sequentially. Object-based languages still do *some* things procedurally; the procedural approach comes in very handy, and there's no point in throwing the baby out with the bathwater (so to speak). But by and large, object-based development is significantly different from the programming that people were doing thirty years ago.

A slight (but very important, if you're interested in such things) difference exists between *object-oriented* languages and *object-based* languages. The primary difference is that object-oriented languages support inheritance, and object-based languages don't. Inheritance in this case has nothing to do with an unexpected windfall. *Inheritance* refers to the ability of you, the programmer, to *derive* (or *inherit*) your own custom classes (a *class* is a category, or type, of object) from existing classes.

For example, in an object-oriented language like C++ or Smalltalk, if you have a class of objects called *employee,* you can inherit from it to define a new class called *part-time employee.* But because JavaScript is object-based and not object-oriented, you can use its built-in objects (all of which are detailed in Chapter 10), and you can create brand-new ones — but you can't create new *types* of objects based on the ones that you're given.

The top ten object-oriented definitions

10. **object:** In the real world, any thing, idea, or concept is an object. Any real-world object can be modeled in JavaScript. Think noun.

9. **attribute:** Sometimes called a property, an attribute is a one-word description of an object. Think adjective.

8. **method:** Sometimes called a behavior, a method is an action that a particular object can perform. Think verb.

7. **function:** A named series of JavaScript statements that can be performed all at once simply by calling the name of the function.

6. **event handler:** A special kind of method associated with certain objects that is called automatically (by the JavaScript interpreter) when an event involving that object occurs.

5. **object model:** A group of objects that work together for a common purpose. The JavaScript object model is an example; the purpose of its objects is to provide Web-building capability.

4. **use case:** A detailed description of a scenario that a system (like a Web page) needs to be able to handle.

3. **object-oriented:** Used to describe a programming language (or approach to analysis and design) that supports modeling real-world objects as accurately as possible in software terms. True object-oriented languages support both polymorphism and inheritance.

2. **object-based:** Very close to object-oriented, except not all of the defining object-oriented characteristics are supported. JavaScript is an object-based language (it doesn't support inheritance).

And the number one object-oriented definition:

1. **polymorphism:** (Greek for "many morphs.") The ability of multiple objects to respond to exactly the same method (like "speak") in different ways ("yell," "chirp," "bark," "whisper," and soon).

Objects Defined

An *object* can be anything — literally. Any person, place, thing, or idea (hey, sounds like a noun, doesn't it?!) can be an object. That's because *objects* are nothing more than computer representations of real-world things. So asking someone to describe what an object is is like asking "How high is up?" The answer to either question is, "It all depends."

Even so, software objects (just like real-world objects) have characteristics and behaviors that you can define that tell us all anyone needs to know about them. Of course, because this is a computer topic, we can't call these bits of information *characteristics* and *behaviors.* No, that would take all the fun out of it. Programmers call characteristics *properties* (or *attributes*) and behaviors *methods.* Properties and attributes are really the same thing, but JavaScript programmers tend to differentiate between properties (which belong to JavaScript objects) and attributes (which are associated with HTML objects). (Don't ask me why — I just work here!)

And to continue with the English parts-of-speech example wherein objects equate to nouns, thinking of properties as adjectives and methods as verbs may help. Now, isn't that simple?

Take a look at Table 4-1 to see examples of some definitions of everyday objects. You may create your own objects soon, so take good notes!

Table 4-1	Example Object Definitions	
Object (noun)	*Property (adjective)*	*Method (verb)*
dog	black	run
	Australian shepherd	bark
	furry	bite
	...	...
customer	name	change address
	address	change name
	credit history	place order
	...	...
order form	title	open
	text input field	close
	submit button	submit
	...	...

After you've finished defining an object (which you do by creating custom JavaScript functions, as explained in Chapter 8), you know exactly what the object is (its name), what it's like (its properties), and what it can do (its methods).

You don't have to create your own objects; for lots of Web pages, the built-in ones will do you just fine. For some pages, though, you'll find yourself wanting to *model* (express in JavaScript statements) the conceptual elements of your Web page in object terms. It'll just pop right out and hit you on the head!

For example: say you're creating a Web page that people can use to purchase your stuffed armadillos (cloth ones, not real ones!). For argument's sake, assume that certain states and countries impose certain restrictions on purchase of said armadillos. California law might require you to charge sales tax, Canada might ban the import of the armadillos altogether, and so on. Well, you think of California and Canada as separate entities, right? Why not model them that way? Why not create, with custom functions, JavaScript objects called California and Canada that each contain the properties and methods particular to the way these jurisdictions affect your business?

Again, there's no law that says you have to create your own JavaScript objects, or that if you do, that you have to do it a certain way. Let's face it: people approach problems differently, and any objects you create to help you build a Web page are correct if they make sense to you. (And don't let anyone tell you any differently!) Just be aware that JavaScript gives you the ability to create your own objects if and when you want to.

Object Models Always Pose Nude

No object is an island unto itself. Think about it: almost every task you can name involves multiple things working together to accomplish it. Well, just like in the real world, software objects can also work together to solve problems. A group of objects that work together is called an *object model*. An example of an object model for an insurance firm may include objects named *customer, policy, agent,* and *underwriter.* Together, all of the objects in the object model represent all the real-world things that have to interact to get something done (to sell an insurance policy to a customer, to pay the agent who sold the policy, to consult with the underwriter to determine policy terms, and so on).

Whoa, there, pardner!

When you create a JavaScript representation of an object (like a dog, a customer, or an order form) via a custom function, it's called *modeling the real-world object in JavaScript.* (I think the term *modeling* comes from statistics, which is a discipline where people are always modeling something or other with really long, indecipherable mathematical equations. Not being particularly handy with statistical formulas, though, I like to think of it in terms of sculpture instead — you know, picturing a little clay model of a dog, or a customer, or whatever, that's easy to work with and manipulate.)

As you begin to model your own objects in JavaScript, it's important to remember that real-world objects need only be modeled if doing so helps you solve the particular problem at hand.

For example, if you've defined a "customer" object for your Web page, you probably need to keep track of the name, address, amount ordered, and payment method for each customer, but you probably *don't* need to model what the customer's favorite flavor of ice cream is (unless you happen to be an ice-cream retail chain!).

Object-oriented analysis and design is so powerful that going hog-wild and modeling everything that exists just because you can is tempting, so try to think of object-oriented analysis and design as an all-you-can-eat buffet: Take all you want, but eat all you take (that is, model everything you need to model, but don't bother modeling things that aren't really necessary for you to use to describe the piece of the world that matters for your application).

If you're creating a Web page and find yourself doing lots and lots of JavaScript calculations (the kind you see in Chapter 5), you, my friend, are programming. (If you're doing tons of calculations, and you plan to have several connected Web pages, you're programming a — sharp intake of breath — Web application!) Sometimes your JavaScript scripts will be short and sweet, with very little logic in them at all, and if that's the case, you really don't need an object model. But if you are programming a good-sized Web page, there's a distinct possibility that the best way to organize your programming (JavaScript) statements is with an object model — a group of objects that you can use to simplify your programming logic.

For example, in Listing 4-1, two objects have been defined: state, and taxTable. In this scenario, a taxTable object contains a list of five state objects. Each state object, in turn, contains the two-digit name of the state and that state's tax percentage. Together, these objects constitute an object model, because they work together to provide a solution — namely, to calculate the sales tax for an order based on the buyer's residence.

Listing 4-1:   Example Object Model Implementation in JavaScript

```
...
...
function state(state, tax){
    this.state=state // fill in each state's name
    this.tax=tax     // fill in each state's tax percentage
}

function taxTable(){
    this[0]=new state("AZ", 1.23) // first taxTable object
    this[1]=new state("CA", 2.24) // second taxTable object
    this[2]=new state("TX", 7.50) // third taxTable object
    this[3]=new state("WA", 8.01) // fourth taxTable object
    this[4]=new state("NY", 0.54) // fifth taxTable object
}
...
...
<BODY onLoad="taxGuide = new taxTable()">
```

See the last line in the listing, the one that starts <BODY onLoad...>? Well, that's the statement that creates the taxTable and state objects. As soon as a user loads this HTML file (see the onLoad event handler on that same line?) JavaScript creates a new taxTable object and names it taxGuide. It does this by executing the function called taxTable(), and when it gets to the first line of the taxTable() function, it sees it has to create a state, so it does this — by hopping up to the state() function and performing the statements it finds there. This process is repeated five times for a total of five states.

The code snippet in Listing 4-1 was taken from list0808.htm. Load it up and take a look!

Object-Oriented Analysis and Design: If You Thought Dissecting Frogs Was Fun, You'll Love This!

Object-oriented analysis and design is the formal term for "figuring out what objects you should create in JavaScript and how they should look," and there are as many ways to approach it as there are to cut an onion. (I can see the cooks among you nodding knowingly.) But the approach that makes the most sense to me (and it's not just my opinion, either; it's caught on very rapidly in the last few years) is to follow some rough version of the following:

1. **Begin with the overall goal that you want to accomplish, and describe it in detail.**

   It's important to get a good, solid grip on what it is you want your Web page to do. What's its purpose? What does it have to keep track of, display, and so forth?

2. **After you have a handle on what you want to achieve, break the goal up into its constituent parts (that is, into several different *use cases*), and define each one in as much detail as possible.**

   This is where you get specific. You're after concrete items here, not vague generalities — for example, "keeping track of orders" is general; it's important, but it's part of Step 1. "Produce an invoice for each order" and "subtract each order from in-stock inventory levels" is more concrete, and it's this type of concrete action that you want to define in this step. The more details, the better, because your use cases are your working blueprints for the rest of the process.

3. **Look at your descriptions (hopefully you wrote everything down!) and pick out all the nouns.**

4. **Write the nouns in one column with a great deal of space around them.**

   These nouns represent your first stab at defining your object model.

5. **Then look at all the related adjectives and verbs and write them next to the noun they go with.**

   This action fleshes out your object model with properties and methods.

6. **Go over real-life examples of use cases with real data to make sure that you haven't missed anything by over-generalizing.**

   Try poking real instances into your model. For example, say you decided that one of your use cases was "A visitor to my Web site orders some of my world-famous Jell-O cookbooks and pays with a credit card." Fine! Now make up a pretend person (call him Bob), and pretend that you're Bob and that you're actually buying six of your own cookbooks. Will the object model you defined in Step 5 support your purchase? Or did you forget to model something crucial, like a credit card expiration date?

What do you want to do?

Pretend for a moment that you're in charge of writing a Web application to handle animal inventories for a public zoo (you're putting it on the Web so other zoos and zoo patrons can have easy access to it). Here's how you might tackle the problem, based on the steps outlined previously:

First, begin with the overall goal that you want to accomplish, and describe it in detail:

Overall goal: handle animal inventories

Handling animal inventories involves the following:

A) You want to be able to track each animal from its point of origin to the specific exhibit housing it.

B) Because keeping the animals healthy is very important, you need to be able to catalog

i) how each animal behaves and

ii) what it typically eats

so if the animal's behavior changes in any way, you have something to compare the changes to.

Okay, exactly what do you want to do?

After you have a handle on what you want to achieve, break the goal up into its constituent parts (that is, into several different use cases), and define each one in as much detail as possible.

A) **Use case number one**: You need to print a report for the zookeeper to take on her daily rounds. For each animal, the following information must be listed:

i) Exhibit number

ii) Type of animal and identifying number

iii) How the animal normally moves

iv) How the animal normally sounds

B) **Use case number two**: You need to print a quarterly report for environmental purposes that shows the following:

i) Type of animal and identifying number

ii) Where the animal lived previously

iii) How many offspring the animal has produced

Shake out the nouns

Next, look at your description and pick out all the nouns, adjectives, and verbs. These are your objects, properties, and methods. An example following from the preceding description is described in Table 4-2.

Table 4-2	Animal Inventory Object Model	
Objects (nouns)	*Properties (adjectives)*	*Methods (verbs)*
animal	species	move
	identification number	make noise
	point of origin	
	number of offspring	
	diet	
	exhibit number	

Get real!

Finally, go over real-life examples of use cases with real data to make sure that you haven't missed anything by over-generalizing. Table 4-3 lists two real-life examples.

If you notice that any two or more objects are suspiciously similar, you can group the objects together and define a *class* of objects.

Table 4-3	Animal Inventory Object Model with Two Examples	
Objects (nouns)	*Properties (adjectives)*	*Methods (verbs)*
animal: elephant	species: *Loxodonta africana*	move: lumber
	identification number: E-123	make noise: trumpet
	point of origin: Africa	
	number of offspring: 1	
	diet: hay	
	exhibit number: 45	

(continued)

Table 4-3 *(continued)*

Objects (nouns)	Properties (adjectives)	Methods (verbs)
animal: mouse	species: *Mus musculus*	move: scamper
	identification number: M-545	make noise: squeak
	point of origin: Mongolia	
	number of offspring: 23	
	diet: seeds	
	exhibit number: 12	

As you can see by the preceding table, both of these objects (the elephant object and the mouse object) have nearly identical properties and methods. Of course, the *values* for their properties are different (hay versus seeds), and the *results* of their behaviors are different (one trumpets, the other squeaks); these differences are what make elephants and mice different. But the *kind* of information we want to keep about these two entities is identical, except for the name.

Instead of having two objects (one called *elephant* and one called *mouse*), you can design one class of object called *animal*. Then you can add one more property (called *name*) to the animal class. Voilà! If you understand this concept — abstracting particular examples of animals (E-123 and M-545) into a type, or class, called *animal* — then you, my friend, understand object technology. All the rest is gravy.

The elephant as object

To recap, this is what our elephant object looks like:

Its class is *animal*, and its name is *elephant*. If you ask the elephant to tell you its species, it answers, *"Loxodonta africana."* If you ask the elephant to move, it lumbers — to make noise, it trumpets.

Be polite

Asking, or telling, objects to do something (I prefer to ask because telling is just plain rude!) is actually common nomenclature among object programmers. Asking an object to do something is a little different from asking a real-world object to do something (yelling "Yo! Dumbo! Speak to me!" rarely works on a software elephant, for example), but it's still pretty easy. Check the section called Methods Defined in this chapter if you're just dying to know how to ask an object to do something.

The mouse as object

The mouse belongs to the animal class, too. If you ask the mouse to tell you its species, it answers, *"Mus musculus."* If you ask the mouse to move, it scampers — to make noise, it squeaks.

A special term is used for the fact that we can say the same thing (make noise) to two different objects (the elephant and the mouse) and get two different answers (trumpet and squeak). The term is *polymorphism,* and it's one of the defining characteristics of object-oriented languages.

Some JavaScript objects

In addition to being able to create your own objects, you can also use any of the built-in JavaScript objects (forms, list boxes, push buttons, and so on).

You can find an exhaustive list of JavaScript objects in Chapter 10. For now, just be aware that the JavaScript designers figured out almost everything a script author would want to do to develop really great interactive Web pages. From the descriptions the designers came up with, they isolated some 20-odd objects that work together (the JavaScript object model) to create these Web pages. Each object contains some properties that describe how it looks as well as some methods that describe how it can act and react. Using these built-in objects will save you tons of time, and if you need one that doesn't already exist, you can create it yourself!

Properties Defined

Properties are attributes that describe an object. Every object that has a property defined for it has a corresponding *value* for that property. For example, if an object's property is `color`, the value for that property may be *red*. If an object's property is `age`, the value for that property may be *29*. If an object's property is `firstName`, its corresponding value may be *Jorge* — and so on. Even built-in objects have properties. For instance, an input field, or `text` object, has the following properties: `name`, `value`, and `defaultValue`.

A property value can be empty (otherwise known as *null)* depending on the situation. If you created a form that defined an input text field called "Spouse," for example, and an unmarried person filled out the form, that person's entry for this field would legitimately be blank. Interestingly enough, null all by itself is considered to be a value in technical circles (pretty Zen-like, huh?).

Are property values going up? Find out by accessing an object's property values

To access the value of a particular object's property in a JavaScript statement, you need to remember to specify the object first, then the name of the property, and then the word *value,* like so:

```
document.myForm.firstName.value
```

This syntax denotes that you're interested in the value of the property called `firstName` contained in the form named `myForm`, which itself is contained in the document `document`.

Most of the time, you'll be accessing property values in your scripts in order to look at them and make a decision. For example, it's quite common to want to examine a value and see if there's anything in it (perhaps your form has a space for e-mail address and you want to make sure that your user enters one). In this case, your JavaScript statement would look something like this:

```
if (document.myForm.emailAddress.value == "") { // it's
            blank!
    alert("Please enter an e-mail address.") //pop up a
            message
}
```

Properties of JavaScript objects

Most of the objects available in JavaScript have their own set of properties; some, like the anchor object, have no properties at all. (Chapter 11 contains a listing of JavaScript properties arranged alphabetically.)

Methods Defined

A *method* by any other name (some programmers call them *behaviors* or *member functions*) is a special sort of function that applies only to an object. A method's name is generally a verb that describes something that object can do.

Take, for example, your soon-to-be old friend the push button. The name of the object is `button`, and it only has one method defined for it – the `click()` method. (That's because clicking a button is pretty much all you can do to it!)

On the other hand, you can do lots of things to the built-in `form` object: you can clear a form (with its `clear()` method), write something on a form (with its `write()` and `writeln()` methods) — even open or close a form (`open()` and `close()` methods, respectively).

Calling all methods

The way that you *call* a method (*calling* means triggering a method in order to make JavaScript perform it) is slightly different than the way that you access the property value of an object. To call a method, you first specify the name of the object you're referring to; then you specify the name of the object's method followed by two parentheses (`()`). Within the parentheses go any parameters the method may require.

For example: say that you're creating a Web page, and you want your users to type in their names so you can customize all of your messages to them (you know, "Well, Tom, I see that you neglected to choose a payment method. Shall I bill you directly?"). Say also that you'd really like to emphasize the user's name: you'd like to make it blink on an off, perhaps. Here's how your JavaScript statement might look:

```
alert("Well, "
    + document.myForm.firstName.blink()
    + ", I see that you neglected to choose a "
    + "payment method. Shall I bill you directly?")
```

This syntax calls the `string` object's `blink()` method (the text field `firstName` contains a string in this case). `firstName` is a text object in the form `myForm`, which is itself located inside the Web `document`. Notice that the `blink()` method doesn't take any arguments; a blink is a blink, and that's that.

Unlike the `blink()` method, some methods do require arguments (sometimes referred to as *parameters*). Case in point: the document's `write()` method lets you write, or display, text anywhere in a document. You pass it the text you want to display as an argument (In this case, the text is "I sure do love JavaScript!"), and it does the rest. Take a look:

```
document.write("I sure do love JavaScript!")
```

Methods of JavaScript objects

Most of the objects available in JavaScript have their own set of methods. There are so many (let's see… 20 objects, each object has a handful or so… that's a lot!) that an entire chapter — Chapter 12 — is devoted exclusively to them.

Functions Defined

Functions are just like methods, except that functions don't *belong* to any particular JavaScript object. Think of a function as a named clump of JavaScript statements that together do a specific thing — say, calculate a total, display a message, or what have you.

When the JavaScript interpreter sees a function definition (you get to see exactly how to define a function in the next section) it loads the function's statements, but it doesn't do anything with them; it just keeps them on hand in case some JavaScript statement later in the file calls the function (*calling* is sometimes referred to as *executing* or *invoking*). Then, when a JavaScript statement calls the function, the JavaScript interpreter swings into action and performs all of the function's statements.

There are two basic types of functions:

 ✔ Built-in functions, which JavaScript defines for you
 ✔ Custom functions, which you have to define yourself

Calling all functions

The only difference between calling a function and calling a method is that because functions aren't attached to objects, there's no object for you to specify when you call a function. Here's an example demonstrating the built-in function called eval:

```
var total, price, numberOrdered, tax
price = 100
numberOrdered = 3
tax = 1.08

total = eval("price * numberOrdered * tax")
```

Don't worry if you see some symbols that aren't familiar to you: all of them (=, ", and *) are described in detail in Chapter 5. All you need to notice about the code snippet above for now is the last line. See how the eval() function is being called? It's being passed one argument ("price * numberOrdered * tax") which is surrounded by parentheses, just the way you'd pass an argument to a method.

Unlike the way you'd call a method, though — which is to say, preceded by a dot and the method's object (remember document.write()?) — you call a function just with its own name, like this: eval().

In addition to using built-in JavaScript functions, you can, and probably will, define your own functions. Functions are a nice way to organize your script into easy-to-manage, reusable chunks. You generally want to define your functions in the header section of your script so they are available to the rest of your script. Listing 4-2 is an example of a programmer-defined, or *custom*, function.

Listing 4-2:   Programmer-Defined JavaScript Function

```
...
...
<SCRIPT LANGUAGE="JavaScript>

function setCase (caseSelection) {
    if (caseSelection == "upper"){
            document.form1.firstName.value =
            document.form1.firstName.value.toUpperCase()
            document.form1.lastName.value =
            document.form1.lastName.value.toUpperCase()
    }
    else {
            document.form1.firstName.value =
            document.form1.firstName.value.toLowerCase()
            document.form1.lastName.value =
            document.form1.lastName.value.toLowerCase()
    }
}
</SCRIPT>
```

The custom function begins on the line that starts `function setCase (caseSelection) {`, and it ends on the line right before `</SCRIPT>`. Don't feel you have to understand everything that's going on in this function; for now, just understand that

- ✔ You define a function inside the `<SCRIPT>`...`</SCRIPT>` tags
- ✔ You let the JavaScript interpreter know a function is coming up by starting it with the special JavaScript keyword `function`, and
- ✔ You can do whatever you like in between

If you're thirsty for knowledge and can't stand not knowing all the nitty-gritty syntax details that you need to follow when you create functions, take a peek at Chapter 5 — they're all there, in living color.

The code snippet in Listing 4-2 was taken from list0707.htm on the companion CD. Check it out!

What's an ASCII? A Hawaiian flower?

Some of the terms in Table 4-4 won't have any relevance to your life until you go to try to use one of the built-in functions (which probably won't be until you're a fairly seasoned JavaScript jockey) — for example, ASCII, float value, and integer value. My motto is, don't clutter up your brain unless there's a darn good reason! So if you're not planning to use one of the functions in Table 4-4 in the next 24-hour period, please feel free to blow off the fact that you don't know what these terms mean. If you are, though, by all means flip to Chapter 13 right away!

Some JavaScript functions

Table 4-4 contains a list of all of the built-in JavaScript functions (there aren't many, are there?):

Table 4-4	Built-in JavaScript Functions
Function	*Purpose*
escape	returns the ASCII representation of the argument sent to it
eval	evaluates an expression
isNaN	evaluates an argument to determine if it's "Not a Number"
parseFloat	accepts a string and returns a float value
parseInt	accepts a string and returns an integer value
unescape	the opposite of escape

Notice that all of these functions, like many methods, return values. (Generally you want to capture the returned value in a variable for use in subsequent computations or display.)

Event Handlers Defined

An *event handler* is a piece of code that (you guessed it!) handles events. When you, as a script author, want to do something that is based on a user event (and you will, because that's where all the fun is), you need to decide two things: what events you care about and what you want to do when they occur. An event handler is attached to any object that a user can potentially interact with (a button, an input text field, a link, and so on). Event handlers are invoked when the event they're set up to handle occurs.

Calling all event handlers

Because event handlers are the software equivalent of bungee cords that are tying events to event-handling functions, you may think that you'd call event handlers in the same way that you'd call any old function, and you'd be right (as you can see from the code in Listing 4-3).

Listing 4-3:   Event Handling in JavaScript

```
...
<SCRIPT>
function setCase (caseSelection) {
    if (caseSelection == "upper") {
        // some code to change the input value to upper case
    }
    else {
        // some code to change the input value to lower case
    }
}
</SCRIPT>
...

<P><INPUT TYPE="button" VALUE="Names to uppercase"
          NAME="upperButton" onClick="setCase('upper')">
<INPUT TYPE="button" VALUE="Names to lowercase"
          NAME="lowerButton" onClick="setCase('lower')">
```

Take a look at the code snippet in Listing 4-3. Do you see where the two buttons are defined near the bottom (one is named *upperButton* and the other is named *lowerButton*)? Each of the these buttons has one event handler associated with it: the onClick event handler. The onClick event handler tells the JavaScript interpreter that when that particular button is clicked, it should call the setCase() function. For example, if a user clicks the push button named *upperButton*, JavaScript will call setCase() and pass it the value 'upper', like this: setCase('upper'). If a user clicks on *lowerButton*, JavaScript will call setCase() and pass it 'lower', like this: setCase('lower').

Event handling is a wonderful thing! With it you can figure out when and precisely how a user interacts with any part of your Web page, and you can respond to that action as you see fit.

Some JavaScript event handlers

All of the event handlers that JavaScript supports, along with the events that they respond to, are listed in Table 4-5.

Table 4-5	JavaScript Event Handlers
Event handler	*Event*
onBlur	a form element loses focus
onChange	a user interacts with a form element
onClick	an element on a form is clicked
onFocus	a form element receives focus
onLoad	Navigator finishes loading a page
onMouseOver	the mouse pointer moves over an element
onSelect	a user selects some text
onSubmit	a user submits a form
onUnload	a user exits a page

Event handlers don't respond to events on *all* form elements, just on those that make sense. See Chapter 14 for a complete list of all event handlers grouped alphabetically and by object.

Chapter 5

JavaScript Language Overview: A Bird's Eye View

*A*s computer languages go, JavaScript is pretty manageable. Okay, you probably can't write the entire language out on the head of a pin, but it's not exactly French, either! All you really need to know are the few basics covered in this chapter, which include

✔ The words in the JavaScript language (valid JavaScript words are the names of objects, methods, properties, variables, and special words called *keywords*)

✔ The punctuation marks JavaScript requires (called *operators*)

✔ How to put words and punctuation together to make complete statements that JavaScript can understand and perform for you

Making a Statement

Statements in JavaScript are just like statements in English: Rules govern parts of speech, punctuation, and syntax, and both JavaScript statements and English sentences are supposed to express a complete thought. Although English statements are made up of words and phrases, JavaScript statements are composed of a combination of expressions, variables, operators, and keywords, all of which are described in detail later in this chapter.

Take a look at a few typical JavaScript statements:

```
alert("Please verify that the following is correct.  You"
     + " have ordered " +
     document.myForm.numberOrders.value +
     " items, at " +
     price +
     "per item.  Do you want to continue?")

if (document.myForm.firstName = "") { displayError() }

onClick="validateFormData(); alert('Submitting the form
         now.');  document.myForm.submit()"
```

Statements can span multiple lines in a script file if they're very long, or they can be bunched together on one line if they're small. If you choose to put more than one statement on a line, though (and frankly, it doesn't do much for the readability of your script), you need to separate the statements with semicolons. Statements that flow onto more than one line don't require any special punctuation, though.

Expressing Yourself

Defining an expression, like defining an English phrase, covers a pretty broad territory. In general, a JavaScript *expression* is made up of *operators* (operators, like + and -, are covered in detail later in this chapter) and *operands* (variables and numbers) that together can be evaluated by the JavaScript interpreter. For example, take a look at the following expressions:

```
new Date()

666 + (123 * 79) + (myAge)

document.myForm.mood.value + " to see you, " +
    document.myForm.yourName.value
```

The three preceding examples are each slightly different, but they all have one thing in common: They can all be evaluated to something. The first example evaluates to a date; the second, to a number (and no, I'm not telling you what that number is!); the third, to a string. That's what an expression is: It's something that can be evaluated by the JavaScript interpreter, and that something can comprise numbers, operators (more on those later on in this chapter), strings, and what have you.

Don't keep your comments to yourself

A *comment* written by a script author isn't interpreted by the JavaScript interpreter; the comment is ignored. Comments are a very useful way, though, to explain things to human readers of your script. (Include yourself in this category, by the way — after you've finished a script and put it aside for a couple of months, you may appreciate those comments yourself!)

You can write comments in two different ways, and either type of comment can appear anywhere — as many times as you like — in your script.

The first type of comment is a single-line comment. It begins with two forward slashes, and it's only good for one line. The second type of comment is a multiple-line comment, and since it spans multiple lines, you have to tell it where to start (you do this with a forward slash followed by an asterisk) and where to end (you do this with an asterisk and then a forward slash). For example:

```
// Single-line comments don't require an ending slash.
/* This comment can span multiple lines.  Always remember to
       close it off, though; if you forget, you'll get
       weird errors when you try to display your script.
       */
```

Remember that JavaScript scripts are the lines that come between the `<SCRIPT>...</SCRIPT>` tags in an HTML file. The HTML comment characters (`<!-` to begin a comment line and `->` to end it) should be used when you want to put comments in your HTML file anywhere *outside* of the JavaScript tags' boundaries.

Mint condition: if...else

The if...else (also called the *conditional*) expression is used to test a condition, which is often another expression (try saying *that* three times fast!). If the condition is true, all the statements that follow the if clause are executed. If the condition is false, all the statements that follow the else clause (if the else clause exists) are executed. Here's the generic description of how to use if...else:

```
if (condition) {
    statements
}
[ else {
    statements
}]
```

The square brackets ([and]) mean that the entire else clause is completely optional. You don't actually put the square brackets in your JavaScript code; you just add the else clause if you want it, or leave it off if you don't. Listing 5-1 shows if...else in action.

Listing 5-1:   JavaScript if...else **Example**

```
if (caseSelection == "upper"){
    document.form1.firstName.value =
        document.form1.firstName.value.toUpperCase()
    document.form1.lastName.value =
        document.form1.lastName.value.toUpperCase()
}
else {
document.form1.firstName.value =
        document.form1.firstName.value.toLowerCase()
    document.form1.lastName.value =
        document.form1.lastName.value.toLowerCase()
}
```

var *(that's variable to you, bud!)*

A *variable* is a named placeholder for a value. Use the var keyword to construct an expression that first declares a variable and then (optionally) initializes its value. To declare a variable, you type something like this:

```
var myCat // variable names can be anything you want
```

This tells the JavaScript interpreter, "Yo, here comes a variable, and name it myCat, will you?"

Initializing a variable means setting a variable equal to some value, which is typically done at the same time you declare it. Here's how you might initialize the variable myCat:

```
var myCat = "Fluffy"
```

After you declare a variable, you can reset its value later in the script by using the assignment operator (=). The name of the variable can be any legal identifier (you want to use letters and numbers, not special characters), and the value can be any legal expression. (A legal expression is any properly punctuated expression that you see represented in this chapter: an if...else expression, a logical expression, and so on.)

A variable is only valid when it's *in scope*. When a variable is in scope, that means it's been declared between the same curly brace boundaries as the statement that's trying to access it.

For example, if you define a variable named firstName inside a function called displayReport(), you can only refer to it inside displayReport()'s curly braces. If you try to use it from inside another function, you'll get an error. If you want to reuse a variable *among* functions (shudder — that way lies madness), you can declare it near the top of your script, before any functions are declared. That way, the variable's scope is the entire script, and all the functions get to "see" it. Take a look at the code example below:

```
...
function displayReport() {
    var firstName = document.myForm.givenName.value

    ...
    alert("Click OK to see the report for " + firstName)
    // Using firstName here is fine; it was declared
    // inside the same set of curly braces.
    ...
}
function displayGraph() {
    alert("Here's the graph for " + firstName) // Error!
      // firstName wasn't defined inside this
      // function's curly braces!
    ...
}
```

As you can see from the comments in the code fragment above, it's perfectly okay to use firstName inside the displayReport() function; firstName is in scope anywhere at all inside displayReport(). It's not okay, however, to use firstName inside displayGraph(). As far as displayGraph() is concerned, no such animal as firstName has been declared inside its scope!

Why, I declare! (functions, that is)

A function declaration requires the function keyword. You'll probably write a great many functions; they're a very good way to organize your script statements into discrete little chunks that each do something specific (instead of having one huge script with dozens of lines, one right after another). Think of a function as a named bundle of JavaScript statements that can be used over and over again just by calling the name of the function.

Organizing your script into functions, like organizing your closet, can seem like a great deal of up-front work for nothing — after all, you don't *have* to. Your script (and your closet) will work as designed, even if they're a mess. The payoff comes when you have a problem (or the perfect brown leather belt) hiding somewhere in all that confusion and you want to find it in a hurry!

Here's the syntax for a function declaration, followed by an example:

```
function name([parameter] [, parameter] [..., parameter]) {
    statements
}
```

```
function calculateTotal(numberOrdered, itemPrice) {
    var result = numberOrdered * itemPrice
    return result
}
```

Your function can take as many arguments as you want it to (including none at all), separated by commas. You generally refer to these argument values in the body of the function (otherwise, why bother to use them at all?), so be sure to name them something meaningful.

Okay, you've seen how a function is declared. Now I'll bet you'd like to see how it's called — and I'd like to oblige you! Here's one way to call calculateTotal() from somewhere else in your script:

```
...
function calculateTotal(numberOrdered, itemPrice) {
    var result = numberOrdered * itemPrice
    return result
} // Now the function is defined, so it can be called
...
alert("Total purchases come to " +
        calculateTotal(inputNumber, inputPrice))
// The statement above calls calculateTotal()
```

A *function call* is the technical term for — what else? — calling a function. See the line of code above that says calculateTotal(inputNumber, inputPrice)? That line is a function call!

Notice also that you can embed a function call within another expression (see how calculateTotal(inputNumber, inputPrice) is actually part of the expression being sent to alert() ?).

return *to sender*

return is used to return a value from a function. Functions don't have to return values, but you'll probably want them to most of the time. The syntax for return is quite simple:

```
return expression
```

I show `return` in action in the function example earlier in this section, so I won't repeat it here. (Hey, I told you that you'd get to see reuse in action!)

random.htm, on the companion CD, contains a function called `generateRandomNumber()` that returns a random number when it's called. Check it out!

The 'for' loop: It's not just for breakfast anymore

The `for` loop looks a little geek-like at first. That's because it hails from the C language, which is known for its brevity (and its power). Here's a copy of the generic form:

```
for ([initial expression]; [condition]; [update expression])
        {
    statements
}
```

The `for` loop introduces three terms that may be new to you: the *initial expression,* the *condition,* and the *update expression.* Here's how it all works:

1. **The JavaScript interpreter first takes a look at the initial expression.**

   The initial expression is almost always a number (usually 0 or 1 — what better place to start than at the beginning?) assigned to a variable; for example, `i=0` or `eachOne=1`.

2. **The JavaScript interpreter then takes a look at the condition to see if the condition is true.**

   (A condition is almost always a comparison; for example, `i<10` or `eachOne<=maximum`).

3. **If the condition is true, the JavaScript interpreter performs all the statements in the body of the `for` loop, and then it evaluates the update expression.**

   The update expression almost always increments the initial expression by one; for example, `i++` or `eachOne++`. (`++` looks kind of funny, but it's not a typo. It's an operator that adds one to the variable it's next to. Think of `eachOne++` as a shorthand way of typing `eachOne = eachOne + 1`.)

4. **Now that the variable has been bumped up, the whole thing starts over again (that's why it's called a loop!). The JavaScript interpreter goes back to Step 2 to see if the condition is true, and if it is. . . .**

   Of course, at some point the condition is no longer true. When that happens, the JavaScript interpreter hops out of the `for` loop and begins at the first statement after the loop.

It's possible to create a `for` loop condition that will always be true. This is known as an *endless loop* because the JavaScript interpreter will never stop evaluating and performing the statements in the body of the loop! (Okay, "never" is a long time; in practice, it'll keep evaluating it until you kill the Web browser session. I've found that turning off the machine works nicely!).

Now here's an example of `for` in action:

```
for (var i = 1; i <= 10; i++) {
    document.writeln(i)
}
```

Here's what's going on:

1. `var i = 1` **creates a variable called** `i` **and sets it to equal 1.**

2. `i <= 10` **tests if** `i` **is less than or equal to 10.**

3. **The first time through,** `i` **is 1, and 1 is less than 10, so the statement in the body of the** `for` **loop (** `document.writeln(i)` **) is performed (the value of** `i` **is displayed).**

4. `i++` **adds one to** `i`**.**

5. `i <= 10` **tests to see if** `i` **is still less than or equal to 10.**

6. **The second time through,** `i` **is 2, and 2 is less than 10, so the statement in the body of the** `for` **loop (** `document.writeln(i)` **) is performed (the value of** `i` **is displayed).**

7. **Now the whole thing repeats from Step 3: one is added to** `i`**, the variable is tested to see if it's still less than or equal to 10, and so on, for as many times as** `i` **satisfies the condition.**

There is certainly nothing magical about the `i` variable name; you could just as easily have named your variable *numberOfTimesToPrint,* or *numberOfPigsOrdered,* or *Fred,* for that matter. `i` in `for` loops just happens to be a convention, nothing more.

As you may expect, the following is what displays on the screen when the `for` loop is executed:

```
1 2 3 4 5 6 7 8 9 10
```

Peeking inside objects with `for...in`

If you like `for`, you'll love `for...in`. `for...in` is used for looping, or *iterating*, through all the properties of an object (see, that object stuff I discuss in Chapter 4 comes in handy after all!), like so:

```
for (var in object) {
```

```
    statements
}
```

Here's a useful function that you can use to loop through all of the properties of a given object and display the property name and the value of that property.

```
function displayProperties(inputObject, inputObjectName){
    var result = ""
    for (var eachProperty in inputObject) {
        result += inputObjectName + "." + eachProperty +
        " = " + inputObject[eachProperty] + "<BR>"
    }
    result += "<HR>"
    return result
}
```

Okay, this code is semi-ugly, but it's pretty straightforward once you understand what the for...in loop does. Here's how it works:

The code above defines the function called displayProperties(). Calling the function from another JavaScript statement might look something like this:

```
document.writeln(displayProperties(document, "document"))
```

The JavaScript interpreter hops up to the displayProperties() definition, only this time it substitutes the document object for the argument inputObject and the string "document" for the argument inputObjectName.

Inside the for...in loop, the JavaScript interpreter loops through all of the properties of the document object. Each time it comes to a new property, it assigns it to the variable called eachProperty. Then it constructs a string and adds the string to the end of the variable called result. After the for...in loop has looped through all of the document's properties, the result variable will hold a nice long string containing the names and values of all the properties in the document object.

Displaying (or *dumping,* as it's commonly called) the property values of an object can be really useful when you're trying to track down an error in your script. A function like this one enables you to know exactly what the interpreter thinks objects look like (which is sometimes quite different from the way *you* think they look!). Bummer, though: note that displayProperties()only displays objects that are one level deep. If you send displayProperties() an object that contains another object, displayProperties() still only displays the top-level object.

while *away the hours*

while is another kind of loop (refer to the for loop). The difference is that while enables you to set up a loop where a statement, or series of statements, is executed until the while condition is no longer true. If the condition is *never* true, the statements are never executed; if the condition is *always* true, well, let me just say that those statements execute for a long, long, long, long time. Obviously, then, you want to make sure that one of the statements in the body of your while loop changes the while condition in some way so that it stops being true at some point.

```
while (condition) {
    statements
}
```

Here's an example of while in action:

```
var totalInventory=700, numberPurchased=200, numberSales=0
while (totalInventory > numberPurchased) {
    totalInventory=totalInventory - numberPurchased
    numberSales++
}
document.writeln("Our stock supply will support " +
numberSales + " of these bulk sales")
```

Step into the JavaScript interpreter's virtual shoes for a minute and take a look at how this all works! (Remember, you're the JavaScript interpreter now, so be serious.)

While the total inventory is more than the number purchased... let's see... 700 > 200....Okay. Subtract the number purchased from the total inventory, and bump up the number of sales by one. That's **one** *loop down.*

While the total inventory is more than the number purchased... hmm....Total inventory is 500 now, and that's still greater than 200, so I'll subtract the number purchased from the total inventory and add another one to the number of sales. **Two** *loops down.*

While the total inventory is more than the number purchased... Okay, total inventory is 300 now, which is still greater than 200. Subtract number purchased from total inventory, add one to the number of sales. **Three** *loops down.*

While the total inventory is more than the number purchased... Hey! It's not! Total inventory is 100, and the number purchased is 200. I'm outta here. Here's what I'll write to the screen: **Our stock supply will support 3 of these bulk sales.**

Nice to know how the other half thinks, isn't it?

Never mind! Changing your mind *with* continue *and* break

Both continue and break are used inside of loops (either while loops or for loops). They do slightly different things, as you'll see shortly, and they can be used in the same loop (although they don't have to be).

When the JavaScript interpreter encounters a break statement, the interpreter breaks out of the loop that it's currently processing and starts interpreting again at the first line *following* the loop.

In contrast, continue also tells the JavaScript interpreter to stop what it's doing, but on a somewhat smaller scale. continue tells the interpreter to stop the loop it's currently processing and hop back up to the beginning of the loop again, to continue as normal.

continue and break are useful for exceptions to the rule. For example, you may want to process all items the same way except for two special cases. Just remember that break *breaks* out of a loop, and continue stops iteration execution, but then *continues* the loop.

Here is an example of break used inside a while loop:

```
var totalInventory=700, numberPurchased=200, numberSales=0
while (totalInventory > numberPurchased) {
    totalInventory=totalInventory - numberPurchased
    numberSales++
    if (numberSales > 2) {
        break
    }
}
```

In the code above, when the number of sales reaches 3, the break keyword causes the JavaScript interpreter to hop out of the while loop altogether.

And here's an example of continue used inside a for loop:

```
for (var i = 1; i <= 20; i++) {
    if (i == 13) {   // superstitious; don't print number 13
        continue
    }
    document.writeln(i)
}
```

In the code snippet above, when the variable called i contains the value 13, the JavaScript interpreter stops what it's doing, without hitting the writeln() method, and continues on with the next loop (that is, it sets i equal to 14 and keeps going).

You can test this scrap of code for yourself; it should produce the following result.

```
1 2 3 4 5 6 7 8 9 10 11 12 14 15 16 17 18 19 20
```

with: *the lazy typist's friend*

with is a kind of shorthand that enables you to save typing when you want to refer to several attributes of the same object. For example, if you want to display several attributes of an object one after the other, instead of writing this:

```
document.writeln(document.lastModified)
document.writeln(document.location)
document.writeln(document.title)
```

you can write this:

```
with (document) {
    writeln(lastModified)
    writeln(location)
    writeln(title)
}
```

In the code scrap above, JavaScript assumes that any property you reference inside the *with* clause belongs to the document object; document doesn't have to be typed out explicitly for each property.

Variables: The More Things Change, the More They Stay the Same

A *variable,* as the name implies, is a placeholder for variable information. A value that is assigned to a variable can be changed as often as you need to change it. And unlike other, more strongly "typed" languages, such as C and Java, you don't need to know ahead of time what kind of value you're going to store in a variable. You can assign a string (a *string* is a bunch of alphanumeric characters surrounded by quotes, such as "howdy!") to a variable, and then turn right around and assign a number to the same variable. The JavaScript interpreter won't complain a bit.

For example, all of the following statements are perfectly valid:

```
var timesThrough = 3 // assigning an integer
timesThrough = "skippy" // assigning a string
timesThrough = 2.2309 //assigning a floating point number
```

If you want to name a variable *number,* and then assign a string value to it, that's fine by the JavaScript interpreter! It does no checking up on you whatsoever.

Operators Are Standing By

Operators are like conjunctions. Remember fifth grade English (or *Conjunction Junction, What's Your Function?* if you were a cartoon connoisseur? "And, but, and or, they'll take you pretty far. . . .") *Operators,* like conjunctions, enable you to join multiple phrases together to form expressions.

Two categories of operators exist: *binary,* meaning two items (or *operands*) must be sandwiched on either side of the operator, and *unary,* meaning only one operand is required.

Table 5-1 gives you a rundown of the basic operators. The JavaScript interpreter always evaluates the expression to the right of the equal sign first, and only then does it assign the evaluated value to the variable — with two exceptions: the unary decrement operator (- -), and the unary increment operator (++).

Table 5-1		JavaScript Operators		
In all of these examples, x is initially set to 11.				
Operator	*Meaning*	*Example*	*Result*	*How come?*
%	modulus	x = x % 5	x = 1	11 / 5 = 2 with 1 remainder
++	increment	x = x++	x = 11	++ after a var is applied after assignment
		x = ++x	x = 12	++ before a var is applied before assignment
- -	decrement	x = x--	x = 11	-- after a var is applied after assignment
		x = --x	x = 10	-- before a var is applied before assignment
-	negation	x = -x	x = -11	turns positive numbers negative and vice versa
+	addition	x = x + x	x = 22	11 + 11 is 22

Some of the operators are pretty normal; most of us are familiar with addition and negation, for example. The increment operators are a little weird, though, because not only are they a new thing (you never see ++ or -- outside of a computer program listing), but depending on whether you put them before or after the variable, they behave differently!

If you want to verify your understanding of how operators work, load the HTML file called operator.htm on the companion CD and play around with it.

Just as in math, an order of evaluation is applied to a statement that contains multiple operators. Unless you set phrases off with parentheses, the JavaScript interpreter observes the precedence order shown in Table 5-2 (from the comma, which has the lowest order of precedence, to the parentheses, which has the highest):

Table 5-2	JavaScript Operator Precedence, from Lowest to Highest
Operator	**Syntax**
comma	,
assignment	=, +=, -=, *=, /=, %=
conditional	? :
logical "or"	||
logical "and"	&&
equality	==, !=
relational	<, <=, >, <=
mathematical	+, -, *, /, %
unary	!, -, ++, -- // negation, increment, and decrement operators
call	( )

So, how exactly does this work? Like this: Say the JavaScript interpreter runs into the following statement in your script:

```
alert("Grand total: " + getTotal() + (3 * 4 / 10) + tax++)
```

The interpreter knows its job is to evaluate the statement, so the first thing it does is scan the whole line. When it finds the first set of parentheses, it knows that's where it needs to start. It thinks to itself, "Okay, first I'll get the return value from getTotal(). Then I'll evaluate (3 * 4 / 10). Within (3 * 4 / 10), I'll do the division first, then the multiplication. Now I'll add one to the *tax* variable. Okay, the last thing I have to do is add the whole thing up to come up with a string to display."

Frankly, if you can't remember the precedence order, that's okay. Just group expressions in parentheses like you did back in high school algebra class. Since parentheses outrank all the other operators, you can force JavaScript to override its default precedence order and do whatever you like!

Your assignment for tomorrow:
(= , += , -= , *= , / - ,%-)

Assignment operators enable you to assign values to variables. Besides being able to make a straight one-to-one assignment, though, you can also use some assignment operators as a kind of shorthand to bump up a value based on another value. Table 5-3 describes how this process works:

Table 5-3	JavaScript Assignment Operators (from Lowest to Highest Precedence)
Assignment	*Meaning*
x = y	the value of y is assigned to x
x += y	x = x + y (addition)
x -= y	x = x - y (subtraction)
x *= y	x = x * y (multiplication)
x /= y	x = x / y (division)
x %= y	x = x % y (modulus)

The order of precedence in Table 5-3 is from lowest to highest, so the JavaScript interpreter will evaluate any modulus operations first, and then division, and then multiplication, and so on.

Compared to what?

When comparing two values or expressions, you can compare for equality as shown in Table 5-4:

Table 5-4	JavaScript Comparison Operators	
Operator	*Example*	*Meaning*
== (two equal signs)	x == y	x equal to y
!=	x != y	x not equal to y

(continued)

Table 5-4 (continued)

Operator	Example	Meaning
<	x < y	x less than y
>	x > y	x greater than y
<=	x <= y	x less than or equal to y
>=	x >= y	x greater than or equal to y
?:	x = (y < 0) ? -y : y	if y is less than zero, assign -y to x; otherwise, assign y to x

It's only logical

Logical operators take logical (also called *Boolean*) operands, and they also return Boolean values. A *Boolean value* is either true or false (no fuzzy logic here!). When you see two expressions separated by a logical operator, the JavaScript interpreter first resolves the expressions to see whether each is true or false, and then resolves the entire statement. If something has a non-zero value, that something is considered to be true; if something has a zero value, that something is considered to be false. Table 5-5 describes the logical operators available in JavaScript.

Table 5-5	JavaScript Logical Operators	
Operator	**Meaning**	**Example**
&&	and	if (x == y && a != b)
||	or	if (x < y || a < b)
!	not	if (!x)

Watch out!

A common mistake, even (especially?) among seasoned programmers, is to use a single equal (=, an *assignment* operator) in place of a double equal (==, a *comparison* operator) or vice versa. JavaScript won't complain if you make this mistake; after all, both (x==6) and (x = 6) are legal, and JavaScript has no way of knowing which you really mean.

```
if (x = 6) { // this doesn't
compare 6 to x, it assigns 6
to x!)

    document.writeln("x is 6,
all right!")
}
```

Creationism: new *and* this

When used in conjunction with a function that defines a type of object, the new operator enables you to create an example (or a dozen examples) of that type of object.

The best way to explain this is by an example:

```
function person(name, age, sex, occupation) {
    this.name = name
    this.age = age
    this.sex = sex
    this.occupation = occupation
}
```

You're already familiar with functions, so this example should look pretty familiar. The person function takes four parameters, one each for name, age, sex, and occupation. Then the person function immediately assigns these input values to its own attributes, which are (coincidentally) named the same thing.

In this example, the this keyword is shorthand for person. The JavaScript interpreter knows that you're inside a function called person, so it automatically substitutes the function name for the this keyword so you don't have to spell out the whole function name yourself.

When you want to create an example of person called Jennifer, here's what you do:

```
jennifer = new person("Jennifer McLaughlan", 33, "F", "lion
            tamer")
```

You're probably thinking to yourself, "Why, that last line of code looks almost like a function call — in fact, it looks exactly like a function call, except for the new keyword." Bingo! It is a function call; you're calling the function named person(). Since this is a special kind of function, though — a function that defines an object — you add in the new keyword to tell the JavaScript interpreter that you want it to create a new instance of person every time you call it. (There wouldn't be much good in overwriting Jennifer with Bob and then Carl and then Robin, would there? No, there wouldn't! You want all of them.)

After the statement above is performed, you have a new instance of the person object whose name is Jennifer McLaughlan, aged 33, is female, and tames lions for a living. At this point, you can use the object jennifer as you would any of the built-in objects in JavaScript.

If you think that objects with properties but no methods are kind of boring, you're right. Here's how you add your own methods to the objects you create:

```
function ftalk(kind){
    if (kind == "dog") {
        document.writeln("bow-wow!")
    }
  else {
        if (kind == "cat") {
        document.writeln("meow-meow-meow")
            }
    }
}
function pet(name, kind, color) {
    this.name = name
    this.kind = kind
    this.color = color
   this.talk = ftalk(kind)
}
```

See the definition of the pet() function above? It has three properties: name, kind, and color. It also has one method, called talk. You know that talk is a method and not a property because it's being assigned a function, not a variable. Bear with me here; it'll all make sense when you see it in action!

Here's how you call it:

```
Boots = new pet("Boots", "cat", "orange striped")
Boots.talk
```

The output from the code above would be the string "meow-meow-meow" written to the screen. That's because the first line of code creates a new instance of pet (which happens to be a cat). When the second line of code asks Boots to talk, the JavaScript interpreter hops to the pet() function and sees it needs to pass the kind variable ("cat") to the ftalk() function, which it does — and the response from ftalk() is "meow-meow-meow."

If creating your own objects and methods isn't clear to you right now, it will be after you've had a chance to load and play with object.htm, located on the companion CD.

Leftovers again?

A couple of JavaScript operators, typeof and void, just don't seem to fit in any other operator category. You'll understand what I mean when you see how each is used.

typeof

The `typeof` operator can be applied to any JavaScript object to find out what type of object that object is. For example, if you apply the `typeof` operator to a string, it will return `"string"`; if you apply it to a number, it will return `"number"`; if you apply it to true, it will return `"boolean"` —and so on, for every kind of object that exists. Here's how `typeof` looks in action:

```
typeof "My friend Flicka"      // returns "string"
typeof false                   // returns "boolean"
typeof 69                      // returns "number"
typeof document.lastModified   // returns "string"
typeof Math                    // returns "function"
typeof someVariable            // returns variable type
```

Take a look at the HTML file typeof.htm to see what `typeof` returns for all kinds of JavaScript objects.

Into the void

The `void` operator is a strange beast; it's used to tell JavaScript to do *nothing*. (Only programmers would make up an operator whose sole purpose in life is to do nothing, don't you think?) Perhaps you think there's not much call for an operator that does nothing. Well, you'd be right — *except* in one pretty important instance: creating an image that does something when a user drags her mouse pointer across it.

Say you'd like to display an image on your Web page. Say you also want to recognize when your users drag their mouse pointers across the image, so that you can display a different message in the status bar for each section of the image they pass over.

Well, you can create an image with the HTML `<IMG>` tag, but in order to recognize when a user's cursor passes over that image, you also need to define an additional object, called an `area`. (You define an area by using the `<AREA>` tag, as shown in the following code fragment. The `area` object is somewhat misnamed, in my opinion; it should have been named bigFatLink instead — because that's exactly what it is.)

Now, the reason you need to define an area *and* an image is because you want to take advantage of the area's `onMouseOver` and `onMouseOut` event handlers, which will allow you to recognize when a mouse pointer is dragged over (or out of, respectively) your image. The catch is, the `area` object (because it's nothing but a big fat link) expects you to define a URL in its HREF attribute to link *to* — and you don't *want* to define a URL to link to. All you want to do is use `onMouseOver` and `onMouseOut`.

The solution? Give the area what it wants — a URL definition — but give it one that does *nothing:* in a word, give it void! Check out the following code to see exactly how that's done. (For more on the event handlers onMouseOver and onMouseOut, see Chapter 14; see Chapter 10 for an in-depth discussion of the area object.)

Confused by the void? Then load the HTML file void.htm located on the companion CD and play around with it (it contains a working example of the source code below). The image file referenced in void.htm, called thistle.gif, can also be found on the CD.

```
<MAP NAME="thistleMap">
<AREA NAME="topThistle" COORDS="0,0,228,318"
          HREF="javascript:void(0)"
onMouseOver="self.status='That mouse pointer sure feels
          nice'; return true"
onMouseOut="self.status='Thanks for visiting; come again!';
          return true">
</MAP>
<IMG NAME="currentImage"
SRC="images/thistle.gif" ALIGN="MIDDLE" ALT="[Scottish
          thistles]" USEMAP="#thistleMap">
```

Part II
JavaScript in Action

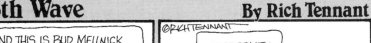

In this part . . .

*I*n this part, you find practical ways to gather and verify user input as well as tips to help you design your own Web page and communicate effectively with your Web page's readers. You see real, live, working examples of all of the techniques that are presented in Part II (and the examples are included on the *JavaScript For Dummies CD-ROM* that is included with this book, so you don't even have to type the code).

Chapter 8 shows you how to use graphics, colors, sounds, hypertext links, and mini-databases in order to add excitement to your documents. And for those of you looking ahead (and *ahead* is, oh, about two months from now in the computer industry), Chapter 9 features a discussion of *server-side* JavaScript as well as the different component services that you can integrate into your *client-side* scripts.

Chapter 6

Talk to Me: Gathering User Input

· ·

· ·

*O*ne of the benefits of using JavaScript is the capability to accept input from the folks who read your Web pages and process the input right there on their Web browsers. If you're familiar with any graphical database application, you know the kinds of tasks that you need to do to make providing input painless for your users; tasks such as

   ✓ Stating clearly the kind of input that's expected

   ✓ Alerting the users immediately (and gently) if they enter an inappropriate value

   ✓ Reassuring them that their order (or whatever) has been transmitted at the end of the process

This chapter outlines the easiest ways to gather and verify input and provide your users with helpful feedback. The listings in this chapter are also on the *JavaScript For Dummies CD-ROM* that came with your book, so you can see them in action without having to type them in yourself. With that said, get cracking!

Harvesting Your Users' Input

Two basic considerations are involved in gathering user input: letting users know what information you expect them to type in, and getting access to the values they provide. The first issue is more a matter of design style than anything else, and books such as *Creating Web Pages For Dummies* by Bud Smith and Arthur Bebak, can give you heaps o' hints in this area. This section focuses instead on the business end of input gathering: the form elements `text`, `textarea`, and `select`.

Oh, no! Everything's blurry!

The name for the `onBlur` event handler is based on the concept of focus (clever, don't you think?). An object is said to receive focus when you click on it; and so, by default, the object becomes *blurry* when you click on something else, and the object *loses* focus. Here's a quick rundown of when the event handling code for the following common event handlers is run:

✔ The *handlerText* for `onBlur` is executed when a user clicks on the element (the element gets focus) and then clicks somewhere else (the element loses focus, or *blurs*).

✔ The *handlerText* for `onChange` is executed when an element loses focus *and* its contents are modified.

✔ The *handlerText* for `onFocus` is executed when an element receives focus (a user tabs to it or clicks on it, but stops short of actually selecting any text).

✔ The *handlerText* for `onSelect` is executed when a user selects some or all of the text in an object. The behavior of `onSelect` is similar to `onFocus`, except that `onSelect` occurs when the element receives focus *and* text is selected.

Let 'em type whatever they want (as long as it's short!)

The `text` element is a form element that lets users type in — you guessed it — text. Typically you'll see `text` elements used as input fields for things like names, ages, phone numbers — anything that can be described in a few words or less.

Because the `text` element is a form element, it (like all the other form elements) must be placed between the `<FORM>`...`</FORM>` tags. `<FORM>`...`</FORM>` tags, as you may recall from Chapter 3, are *inherited* from HTML — that is, you can display these tags on your Web page and use the input data in JavaScript calculations, but the `<FORM>`...`</FORM>` tags themselves (and everything in between them) need to be placed outside the `<SCRIPT>`...`</SCRIPT>` declaration.

Listing 6-1 shows an example of a text element that prompts a user for his or her name. When the user clicks elsewhere on the page, causing the text element to *blur* (see the nearby sidebar, "Oh, no! Everything's blurry!"), a message appears in the text field.

Listing 6-1:   Example of `onBlur` **Event Handler**

```
<HTML>
<HEAD><TITLE>Single Input Field Example</TITLE>
<SCRIPT LANGUAGE="JavaScript">
```

```
function display() {
    document.feedbackForm.firstName.value="Name accepted."
}
</SCRIPT>
</HEAD>
<BODY>
<BR>
<FORM NAME="feedbackForm">
<BR>Please enter your name:
<INPUT TYPE="text" NAME="firstName" VALUE="your name here"
        SIZE=25 onBlur="display()">
</FORM>
</BODY>
</HTML>
```

Let 'em type whatever they want, as much as they want

Use a `textarea` element if you need to ask users for input that you expect to span multiple lines. You see an example in Listing 6-2.

Listing 6-2: `textarea` **Form Element Example**

```
<HTML>
<HEAD><TITLE>Multi-Line Entry Field</TITLE>
<SCRIPT LANGUAGE="JavaScript">
function display() {
    document.feedbackForm.directions.value=""
}
</SCRIPT>
</HEAD>
<BODY>
<BR>
<FORM NAME="feedbackForm">
<BR>Enter any comments:
<TEXTAREA NAME="directions" ROWS=4 COLS=60
onChange="display()">
This is default text. You can type right over it,
add to it, cut it, paste it, or copy it. If you
make a change and then click somewhere else on the
page, though, the text will disappear.
</TEXTAREA>
</FORM>
</BODY>
</HTML>
```

When loaded, this script looks as it does in Figure 6-1. Notice that if users type in more information than can be displayed, the control automatically enables scrolling.

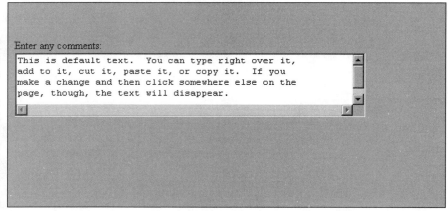

Figure 6-1:
The
textarea
form
element
enables
multiple-line
input — and
scrolling is
free!

Give 'em a choice

The select element can be used two ways: to display a selection list, or to display a scrolling list. A *selection list* enables a user to make one selection from a drop-down box; a *scrolling list* enables a user to select multiple entries. The `<SELECT>`...`</SELECT>` tag is the same in both cases — the only difference is whether the MULTIPLE keyword is present (if the select declaration contains the MULTIPLE keyword, the list is a scrolling list; otherwise, the list is a simple selection list). Two input controls for the price of one! Listing 6-3 shows an example.

Listing 6-3:   **JavaScript Source to Implement a Single Selection List**

```
<HTML>
<HEAD><TITLE>Single Selection Input Field</TITLE>
<SCRIPT LANGUAGE="JavaScript">
function display(selection) {
    var tempIndex, selectedFlavor

    tempIndex=selection.selectedIndex
    selectedFlavor=selection.options[tempIndex].text

    if (selectedFlavor != "chocolate") {
    document.feedbackForm.opinion.value=selectedFlavor +
            " is okay"
    }
    else {
      document.feedbackForm.opinion.value=
            "chocolate's my favorite, too!"
    }
}
</SCRIPT>
</HEAD>
```

```
<BODY>
<BR>
<FORM NAME="feedbackForm">
What's your favorite ice cream flavor?  Pick one:
<SELECT NAME="favoriteOne" onChange="display(this)">
<OPTION SELECTED> chocolate
<OPTION> vanilla
<OPTION> pistachio almond fudge
<OPTION> pink peppermint
<OPTION> caramel/marshmallow swirl
</SELECT>
<INPUT NAME="opinion" VALUE="" SIZE=35>
</FORM>
</BODY>
</HTML>
```

Notice the gyrations going on in the display(selection) function? All the
data you need to get at in a list is accessible; some bits are just, well, more
accessible than others. The display(selection) function is a good function
to have lying around. Face it: You usually give folks a list to pick from because
you want to *do* something with the value they choose! And that's what this
function does: It isolates the text value for the item the user selects. Figure 6-2
shows how this script displays when it's loaded.

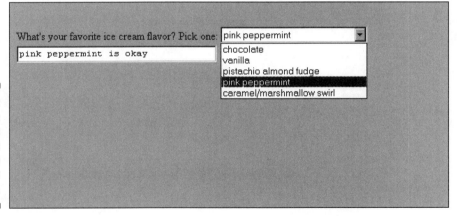

Figure 6-2:
With a
single
selection
list, there's
only one to
a customer.

Now comes even more fun! The same select element is used, but this time
with the MULTIPLE keyword. Check out the source in Listing 6-4 and notice the
MULTIPLE keyword.

Listing 6-4:   JavaScript Source for Multi-Selection Scrolling List

```
<HTML>
<HEAD><TITLE>Multiple Selection Input Field</TITLE>
<SCRIPT LANGUAGE="JavaScript">

function displayResult(selection) {
    var numberPicked=0
    for (var i=0; i<6; i++) {
        if (selection.options[i].selected) {
            numberPicked++
        }
    }
    document.feedbackForm.result.value=numberPicked
}
</SCRIPT>
</HEAD>
<BODY>
<BR>
<FORM NAME="feedbackForm">
What kinds of music do you like?
<SELECT NAME="favoriteOne" MULTIPLE
            onChange="displayResult(this)">
<OPTION SELECTED> jazz
<OPTION> rock
<OPTION> blues
<OPTION> Gregorian chants
<OPTION> California beach tunes
<OPTION> anything that involves bagpipes
</SELECT>
<BR>
Here's how many you selected:
<INPUT TYPE="text" NAME="result" VALUE="" SIZE=5>
</FORM>
</BODY>
</HTML>
```

Notice how, in the `displayResult(selection)` function (replicated below), the entire list is cycled through.

```
for (var i=0; i<6; i++) { // loops through 6 times
    if (selection.options[i].selected) { // if selected
        numberPicked++  // add one to the count
    }
}
```

Only the music types that were selected cause the number one to be added to the counter. A bit clunky? Maybe. . . . But it works! Figure 6-3 shows how this script displays.

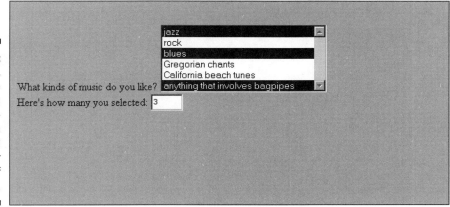

Figure 6-3:
Take three, they're small: using a multiple-selection control gives your users lots of choices.

Keeping 'em Honest

In many cases, you may have something definite in mind for a value. If you ask for someone's e-mail address, for example, you may want to make sure not only that an address is typed in, but that the address follows a convention that you know to be standard for all e-mail addresses (for example, that it contains the @ symbol). Verifying user input immediately, before the values are sent to a Web server for calculation, can save a great deal of time. Input verification generally falls somewhere in the following three categories: *existence* (whether or not a value exists at all), *numeric* (numbers only), and *pattern* (a specific convention, such as is found in a phone number, a social security number, a date, and the like).

If a variable falls in the middle of a forest, does it make a sound?

Sometimes, when you provide a text input field on a Web page, you want to be absolutely sure that your users fill it in. For example, if the purpose of your Web page is to solicit feedback on your online e-zine, and you provide a "comments" field, it doesn't make much sense for you to accept a user's name and e-mail address if the user neglects to type in a comment! In a case like this, you want to be able to check for the existence of a value in the "comments" field before you go to the trouble of accepting any input information.

Listing 6-5 shows one way to test for existence of a value (in this case, a company name):

Listing 6-5:   Test for Existence of an Input Value

```
<HTML>
<HEAD>
<TITLE>Existence</TITLE>
<SCRIPT LANGUAGE="JavaScript">
function verify() {
    aCharExists=0
    entry=document.feedbackForm.companyName.value
    if (entry) {
        window.alert("entry.length is " + entry.length)
        for (var i=0; i<entry.length; i++) {
            if (entry.charAt(i) != " ") {
                aCharExists=1
            }
        }
    }
    if (!aCharExists) {
        window.alert("Please enter a company name.")
    }
}

</SCRIPT>
</HEAD>
<BODY>
<BR>
<FORM NAME="feedbackForm">
<BR>Company name:
<INPUT TYPE="text" NAME="companyName" VALUE="" SIZE=35
onBlur="verify()">
</FORM>
</BODY>
</HTML>
```

Here's how the test works. If you take a look at the `verify()` function definition, you see that it pops up a warning in two cases: First, when a user switches
focus away from the input field without first having typed something in (the `if
(entry)` condition checks for that), and second, when a user types in only
spaces (the code fragment below checks for that):

```
for (var i=0; i<entry.length; i++) {// Check every digit.
    if (entry.charAt(i) != " ") { // If it isn't a space,
        aCharExists=1  // it's a valid character.
    }
}
```

If an entry exists at all, the function loops through it, character by character,
looking for a non-blank symbol. If the function doesn't find a non-blank symbol,
or if the entry is null, the function displays a pop-up window that requests that
the user enter a non-blank value.

Running numbers

Depending on your needs, the JavaScript functions parseInt, parseFloat, and isNaN (all of which are discussed at length in Chapter 13) may be just what the doctor ordered if you want to verify that a user has entered numeric information into a specific field. These functions, however, return the computer equivalent of a thumbs-up if the first digit is numeric, regardless of what the user types in after that. So if a user types in **8abcd**, parseInt, parseFloat, and isNaN would give that entry their blessing! If you want to do a more thorough check (or *data scrub,* as the computer scientists among us call it), you can check with a homemade function, such as the one in Listing 6-6. Notice that this function ignores any blank spaces that the user might accidentally type next to a number.

Listing 6-6: Function to Verify Numeric Input

```
<HTML>
<HEAD>
<TITLE>Numeric Verification</TITLE>
<SCRIPT LANGUAGE="JavaScript">
function isANumber(){
    entry=document.feedbackForm.numberItems.value
    if (!parseFloat(entry)) {
        window.alert("Please enter a numeric value.")
    }
    else {
        for (var i=0; i<entry.length; i++) {
            if (entry.charAt(i) != " ") {
                if (!parseFloat(entry.charAt(i))) {
                    window.alert("Please enter a numeric value.")
                    break
                }
            }
        }
        document.feedbackForm.numberItems.value =
            parseFloat(entry)
    }
}
</SCRIPT>
</HEAD>
<BODY>
<BR>
<FORM NAME="feedbackForm">
<BR>Number of items you wish to purchase:
<INPUT TYPE="text" NAME="numberItems" VALUE="" SIZE=5
onBlur="isANumber()">
</FORM>
</BODY>
</HTML>
```

This is a long one (but worth every line!). The real meat of the script is in the if...else expression inside isANumber(). First it checks whether or not anything was entered (the *if* part). If something was entered, the *else* part kicks in and begins to check the digits one at a time to make sure they're numeric.

The only slightly weird statement in this function is this one:

```
if (entry.charAt(i) != " ") { // why is this here?
    if (!parseFloat(entry.charAt(i))) {
        window.alert("Please enter a numeric value.")
    break
    }
}
```

parseFloat() returns a "NaN" (which satisfies the *if* condition) if the incoming digit is a space. Well, okay, technically a space isn't a number; I'll give parseFloat() that. But in this scenario, I want the user to be able to put in a space and not get an error. What if someone types in **123**, followed by a space? I don't want to pop up an error that says "Please enter a numeric value," because the user would think I was crazy — as far as she can see on her screen, she *did* enter a number! So the clause if (entry.charAt(i) != " ") ensures that if a user types in a space, the JavaScript interpreter doesn't bother asking parseFloat() for its opinion.

I think I see a pattern here!

A phone number is a common pattern, and it's conceivable that you would want to make sure that what your user enters into a phone number field is valid. (Of course, by *valid* I mean a series of digits, a couple of parentheses, and a dash — not that the phone number is actually in service!)

Notice that two functions are used in the following example. The example illustrates the practice of breaking things up into manageable chunks (with a side benefit that you can reuse isANumber() in another program). Notice also that the isANumber() function is very similar to the one used as an example earlier in this chapter. The difference here is that I want to enable users to type in phone numbers that contain zeros; before, I didn't want someone to be able to type in a zero (the earlier function verified an order number, and what would be the point of allowing someone to fill out an order form for zero items?).

The example in Listing 6-7 can be adapted to any pattern you can think of. As long as you can describe the pattern precisely, you can break it into meaningful chunks with the substring() method of the built-in JavaScript string object and examine each chunk. As soon as you find a chunk that doesn't match your expectations, you can respectfully request that the user modify the input.

Listing 6-7:   Pattern Verification: Phone Number

```
<HEAD>
<TITLE>Pattern Verification</TITLE>
<SCRIPT LANGUAGE="JavaScript">

function  isANumber(number){
    answer=1
    for (var i=0; i<number.length; i++) {
        if ((number.charAt(i) != "0") &&
            !parseFloat(number.charAt(i))) {
                answer = 0
                break
        }
    }

    return answer
}

function  isAPhoneNumber(){
    entry=document.feedbackForm.homePhone.value
    if (entry) {
        var openParen = entry.substring(0,1)
        var areaCode = entry.substring(1,4)
        var closeParen = entry.substring(4,5)
        var exchange = entry.substring(5,8)
        var dash = entry.substring(8,9)
        var line = entry.substring(9,13)

        if (
            (openParen != "(")        ||
            (!isANumber(areaCode))    ||
            (closeParen != ")")       ||
            (!isANumber(exchange))    ||
            (dash != "-")             ||
            (!isANumber(line))
            ){
            window.alert("Please enter phone number in the
                following format: (123)456-7890")
        }
    }
}
</SCRIPT>
</HEAD>
<BODY>
<BR>
<FORM NAME="feedbackForm">
<BR>Please enter your home phone number
<BR>in the following format: (123)456-7890
<INPUT TYPE="text" NAME="homePhone" VALUE="" SIZE=13
onBlur="isAPhoneNumber()"
```

(continued)

(continued)

```
>
</FORM>
</BODY>
</HTML>
```

All the really interesting stuff is taking place inside the isAPhoneNumber() function. See all those statements that contain calls to entry.substring() (there are six of them)? Following is what the JavaScript interpreter does when it encounters them. Assume a user typed in the phone number (512) 555-1212, so that's what the value of entry is. The numbers below the phone number represent the order of the digits in the phone number, which can be mighty helpful when you're trying to figure out what the substring() method is actually doing!

(	5	1	2	)	5	5	5	-	1	2	1	2
0	1	2	3	4	5	6	7	8	9	10	11	12

```
var openParen = entry.substring(0,1)
```

openParen gets the digit that starts at 0 and ends before 1. That means it gets this: **(**

```
var areaCode = entry.substring(1,4)
```

areaCode is assigned all the digits starting at 1 and ending before 4: **512**

```
var closeParen = entry.substring(4,5)
```

closeParen is assigned the digit that starts at 4 and ends before 5: **)**

```
var exchange = entry.substring(5,8)
```

exchange gets the digits that start at 5 and end before 8: **555**

The whole phone number is split apart just like that, and then each piece is tested (still in isAPhoneNumber()) to see if each meets the criteria for that piece. The first digit must be an open parenthesis, the next three digits must be numeric, and so on — and if any of the pieces fail, then the entire phone number is invalid, and the user is requested to enter another.

Giving 'em a Piece of Your Mind

You may want to consider the following feedback-related issues while you're designing your form:

> ✔ *Design,* which relates to how you approach feedback in general; and
>
> ✔ *Implementation,* which has to do with the specific JavaScript mechanisms you use to implement your design.

Plan your attack

Giving feedback to your users is helpful to you as well as to the people who visit your Web page. You benefit because, when you give users clear instructions on what kind of information to give you, you get good data — and that means fewer mistakes when it comes time to process the information (fill their order, send them information, or whatever it is your page is designed to do). Your users benefit because they *want* to give you the correct information. They're taking the time to fill out your form, and they want to do it correctly.

So feedback is a Good Thing. Following are a few things to keep in mind, though, as you decide when and how to interact with your users.

DON'T SHOUT!!!!!

Nobody likes being yelled at, and messages THAT ARE ALL IN UPPERCASE LIKE THIS AND END IN EXCLAMATION POINTS ARE YELLS!!!!!!!! Admit it. When you were reading that line just now, didn't your internal voice take on a more strident tone? That's exactly what your users experience. Say what you need to say; just use normal capitalization and punctuation.

Be specific

Sometimes, you don't particularly care what a user types in (for example, if you're asking for comments on your product). (Okay, you may *care,* but not about whether the data is alphabetical or numeric or contains the word *fantastic!*) At other times, what the user types in is crucial. For the times when it's crucial, be sure to let the user know up front what format is expected.

When you *do* need to pop up an error message, make sure that it tells users precisely what's wrong with their input. You know *exactly* what's wrong (that's why you're displaying an error message), so tell your user. This is your chance to outshine the !%^*## programmers who respond to incorrect input values with nothing more helpful than an `Invalid format. Please retry.` message. Sheesh!

Give your users a break

Just because you're now a card-carrying expert at verifying user input doesn't mean that you have to pop up an error message *every* time that you detect an error. In some cases, you may be able to *massage* (geek-speak for *modify*) the input data to suit yourself without bugging the user at all. For example, just because you'd *like* to see a value in uppercase letters doesn't mean the user *has* to enter it in uppercase letters. Instead of displaying an error and requesting that the user retype the entry, you can just as easily take the input and change it to uppercase yourself.

To see an example of massaging input data, take a look at the file list0707.htm.

Also (and this probably goes without saying, but you never know), make sure that you test your form carefully for every conceivable error (and series of errors) that a user might reasonably be expected to make. Few things are more frustrating to users than getting tangled in an endless loop of errors that refuse to go away, even *after* the user has figured out what's wrong and corrected it!

Make 'em sit up and take notice

After you know what you want to tell your users and when you want to tell them, all you need to know is how. Here are some of the easiest ways to notify a user that something has gone awry:

Pop-up messages: cute the first time!

Pop-up messages (the most common of which is known as an *alert*) are a great way to get a user's attention. Pop-up messages are fairly intrusive, though, because users have to stop what they're doing and deal with a pop-up message before they can continue what they were doing. Because of this intrusive delay, using pop-up messages sparingly is a good idea. Figure 6-4 shows an alert pop-up message in action. Following is the general syntax for creating an alert box.

Figure 6-4: Be alert and use the `alert()` method! (The world needs more lerts.)

> Please enter your home phone number
> in the following format: (123)456-7890 `5125551212`
>
> **Netscape** ☒
> ⚠ JavaScript Alert:
> Please enter phone number in the following format: (123)456-7890
>
> [OK]

```
window.alert("message text")
```

Status bar messages: subtle, yet elegant

The status bar, at the bottom of a page, is often used for — well — status information. You may notice text appearing and disappearing in this area when you load a Web page or move your mouse pointer over a link.

Displaying your own text in the status bar is pretty easy to do. Just keep in mind that you generally want to display text in response to some kind of event. And remember to clean up after yourself, too. As soon as your user stops doing whatever caused the text to display, clear it out to avoid confusion.

You can display text in the status bar whenever you like: when a user opens your page, moves the mouse over a link or a graphic, and so on. You can even scroll the text if you're really feeling frisky! In Listing 6-8, two buttons have been defined: one that displays a status bar message, and one that erases it.

Listing 6-8:   Status Bar Display Example

```
<HTML>
<HEAD>
<TITLE>Status Bar Display</TITLE>
<SCRIPT LANGUAGE="JavaScript">

function writeToStatusBar(text) {
    window.status = text
}

</SCRIPT>
</HEAD>
<BODY>
<BR>
<FORM NAME=myForm>
<INPUT TYPE="button" NAME="look" VALUE="Display"
onclick="writeToStatusBar('This is a good way to display help
            information.')">
<INPUT TYPE="button" NAME="stopLook" VALUE="Erase"
onclick="writeToStatusBar('')">
</FORM>
</BODY>
</HTML>
```

Figure 6-5 shows a message displaying in the status bar. See how tiny the message is?

You can make the message blink or scroll if you want to draw attention to it, but keep in mind that what seems like a novel idea the first time a user sees it can get mighty old by the hundredth time. See the following section for more ways to spice up your text messages.

Not your ordinary text

To emphasize a word or sentence that you're displaying, you can make it blink, change color, or appear bold so it immediately draws your users' attention. As you might expect, because these eye-catchers are all *behaviors* of text, they're implemented as *methods* on the `string` object. You can find a complete list of `string` methods in Chapter 10. All of the `string` methods listed in Chapter 10 work pretty much the way the following examples work:

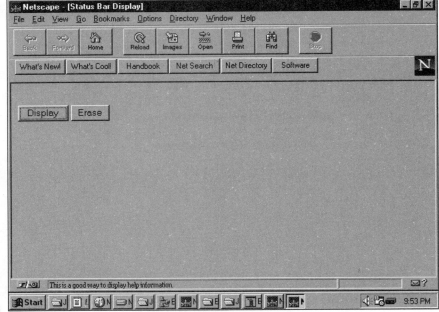

Figure 6-5:
Take a look at this example of status bar display text. Simple to do and low-key, too.

```
blink()
document.write("JavaScript's the " + "Coolest".blink())
```

The preceding statement causes the word "Coolest" in the sentence "JavaScript's the Coolest" to blink on and off.

```
bold()
document.write("JavaScript".bold()+
    "is more fun than humans should be allowed to have")
```

The preceding statement makes the word "JavaScript" display in bold; the rest of the text displays normally.

```
fontcolor(color)
document.write("Java".fontcolor("green") +
    "Script".fontcolor("red"))
```

The result of the preceding statement is the displayed word "JavaScript," half ("Java") colored green and the other half ("Script") colored red.

I encourage you to try out all the fun things you can do with text. For a quick leg-up, load one of the following HTML files from the companion CD: blink.htm (blinking text example), list0808.htm (color example), or font.htm (font example).

Chapter 7

Take Control!

Controls (or *widgets,* as they're sometimes called) enable viewers of your page to reach out and touch you. A *control* is anything that a user can click on or type inside. Controls are defined with HTML forms statements, but you access them with JavaScript statements.

Navigator and Internet Explorer both support standard HTML (standard HTML includes all the form elements). In addition, they both support the `<SCRIPT>...</SCRIPT>` extension that allows you to include JavaScript statements in your HTML files — and it's the JavaScript statements that enable you to access and manipulate the values that users enter into the form elements. This chapter shows you both sides of the coin: how to use HTML to define form elements, and also how to use JavaScript to capture values and respond to your users.

If you want to see the example files for the listings mentioned throughout this chapter, check out the files on this book's companion CD. The files are named appropriately—for example, Listing 7-1 can be found in the file named list 0701.htm.

Check Your Box at the Door, Please

A *checkbox* is like a toggle switch that turns off or on each time a user clicks on it. Like multiple-selection list boxes, checkboxes can be grouped together to enable users to select multiple values (as opposed to single-selection list boxes and radio buttons, which restrict users to one choice).

To define a checkbox, you use standard HTML syntax with the addition of the `onClick` event handler. (Remember, form elements are HTML constructs; JavaScript adds the capability to work with the user-supplied values.)

Listing 7-1 shows a way that you can define a checkbox and access its properties. I have defined several checkboxes in this example because most of the time you want to display groups of checkboxes, not just one.

The `CHECKED` attribute defaults the checkbox to *checked* so that the checkbox appears with a check mark when it's initially displayed.

Listing 7-1:   JavaScript Source Code for Checkbox Example

```
<HTML>
<HEAD>
<TITLE>Checkbox Example</TITLE>
<SCRIPT LANGUAGE="JavaScript">

function display(checkboxSelected) {
    var contents = ""
    contents +="\r\n"
    contents +="name of checkbox selected is ---> "
    contents += checkboxSelected.name
    contents += "\r\n"
    contents += "is checkbox checked on or off? ---> "
    contents += checkboxSelected.checked
    contents += "\r\n"
    contents +=
            "was this checkbox defaulted to 'checked'? --->"
    contents += checkboxSelected.defaultChecked
    contents += "\r\n\r\n"
    contents +=
            "function defined for event handler onclick --->"
"
    contents += checkboxSelected.onclick

    document.bookForm.result.value = contents
}

</SCRIPT>
</HEAD>
<BODY>
<BR>
<FORM NAME="bookForm">

<BR><BR>
```

```
<B>What type of book are you most likely to buy?  Check all
        that apply:</B>
<BR><BR>
<INPUT TYPE="checkbox" NAME="fiction"
        onClick="display(this)">
Fiction
<INPUT TYPE="checkbox" NAME="non-fiction"
        onClick="display(this)">
Non-Fiction
<INPUT TYPE="checkbox" NAME="autobio"
        onClick="display(this)">
Autobiography

<BR>
<TEXTAREA NAME="result" ROWS="6" COLS="60">Your result will
        be shown here
</TEXTAREA>
</FORM>
</BODY>
</HTML>
```

Notice, in Listing 7-1, that the values for name, checked, defaultChecked, and onclick are being accessed. In this example, the values for the very last item clicked are displayed in a multiline text window so that you can see exactly what JavaScript records for each checkbox. In your own applications, you can do anything that you like with the values. For example, if a user selects the fiction checkbox, you may want to display a list of fiction titles.

Figure 7-1 shows what you see after you load the source in Listing 7-1. Notice that the \r\n in the source causes the next line of text to display on a new line (hey, that's pretty intuitive, huh? Not.).

Thank You for Sharing

Input fields are areas where you want users to type in information on a form. Depending upon your application, you may want users to type a single word or several sentences. You may even want users to type in something that doesn't display, but that you can access programmatically (typically a password). Each of these situations calls for a different input element (each of which, as you know, is implemented as an object — JavaScript is object-based, after all!), as described in the following sections.

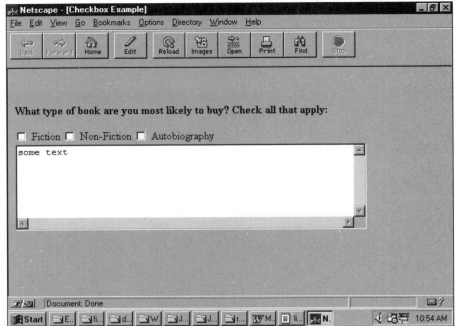

Figure 7-1:
Pick a
category,
any
category!

Short and sweet: the text *element*

The text object is probably the simplest control. The text object enables you to define a single text field, as shown in Listing 7-2. Even though the text field can be virtually any size you want and comes with a built-in scrollbar, you probably want to consider using textarea instead of text if you expect users to type in more than a word or two.

Special characters for special strings

You know that a *string* is a series of characters. But what character do you type in to get a carriage return embedded in your string? If you hit the carriage return on your keyboard, you simply break the string in half. Here's the solution: Use a special character to represent a carriage return. For PCs running Windows, the special character is \r\n. For the Mac, \n does the trick.

Listing 7-2:   Source for Single-Field Text Entry Example

```
<HTML>
<HEAD>
<TITLE>Text Entry Field Example</TITLE>
<SCRIPT LANGUAGE="JavaScript">

function display(textField) {

    alert("\nname is --->" + textField.name +
          "\nvalue is --->" + textField.value +
          "\ndefaultValue is --->" +
          textField.defaultValue +
          "\n\nonBlur is --->" + textField.onblur)
}

</SCRIPT>
</HEAD>
<BODY>
<BR>
<FORM NAME="entryForm">

<BR>
<B>Please enter your company's name and then click somewhere
          else on the page:</B>
<BR><BR>
<INPUT TYPE="text" NAME="companyName" SIZE="25"
          onBlur="display(this)">

</FORM>
</BODY>
</HTML>
```

See the statement near the bottom of Listing 7-2 that says `<INPUT TYPE= "text" NAME="companyName" SIZE="25" onBlur="display(this)">`? That's the statement that defines the `text` element called `companyName`. When a user blurs this element (clicks on it and then clicks somewhere else), the JavaScript interpreter will perform all of the statements in the `display()` function. The result is that the guts (properties, to be more precise) of the `companyName` field are displayed to the screen.

Figure 7-2 shows what's displayed when the source in Listing 7-2 is loaded.

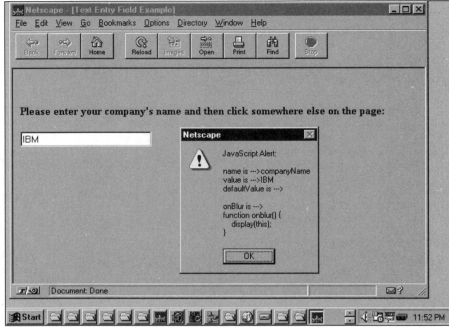

Figure 7-2:
It just
doesn't get
any simpler
than this!

For the long-winded: the `textarea` element

At times, a single text entry field just isn't big enough, and those times are when `textarea` comes in handy. The `textarea` control enables you to specify a scrolling field that your users can use to input several lines of text. Because `textarea` is automatically set up with horizontal and vertical scrollbars, if users type in more text than can fit in the displayed field, all they need to do to see it is scroll up and down or side to side. Listing 7-3 shows you how to define a `textarea` control and also how to access its properties.

Listing 7-3:   Source for Multiple-Line Entry Field Example

```
<HTML>
<HEAD>
<TITLE>Example of Multiple-Line Entry Field</TITLE>
<SCRIPT LANGUAGE="JavaScript">

function display(multiLineTextField) {

    alert("\n" + "name is --->" + multiLineTextField.name
        + "\n" + "value is --->" +
        multiLineTextField.value +
        "\n" + "defaultValue is --->" +
        multiLineTextField.defaultValue +
```

```
              "\n\n" + "onchange is --->" +
              multiLineTextField.onchange)

   }

</SCRIPT>
</HEAD>
<BODY>
<BR>
<FORM NAME="feedbackForm">
<BR>Enter any comments:

<TEXTAREA NAME="directions" ROWS="4" COLS="60"
onChange="display(this)">
This is default text.  You can type right over it,
add to it, cut it, paste it, or copy it.
</TEXTAREA>

</FORM>
</BODY>
</HTML>
```

Figure 7-3 shows the multiline entry field in action.

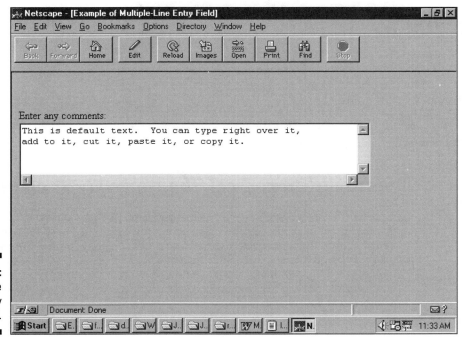

Figure 7-3:
Multiple-line
text entry
field.

How do you know what properties are available for a form element? (I mean, you can't very well ask for the value of a property if you don't know what the property is called!) In the code example in Listing 7-3, I displayed the value, defaultValue, and onchange properties by name. There's a quick way to see all of the names and their associated values for an object all at once, though, and that's by using the this keyword.

You can get up-close and personal with the this keyword in Chapter 5, but for now, just think of it as JavaScript's shorthand for "whatever the thing is that I'm in when I encounter the this keyword." Confused? You won't be when you see how simple this is!

To check out an example of the this keyword in a real, live, honest-to-goodness script, load the HTML file called this.htm located on the companion CD.

```
<TEXTAREA NAME="directions" ROWS="4" COLS="60"
onChange="alert('Here is the object:\n' + this)">
```

The code fragment above does a pretty amazing thing: it pops up an alert dialog box that says "Here is the object:" and then it dumps out the contents of the object — automatically! Figure 7-4 shows you what the result looks like.

Figure 7-4: Letting JavaScript do the legwork: the this keyword.

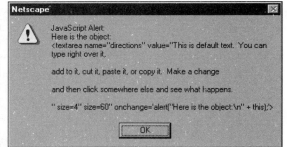

Shhh! It's a secret! The password element

A password object is just like a text object, except that a password *field* displays asterisks instead of the characters the user types in order to conceal its value from the user. If you ask users to enter sensitive information, such as a password or financial information, you may use a password field so that folks looking over their shoulders can't see the value that the users type. You can find a script that declares a password and then accesses the password's properties in Listing 7-4.

Listing 7-4:   Source for Password Input Field Example

```
<HTML>
<HEAD>
<TITLE>Password Entry Field Example</TITLE>
<SCRIPT LANGUAGE="JavaScript">

function displayPassword(){
    alert("\nname is --->" +
        document.entryForm.secret.name +
        "\nvalue is --->" +
        document.entryForm.secret.value +
        "\ndefaultValue is --->" +
        document.entryForm.secret.defaultValue)
}

</SCRIPT>
</HEAD>
<BODY>
<BR>
<FORM NAME="entryForm">

<BR>
<B>Please enter a secret password and then click the
            button:</B>
<BR><BR>
<INPUT TYPE="password" NAME="secret" SIZE="15"
            VALUE="bosefus">
<INPUT TYPE="button" NAME="passwordViewer"
VALUE="Push To View" onClick="displayPassword()">

</FORM>
</BODY>
</HTML>
```

See where the button is hooked up to the `password` control? (The statement that does this is repeated below). The button is connected because `password` itself doesn't have any event handlers, so something else (a push button, in this case) has to act as the trigger to display the password text.

```
<INPUT TYPE="button" NAME="passwordViewer"
VALUE="Push To View" onClick="displayPassword()">
```

Figure 7-5 shows what's displayed when a user types something in the password field.

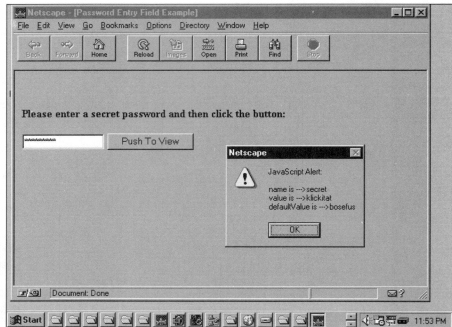

Figure 7-5:
Shhh! Can
you keep a
secret?

Button, Button, Who's Got the Button?

Push buttons are such handy little controls that no form is complete without one. Push buttons are typically set up with an onClick event handler, so that when a user clicks on a push button, something happens. Two built-in push buttons perform two of the most common functions you're likely to need: reset and submit. The reset button automatically clears out all the user-defined values in a form and resets any defaults; the submit button submits the form to the URL specified in the form's action property. Besides these two fast-food buttons, you can create your own custom buttons to do whatever you like. You can also use radio buttons to enable your users to choose one option from a group of options.

Starting over with the reset button

A reset button is a special type of push button. The reset button is hard-wired to reset all of the elements in a form to their default values when it's clicked. reset supports the onClick event handler, but be aware that once the user clicks on the reset button, those form values are going to be reset. Period. And nothing you put in the reset button's onClick event handler can bring back the values once they're reset.

Because the reset object is so specialized, its declaration is fairly simple as you can see in Listing 7-5.

Listing 7-5:   Source Code for reset Button Example

```
<HTML>
<HEAD>
<TITLE>reset Button Example</TITLE>
</HEAD>
<BODY>
<BR>
<FORM NAME="entryForm">

<BR>Please check all of the following sport-related
           activities you enjoy:<BR>
<INPUT TYPE="checkbox" NAME="play"> play
<INPUT TYPE="checkbox" NAME="watch"> watch
<INPUT TYPE="checkbox" NAME="coach"> coach

<BR>
<B>Please enter your favorite sport and then click the
         'Reset' button:</B>
<BR><BR>
<INPUT TYPE="text" NAME="sport" SIZE="15" VALUE="none">
<INPUT TYPE="reset" NAME="resetButton" VALUE="RESET">

</FORM>
</BODY>
</HTML>
```

Notice in Listing 7-5 that there are no JavaScript statements (no <SCRIPT>... </SCRIPT> tags). That's because the reset button is an HTML construct. If you were to add an onClick event handler, though, you *would* need to put in some JavaScript statements in order to declare a function to use as an event handler.

When you click on the button marked Reset, all of the values you entered — check marks as well as text — are cleared out and the form is reset to the way it looked at the time that you entered it.

Submit? Never!

I know exactly what you're thinking. I, too, have longed for a button that I can push that would make my computer submit! If only it were that easy. Actually, the submit button *is* pretty easy, although it has to be used in conjunction with a more complete <FORM>...</FORM> declaration than you've seen up to now. No sweat, though; you'll be amazed at what you get for the little amount of effort required.

Here's how the procedure works: In the <FORM>...</FORM> definition, you specify a value for the ACTION property. This value identifies the program that you want to send the form information to when a user clicks the submit button. Typically, the value for ACTION is one of two things:

✔ The URL for a CGI program (All you ever wanted to know about CGI programs, but were afraid to ask, is in Chapter 19.)

✔ A mail to link on a Web server (A mail to *link* starts an e-mail program on some — not all — Web servers.)

Before JavaScript, submitting data to a server like this was the only way that you could process input data.

Listing 7-6 shows how you set up a submit button. Notice the <FORM>...</FORM> section? (For a complete blow-by-blow on <FORM>...</FORM>, see Chapter 10.) For now, pay special attention to the ACTION property. ACTION is the specific name of the program or mail to link that you want to send the form data to. (The code in Listing 7-6 is a bare-bones version of submit, so the ACTION property is the only form property that's defined.) Take a look:

Listing 7-6:   Source for submit **Button Example**

```
<HTML>
<HEAD>
<TITLE>submit Button Example</TITLE>
</HEAD>
<BODY>
<BR>
<FORM NAME="entryForm"
ACTION="mailto:emilyv@vnet.ibm.com">

<BR>Please check all of the following sport-related
            activities you enjoy:<BR>
<INPUT TYPE="checkbox" NAME="play"> play
<INPUT TYPE="checkbox" NAME="watch"> watch
<INPUT TYPE="checkbox" NAME="coach"> coach

<BR>
<B>Please enter your favorite sport and then click the
        'Reset' button:</B>
<BR><BR>
<INPUT TYPE="text" NAME="sport" SIZE="15" VALUE="none">
<INPUT TYPE="reset" NAME="resetButton" VALUE="Reset">
<INPUT TYPE="submit" NAME="submitButton" VALUE="Submit"

</FORM>
</BODY>
</HTML>
```

When you press the button marked Submit, Netscape or Internet Explorer e-mail is launched (depending on which browser you're running), pre-filled with the e-mail address specified in the ACTION property. Figure 7-6 shows how it looks from Navigator.

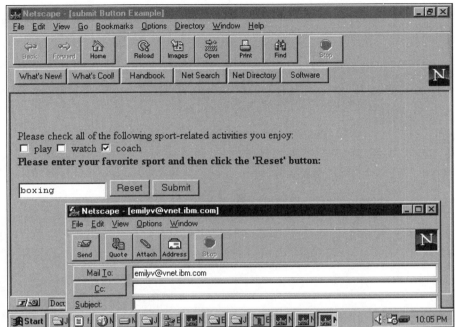

Figure 7-6:
Submit button example.

No matter what code you call when the submit button's onClick event handler is invoked, the code can't stop the form from being submitted. If that's what you're trying to do, use the form object's submit() method or the onSubmit event handler instead.

Tailored buttons

If you want to create a button that does something other than reset or submit your form, you can define your own custom button. As you may expect, the only event that the event handler button supports is the onClick event handler (buttons are rather one-dimensional — all you can do is push 'em). Listing 7-7 shows the source code for a custom push button.

Listing 7-7: **Source for Custom Push Button**

```
<HTML>
<HEAD>
<TITLE>Push Button Example</TITLE>
</HEAD>
<SCRIPT>
function setCase (caseSelection) {
    if (caseSelection == "upper") {
        document.form1.firstName.value =
            document.form1.firstName.value.toUpperCase()
        document.form1.lastName.value =
            document.form1.lastName.value.toUpperCase()
    }
    else {
        document.form1.firstName.value =
            document.form1.firstName.value.toLowerCase()
        document.form1.lastName.value =
            document.form1.lastName.value.toLowerCase()
    }
}
</SCRIPT>
<BODY>
<FORM NAME="form1">
<B>First name:</B>
<INPUT TYPE="text" NAME="firstName" SIZE=20>
<BR><B>Last name:</B>
<INPUT TYPE="text" NAME="lastName" SIZE=20>
<P><INPUT TYPE="button" VALUE="Names to uppercase"
            NAME="upperButton"
   onClick="setCase('upper')">
<INPUT TYPE="button" VALUE="Names to lowercase"
            NAME="lowerButton"
   onClick="setCase('lower')">
</FORM>
</BODY>
</HTML>
```

The code in Listing 7-7 defines two custom buttons: one called `lowerButton`, and one called `upperButton`. When a user clicks on `lowerButton`, the JavaScript interpreter calls the `setCase()` function, passing it the string `"lower"`; the result is that the text the user entered in the `firstName` and `lastName` fields will all be changed to lowercase.

When a user clicks on `upperButton`, the same thing happens — almost. This time, the JavaScript interpreter passes the string `"upper"` to the `setCase()` function, which causes the text in the `firstName` and `lastName` fields to be displayed all in uppercase — regardless of how they looked when the user typed them in initially.

Kickin' back with the radio

Radio buttons are mutually exclusive buttons that are grouped so that a user can choose only one. Listing 7-8 is a script that displays three radio buttons and then displays the chosen value via a pop-up prompt, as shown in Figure 7-7. Notice that the NAME property of all three buttons is set to the same value, chickenChoice. This value is what makes the choices mutually exclusive.

Listing 7-8: Source for Radio Buttons

```
<HTML>
<HEAD>
<TITLE>Radio Button Example</TITLE>
<SCRIPT LANGUAGE="JavaScript">

function display(choice) {
    window.alert("Your choice: " + choice.value)
}

</SCRIPT>
</HEAD>
<BODY>
<FORM>
<BR><BR><BR><B>Which is your favorite part of the
            chicken?</B>
<BR><BR><INPUT TYPE="radio" NAME="chickenChoice"
            VALUE="white"
onClick="display(this)"> white meat
<BR><INPUT TYPE="radio" NAME="chickenChoice" VALUE="dark"
onClick="display(this)"> dark meat
<BR><INPUT TYPE="radio" NAME="chickenChoice" VALUE="veggie"
onClick="display(this)"> Flesh! Yuck! I'm vegetarian
</FORM>
</BODY>
</HTML>
```

The code in Listing 7-8 defines three radio buttons:

1. White meat.

2. Dark meat.

3. Flesh! Yuck! I'm vegetarian.

As I said, the weird thing about radio buttons — which you probably noticed if you took a good look at Listing 7-8 — is that each of their names is the same (chickenChoice). This isn't a typo, and it isn't an accident. The names of radio buttons have to be the same — that's how the interpreter knows that they're a group.

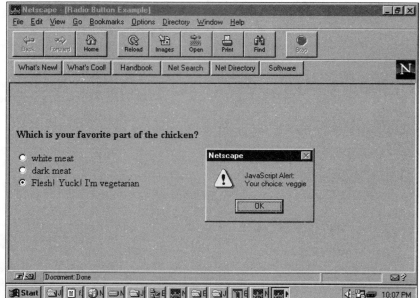

Figure 7-7:
Radio button
example.

Making a List and Checking It Twice

Two kinds of list boxes are available in JavaScript. One list box enables a user to choose a single selection from a drop-down box, and the other list box enables a user to make multiple selections from a scrolling list box. The form element select is used to define both types.

First check: single selection (drop-down box)

Listing 7-9 is an example of how to define a single-selection list box:

Listing 7-9:   Source for Single-Selection List Box

```
<HTML>
<HEAD>
<TITLE>Single Selection Listbox Example </TITLE>
<SCRIPT LANGUAGE="JavaScript">
function display(selection) {
    var tempIndex, selectedFlavor, myFave
    myFave="vanilla"

    //get index # of selection
    tempIndex=selection.selectedIndex
```

```
    // now get text
    selectedFlavor=selection.options[tempIndex].text

    if (selectedFlavor != myFave) {
    document.feedbackForm.opinion.value =
        selectedFlavor + " is okay"
    }
    else {
        document.feedbackForm.opinion.value=myFave
        += "'s my favorite, too!"
    }
}
</SCRIPT>
</HEAD>
<BODY>
<BR>
<FORM NAME="feedbackForm">
What's your favorite ice cream flavor?  Pick one:
<SELECT NAME="favoriteOne" onChange="display(this)">
<OPTION SELECTED> chocolate
<OPTION> vanilla
<OPTION> pistachio almond fudge
<OPTION> pink peppermint
<OPTION> caramel/marshmallow swirl
</SELECT>
<INPUT NAME="opinion" VALUE="" SIZE=35>
</FORM>
</BODY>
</HTML>
```

As you can see from the preceding code, the `select` element has five options
defined that the user can pick from: chocolate, vanilla, pistachio almond fudge,
pink peppermint, and caramel/marshmallow swirl. All of these options are kept
inside an array — the `<OPTION>` array. (An *array* is a numbered, or *indexed*, list
of variables.) When the time comes to figure out which option a user picked,
the `display()` function takes a look at each of the options in turn and exam-
ines it to see if it was the one picked.

The `<OPTION>` array looks like this (the numbers inside the square brackets are
called *index* numbers because they represent what place each option occupies
in the index):

option[0] = "chocolate"

option[1] = "vanilla"

option[2] = "pistachio almond fudge"

option[3] = "pink peppermint"

option[4] = "caramel/marshmallow swirl"

Figure 7-8 shows an example of a single-selection list box.

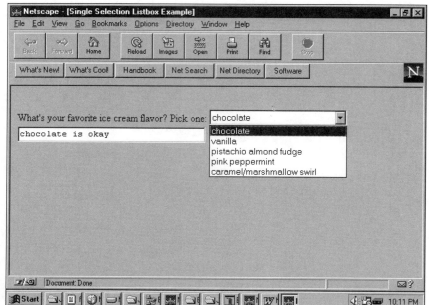

Figure 7-8:
Sorry, you
have to pick
just one
favorite!

Second check: multiple selection (scrolling list box)

Using the same form element, `select,` here's how to define a multiple-selection list box (and, just as important, how to access the values your user has chosen). Notice the addition of the `MULTIPLE` keyword in Listing 7-10.

Listing 7-10: Source for Multiple Selection List Box

```
<HTML>
<HEAD>
<TITLE>Multi-selection List Box Example</TITLE>
<SCRIPT LANGUAGE="JavaScript">

function displayResult(selection) {
    var theResult = ""

    var numberPicked=0
    for (var i=0; i<selection.length; i++) {
```

```
            if (selection.options[i].selected) {
              numberPicked++
              theResult += selection.options[i].text + " "
            }
        }
      document.feedbackForm.result.value=numberPicked
      alert("Here's what you picked: " + theResult)
}
</SCRIPT>
</HEAD>
<BODY>
<BR>
<FORM NAME="feedbackForm">
What kinds of music do you like?
<SELECT NAME="favoriteOne" MULTIPLE
            onChange="displayResult(this)">
<OPTION SELECTED> pop
<OPTION> rock
<OPTION> dogs barking Jingle Bells
<OPTION> rap
<OPTION> show tunes
<OPTION> African classical
</SELECT>
<BR>
Here's how many you selected:
<INPUT TYPE="text" NAME="result" VALUE="" SIZE=5>
</FORM>
</BODY>
</HTML>
```

Why not break with tradition and start with the number one?

You may wonder why the first element in the <OPTION> array isn't referred to as — oh, I don't know — the element number *one*. Beats me. My guess is that the situation is some really old programmer's idea of a joke. Having the first element of an array be the *0th* element is a carryover from C language, and by now folks are probably so used to it that they wouldn't know

what to do if arrays suddenly started with the number one. Unfortunately, this convention is so counter-intuitive that if you create more than two scripts in your programming life and never spend any time tracking down a bug caused by misnumbering array elements, I guarantee that you'll be the first person to do so!

The code in Listing 7-10 is fairly similar to that in Listing 7-9, with one big difference: this `select` definition includes the `MULTIPLE` keyword, so users can pick as many options as they like. (In Listing 7-9, users could only select one option). Figure 7-9 shows an example of a multiple-selection list box.

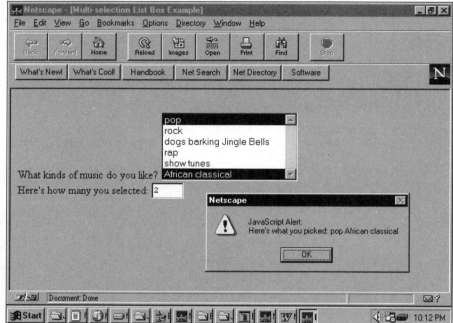

Figure 7-9:
Take as
many as you
want;
they're
small!

The Whole Shootin' Match: The Elements *Array*

Finally, for those of you who aren't content with manipulating measly form element by measly form element, here's a way to access all of the elements on a form, all at once. Oh, the power!

As you know, an array is nothing more than a list (actually, a numbered, or *indexed*, list), and you access the `elements` array like this: `formName.elements[index].value`. Clear as mud? Here's an example, courtesy of Listing 7-11, to help you make sense of it:

Listing 7-11: Source for elements **Array Example**

```
<HTML>
<HEAD>
<TITLE>elements Array Example</TITLE>
<SCRIPT LANGUAGE="JavaScript">
function displayElements(aForm) {
    var resultName = ""
    var resultValue = ""

    for (var i=0; i<aForm.elements.length; i++) {
        resultName += aForm.elements[i].name + " "
        resultValue += aForm.elements[i].value + " "
    }

    alert("There are " + aForm.elements.length +
        " elements contained in this form:\n" +
        resultName + "\nwith values of\n" + resultValue)
}
</SCRIPT>
</HEAD>
<BODY>
<FORM NAME="inputForm">

<INPUT TYPE="button" VALUE="Push Me" NAME="pushButton"
onClick="displayElements(inputForm)">
<BR><BR>
<B>How does programming JavaScript make you feel?  Check all
        that apply:</B>
    <BR><BR><INPUT TYPE="checkbox" NAME="liveAgain"> I can
        live again.
    <BR><INPUT TYPE="checkbox" NAME="mooseKiss"> Better than
        kissing a moose!
    <BR><INPUT TYPE="checkbox" NAME="brainHurts"> My brain
        still hurts.
    <BR><BR><B>How much time have you spent surfing the Web
        in the last week?</B>
    <BR><BR><INPUT TYPE="radio" NAME="timeSpent"
        VALUE="small"> 0 to 2 hours
    <BR><INPUT TYPE="radio" NAME="timeSpent" VALUE="med"> 3
        to 13 hours
    <BR><INPUT TYPE="radio" NAME="timeSpent" VALUE="large">
        More than 76 hours
</FORM>
</BODY>
</HTML>
```

The elements in the elements array are in *source code order;* that is, the 0th element is the first one defined, the 1st element is the second one defined, and so on, like this:

elements[0] = first element defined

elements[1] = second element defined

elements[2] = third element defined

...

Figure 7-10 shows you what the contents of an elements array look like:

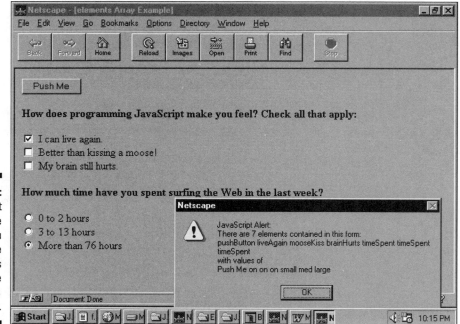

Figure 7-10: No element can hide when you display the contents of the elements array.

Chapter 8

Spicing Up Your Pages with Multimedia and More

. . . .

In This Chapter

▶ Adding hypertext links

▶ Displaying images

▶ Creating color

▶ Generating sound

▶ Adding animation

▶ Using a database

. . . .

*B*ecause displaying forms and form elements is the job of HTML (JavaScript comes into play when you want to work with the data that folks type into your form), I won't go into all the magnificent details of form display here. After all, you bought this book to find out more about JavaScript, not HTML! However, JavaScript *is* embedded in HTML — they work hand-in-glove — so you do need to have a grasp of some basic HTML syntax. In the spirit of *batteries included,* then, here's a useful smattering of HTML *and* JavaScript techniques to help you design attractive, useful Web pages. (Check out Chapter 3 if you need remedial HTML help, or *HTML For Dummies,* 2nd Edition for even more in-depth coverage.)

All the source code listings throughout this chapter are included on this book's companion CD. The files are named appropriately (for example, the code for Listing 8-1 is listed under the filename list0801.htm). Feel free to load them and play around with them. Doing so is lots of fun and can really help increase your understanding!

Layout and Design Tips, No Extra Charge

You've got a great deal of flexibility when it comes to designing Web pages. With a little perseverance, you can do pretty much anything you want. The first tip, then, is to decide what it is you *want* to do. Throwing a huge amount of *flash* (color, outrageous fonts, and images) into a document *just because you can* may backfire. People tend to enjoy pages that are interesting and quietly inviting more than ones that assault their senses.

Hypertext links are almost always a good idea, though. (I say *almost* because anything can be overdone!) You'll get lots of tips on the best way to approach building links in the "Spinning Your Web: Linking Pages" section below.

Remember, too, that added features (such as images and sound) are generally so large that they can take forever to download. Go ahead and use them if they're appropriate to your message; just be aware that some folks aren't blessed with an overabundance of patience and may choose to bypass your content if the load time is too great. Consider giving folks an option: Instead of setting up your page to load images automatically, provide a link instead (an <A>...</A> tag with the HREF property set to a gif file, for example, as described in Chapter 10). When you provide such a link, folks can see your goodies if they're of a mind to; but if not, they can quickly see what else you have to offer.

Finally (and this falls under the "figure out what you want to do" category), consider that JavaScript gives you the flexibility to create more than garden-variety Web pages. JavaScript enables you to create *actual applications*. On the client, you can create your own functions and your own objects, complete with built-in data and rules. If you need more power, you can create (or purchase) other programming components and integrate them into your scripted application (tons more about this in Part IV). The sky's the limit!

Spinning Your Web: Linking Pages

You undoubtedly want to link your JavaScript-enabled Web pages to other people's Web sites. After all, that's why they call it a *web* instead of a *strand*, right? You can think of a link as a phone line connecting you and your mom. In order to make the link, you have to know your mom's telephone number and you need your own phone number (so in case you get cut off, Mom can call you back).

Pretty straightforward, don't you think? The links in your Web pages work the same way. You need a destination point (called an *anchor*), and you need a starting point (unfortunately, also called a *link*). In our phone-home example, the destination point (anchor) would be your mom, and you would be the starting point (link).

Three possible permutations exist for linking Web page locations together:

✔ Linking from one specific location on a page to another specific location on the same page (called *intradocument* linking)

✔ Linking from one specific location on a page to the top of another page (called *interdocument* linking)

✔ Linking from one specific location on a page to another specific location on another page (a combination of *intradocument* and *interdocument* linking)

The specifics for each type of linking are listed in a following section. While you read through, though, keep in mind that no matter what kind of link you're creating, the following tips apply:

✔ Make sure that the links are appropriate for your content.

✔ Make sure that the links are organized so that they're easy to read. (Consider color and placement within the body of your document. A *jump page*, or page devoted to nothing but lists of links, is one way to go.)

✔ Make sure that you give users a way to return to your home page from every other page in your hierarchy. Few things are more frustrating than having to click the left-arrow key three dozen times when all you want to do is get back to where you started!

Linking two specific locations in the same document (intradocument)

Listing 8-1 shows how to link two locations in the same document. You may have seen this technique in your Web travels; it's often used to organize one large HTML file into manageable chunks, so that users can read the table of contents for a page, hop down to the section they're interested in, and hop back up to the table of contents after they have finished checking the section.

Listing 8-1:   Source for Intradocument Linking

```
<HTML>
<HEAD>
<TITLE>Example of Linking Locations Within the Same
          Document</TITLE>
</HEAD>
<FORM NAME="aForm">
<H1><CENTER>How to Stay Fit in Your 100s</CENTER></H1>
<A NAME="TOC"><H2>Table of Contents</H2></A>
<P>
```

(continued)

(continued)

```
<A HREF="#CHAP1">Chapter 1.</A><BR>
<A HREF="#CHAP2">Chapter 2.</A><BR>
<A HREF="#CHAP3">Chapter 3.</A><BR>

<A NAME="CHAP1"><H3>Chapter 1: Aerobic Fitness</H3></A>
<P>Chapter 1 text would go here, and it might be
several paragraphs (even pages) long.
<BR>

<A NAME="CHAP2"><H3>Chapter 2:  Eating Well</H3></A>
<P>Chapter 2 text would go here.  Pretend that
this chapter is really long.  What if someone read
through Chapter 2 and then decided to read Chapter 1?
Unless there was a link back to Chapter 1 (more
likely, a link back to the Table of Contents) it
would be hard for the user to scroll to the
correct starting point.
<BR><BR>
<A HREF="#TOC">Back to Table of Contents</A>
<P>

<A NAME="CHAP3"><H3>Chapter 3: Stress Reduction through Pet
          Ownership</H3></A>
<P>Chapter 3 text would go here.  When you're
designing multiple Web pages, consider putting a
button at the bottom of each page that lets the
user pop back to the first page (your <I>home</I> page).
<BR><BR>
<A HREF="#TOC">Back to Table of Contents</A>
</FORM>
</HTML>
```

Notice in this example that both anchors and links are defined with the `<A>`...`</A>` tag. The difference between anchors and links is that if you assign a value to the `HREF` property, you're defining a *link* (in other words, you're telling the interpreter where you want your users to go when they click on the text that you've defined). If you assign a value to the `NAME` reference instead, you're defining an *anchor* (a place other links can jump to).

Linking two different documents (interdocument)

You can see how to create links between two different Web pages in Listing 8-2. This type of link takes you from a specific location on one Web page straight to the top of another Web page.

Listing 8-2:   **Source for Interdocument Linking**

```
<HTML>
<HEAD>
<TITLE>Example of Linking Documents</TITLE>
</HEAD>
<FORM NAME="aForm">
<BR><H2>Click on any of the links listed:</H2><BR>

<A HREF="http://home.netscape.com/eng/mozilla/2.01/handbook/
            javascript/index.html">
JavaScript Handbook</A><BR>
<A HREF="http://www.idgbooks.com">IDG Books' Home Page
            </A><BR>
<A HREF="http://www.netscape.com">Netscape's home page
            </A><BR>
<A HREF="http://www.sun.com">Sun's home page</A><BR>

</FORM>
</HTML>
```

As Listing 8-2 shows, all you need to do to link to another Web page is specify the other page's URL as part of the <A>...</A> tag. To return to the original page from a link page, use the Back button on the browser menu bar.

Notice what happens when you move your mouse over a link: The URL of the link that your mouse pointer is passing over automatically appears in the status bar! JavaScript automatically includes that feature for you; you don't need to program it explicitly.

The whole enchilada: linking two specific locations in two separate documents

If you want to combine intradocument and interdocument linking, take a look at Listing 8-3. The code is similar to Listing 8-2. This type of linking is handy if you want to link to a specific piece of information buried deep in someone else's page (or another page of your own, for that matter).

If you want to link two of your own pages, all you need to do is define an anchor in one page and a link to that anchor from another. Unfortunately (or fortunately!) you can't very well stick anchors in other people's pages just so you can link to them; you have to use what's there or go without.

You can figure out if there are any anchors available for you to link to in someone else's document in a couple of ways, but by far the easiest way is to load the document that you're interested in and view the source (select View⇨

Document Source from the Navigator menu or View⇨Source from the Internet Exlorer menu). Anything you see that contains `<A NAME="someTextHere"...>` `</A>` is an anchor, and you can link to it as shown in Listing 8-3.

Listing 8-3: Source for Intra- and Interdocument Linking

```
<HTML>
<HEAD><TITLE>Linking Example: to a Specific Location in
            Another Document</TITLE></HEAD>
<BODY>
<FORM NAME="myForm">
<BR><H2>Click on the following link and notice where you jump
            to:</H2><BR>

<A HREF="http://home.netscape.com/comprod/at_work/
            white_paper/intranet/vision.html#enterprise">
Netscape's Enterprise Server</A><BR>

</FORM>
</BODY>
</HTML>
```

The code in Listing 8-3 defines a link which displays on the screen as `Netscape's Enterprise Server`. When a user clicks on the link, the URL assigned to the `HREF` property is loaded. Notice that the `HREF` property is composed of three things:

✔ The URL for the page to which you want to link

✔ A hash symbol (#) that lets the JavaScript interpreter know that an anchor name is coming up (some people call this character a *pound* sign, but that's pretty North America-centric — which I found out the first time I visited the U.K., where they have a slightly different idea of what a "pound" sign is!)

✔ The name of the anchor to which you want to link

Graphics, Colors, Sound, and Other Neat Stuff

One of the cool things about Web pages is that they're light years beyond what used to be considered "normal" for computer interfaces. You know — ugly green monochrome displays with cryptic messages all in uppercase? Well, that was then, and this is now. Not only do you not have to settle for plain-colored text, you don't have to settle for text at all! You can add images, all kinds of different colors, sounds, and custom software components to your Web pages. Read on for details.

A picture is worth 868 words (inflation, you know)

Inserting pictures into your Web page is brought to you courtesy of HTML. Inserting pictures is quite simple to do; all you need to do is remember that unless you specify a complete pathname (such as `http://www.what.com/ images/filename.gif`), both Navigator and Internet Explorer look for your image file by starting in the directory where your HTML file is located.

Take a look at Listing 8-4 to see how you can incorporate nifty graphics into your own Web pages.

Like all of the listings in this book, Listing 8-4 is available for you in ready-to-use HTML format on the companion CD. The name of the file containing listing 8-4 is list0804.htm. The image file, castle.gif, is also included on the CD.

Listing 8-4:   Source for Inserting an Image into a Web Page

```
<HTML>
<HEAD>
<TITLE>Example of Inserting an Image into a Web Page</TITLE>
</HEAD>
<BODY>
<BR>
<FORM>
<IMG SRC="images/castle.gif" ALIGN="TOP" ALT="[Picture -
          Scottish ruin]">
</FORM>
</BODY>
</HTML>
```

Notice the ALIGN and ALT keywords in Listing 8-4. ALIGN tells the interpreter where you want the picture to be placed on your page. (See Chapter 10 for a complete run-down on defining an image in HTML). The ALT keyword enables you to provide a text string to display when someone without a graphics-supporting browser tries to look at your page (always a good idea). Figure 8-1 shows how an image looks to someone without image capability.

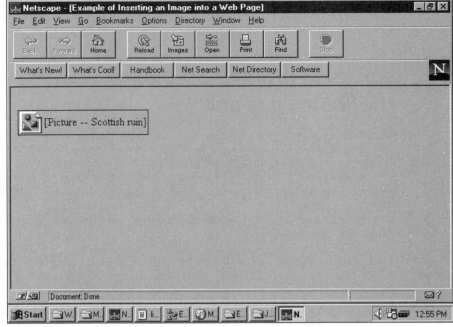

Figure 8-1:
Beware: this is how your image looks to someone without image capability.

The value for the SRC property in this example represents an incomplete pathname. (One tip-off is that the pathname doesn't start with http://.) If Listing 8-4 is stored in an HTML file located on d:\javascripts, the interpreter will try to find castle.gif in d:\javascripts\images. If that's where it is, great! If not, the image won't load.

Figure 8-2 shows how an image looks to someone with image capability.

If Navigator can't load your graphic for any reason, it displays an icon with a big question mark on it instead. A few things could cause this; a misspelled filename, a missing file, and the incorrect pathname are a few likely culprits. If this situation happens to you, click your right mouse button on the question mark icon and select View this image. A window pops up and tells you exactly what the Navigator program is looking for, which should help you pinpoint the problem.

If Internet Explorer can't find your graphic, it won't load it (obviously; I just said it couldn't find it!) but unfortunately, it doesn't give you a visible clue that it has tried and failed, either. Unless the generally available version of Internet Explorer 3.0 behaves differently, your only bet is to left-click on the image a few times and if nothing happens, view the source (View⇨Source) to see what image file it can't find — and take it from there.

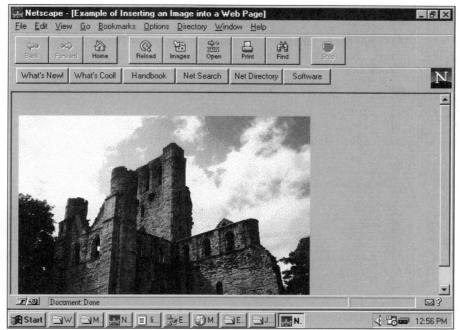

Figure 8-2:
Here's an
image the
way it was
meant to be
seen!

Color me happy

Using color is a good way to spice up your pages. You can specify different
colors for any or all of the items in Table 8-1.

Table 8-1   Properties (And One Method) You Can Color

Item	Type	Description
BGCOLOR	property (of document)	background color
TEXT	property (of document)	foreground color
LINK	property (of document)	unfollowed link color
ALINK	property (of document)	activated link color
VLINK	property (of document)	followed link color
fontcolor	method (of string)	changes string color

These properties (and method) accept *strings* and *hexadecimal RGB triplets* as
values. A complete list of all the color choices available appears in Chapter 16
(along with an exhaustive explanation of RGB triplets, if you're interested!).

The code in Listing 8-5 produces a very colorful Web page. The background is colored lime green and the default text color is dark blue. All of the links start life out black, and then turn chocolate brown when they're being accessed, and then change to maroon after the link has been loaded. This may not be the most soothing color scheme you've ever seen, but it does show you how easy it is to add color to your Web pages!

Unfortunately, the black-and-white format of this book just doesn't do justice to the Web page produced by Listing 8-5. If you'd like to see what it looks like in color, load the HTML file list0805.htm off the companion CD. Then play around with it!

Listing 8-5:   Source for Color Example

```
<HTML>
<HEAD><TITLE>Color Example</TITLE></HEAD>
<SCRIPT LANGUAGE="JavaScript">
    document.write("This is dark
            orchid.".fontcolor("darkorchid"))
</SCRIPT>
<BODY BGCOLOR="lime" TEXT="darkblue" LINK="black"
            ALINK="chocolate"
VLINK="maroon">
<FORM NAME="colorForm">
<BR><H2>Click on the links and watch the colors change:
            </H2><BR>
<A HREF="http://home.netscape.com/eng/mozilla/2.01/handbook/
            javascript/index.html">
JavaScript Handbook</A><BR>
<A HREF="http://www.idgbooks.com">IDG Books' Home Page
            </A><BR>
<A HREF="http://www.netscape.com">Netscape's home page
            </A><BR>
<A HREF="http://www.sun.com">Sun's home page</A><BR>
</FORM>
</BODY>
</HTML>
```

Pay special attention to the color of the links referenced in the preceding code. It's common practice in Web circles to choose contrasting colors (maybe even more contrasting than black and maroon) for the properties LINK and VLINK. That's because doing this makes it easier for your users to recognize at a glance which links they've already followed, and which represent new territory — especially when there are a handful of related links on one page.

Sounds great!

Adding sounds to your Web page can be fun. Adding sounds can also be very expensive in terms of download time, because sound files (which typically have extensions of ra, sbi, snd, au, or wav) are notoriously huge. Add to that the fact that not everyone is equipped with sound-playing software and speakers (hard to believe in this day and age, I know), and the attraction of making sound a big priority for your Web creation begins to pale.

In some cases, though, sound is the perfect medium for your content. A good example can be found on the following Web site for a popular record label:

```
http://www.windham.com/ourmusic/lr/index.html
```

The best way to add sound is to specify a link to a sound file. That way, folks who know that they aren't set up for sound (or who are in a hurry) can choose not to hear the sound.

When a user clicks on a sound link, the Web browser loads the sound file, recognizes that it needs to invoke a sound player, automatically launches a sound player, and (depending on the sound player) plays the file immediately. Take a look at the example in Listing 8-6.

Not only is the source code in Listing 8-6 available on the companion CD, the referenced sound file is also available for your convenience. The name of the HTML file is (of course) list0806.htm; the name of the sound file is dog.wav.

Listing 8-6:   Source for Sound Example

```
<HTML>
<HEAD><TITLE>Sound Example</TITLE></HEAD>
<BODY>
<FORM NAME="myForm">
<BR><H2>Click on the following link and see what happens
          </H2><BR>

<A HREF="dog.wav">
Ferocious 10 lb. puppy growl</A><BR>

</FORM>
</BODY>
</HTML>
```

If you're using Navigator and you try to download a sound file that your configuration of Navigator isn't familiar with, a pop-up message will appear that asks for directions on where to find an application to use. Follow the instructions on the message. If you don't know the name of a sound player off the top of your head, you can browse your program icons to find one. Figure 8-3 shows part of the process of associating sound files with a sound player.

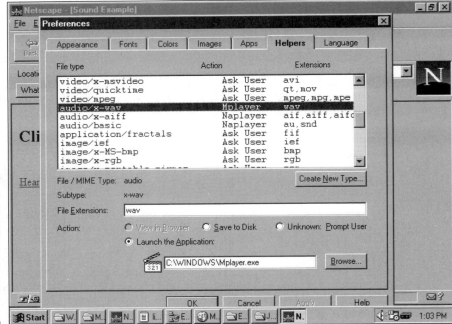

Figure 8-3:
Then:
picking out
a hi-fi. Now:
associating
sound files
with a
sound
player.

Another way to associate a sound file with a particular media player is to select Options➪General Preferences➪Helpers from the Navigator menu bar. (There's a Help button on the bottom right hand side of the Preferences window you can click to help you figure out exactly how to set up a new association). If you're running Internet Explorer, select View➪Options➪Programs, and then in the Viewers section, select File Types.

Moving Pictures

You can add animation to your document in several ways. One way is to follow the same formula as for sound; that is, create a link to an animation file (typically identified with avi, dvi, fli, mov, or mpg file extensions).

Another way to add animation is to integrate your script with a Netscape plug-in, such as Shockwave for Director from Macromedia. Shockwave enables you to play Director movies inside your Web pages.

Still another way to animate your document is to integrate your script with a Java applet or other program that displays animated graphics.

Linking 'em in

Here's an example of integrating an animated sequence into a Web page. If you've read the sound example, this example should look quite familiar to you! If you haven't, here's the lowdown: when you assign the name of an animation file to the HREF attribute of the link tag (<A>...</A>), the animation file loads automatically when a user clicks on that link. Check out the example code in Listing 8-7 to see what I mean.

Both the code in Listing 8-7 and the referenced animation file are available on the companion CD. The name of the HTML file is list0807.htm, and the name of the animation file (as you can see below) is smiling.gif.

Listing 8-7:   Try Linking Animation into Your Web Pages!

```
<HTML>
<HEAD><TITLE>Animation Example</TITLE></HEAD>
<BODY>
<FORM NAME="aForm" METHOD=POST>
<BR><H2>Click on the following link to see an animated .gif
          file in action!</H2><BR>
<A HREF="images/smiling.gif">
Smile </A> and half the world smiles with you (the other half
          thinks you're up to something)...
</FORM>
</BODY>
</HTML>
```

To see this example in action, make sure that the file smiling.gif is in the same directory as the HTML file when you load the HTML file. You may expect a gif file to represent a static image only. This file is actually an *animated* image file. Give it a whirl!

Plugging 'em in

Plug-ins are software components, some of which support animation that enable you to *plug in* other applications to your Web pages. You can download free plug-ins — Shockwave for Director, from Macromedia, is a popular example — from many sites on the Web. Because this book focuses on JavaScript, I won't bore those of you who aren't interested with the details; just be aware that the capability is there if you ever decide you need it (and more besides). If you *are* interested, visit the following for a list of available plug-ins:

```
http://home.netscape.com/comprod/mirror/
          navcomponents_download.html
```

Integrating 'em in

Two of the most popular ways to animate a Web page are to make calls to Java applets and to use CGI programs that run animated sequences. You can read about Java applets and CGI programs in Chapter 9, but to whet your appetite, take a look at Listing 8-8. Listing 8-8 shows how to integrate a Java applet into HTML. This particular Java applet displays an animated figure when it's invoked. Notice the `<APPLET>...</APPLET>` tags? They're like `<SCRIPT>...</SCRIPT>` tags, only they define Java applets instead of JavaScript scripts. (As you see in Chapter 10, there's a corresponding JavaScript object called `applet` that you can reference in your JavaScript scripts.)

Listing 8-8:   Source for Animation via Java Applet

```
<HTML>
<HEAD><TITLE>Animation via Java Applet Example</TITLE>
</HEAD>
<BODY>

<APPLET CODE=Animator.class CODEBASE="http://java.sun.com/
          books/Series/Tutorial/example" WIDTH=55

HEIGHT=68>
       <PARAM NAME="imagesource" VALUE="images/duke">
       <PARAM NAME=endimage value=10>
       <PARAM NAME=pause VALUE=100>
       <PARAM NAME=pauses
          VALUE=2500|100|100|100|100|100|100|100|100|100>
  <APP CLASS="Animator" IMG="http://java.sun.com/tutorial/
          images/duke" WIDTH=55 HEIGHT=68

     OR-
            DER=1:2500|2:100|3:100|4:100|5:100|6:100|7:100|8:100|9:100|10:100>
</applet>

</BODY>
</HTML>
```

Hey! What's all this stuff got to do with JavaScript?

Up until now, many of the examples in this chapter have focused on HTML. No JavaScript at all in some of them! Well, now that you're comfortable with the concept of anchors and links and such and have had a chance to get your feet wet, so to speak, you get to see how invaluable JavaScript can be when it's used in conjunction with HTML display statements.

Suppose that you're building a Web page that enables folks to order personalized scarves. Suppose also that you'd like to be able to give your customers an accurate total for their purchase, including state sales tax (if applicable). You can do this simply by using the object-creation techniques that JavaScript provides. Listing 8-9 shows you how.

If you check out the HTML file for the source code in Listing 8-9, notice that the "state" input field has focus the second you load up the page. That's because the onLoad event handler contains this statement: document.taxForm. stateField.focus(). If you're feeling feisty, remove the statement, reload list0809.htm, and see what happens.

Listing 8-9:   Source for Database Example

```
<HTML>
<HEAD><TITLE>JavaScript Database Example</TITLE>
<SCRIPT LANGUAGE="JavaScript">

function state(state, tax){
    this.state=state
    this.tax=tax
}

function taxTable(){
    this[0]=new state("AZ", 1.23)
    this[1]=new state("CA", 2.24)
    this[2]=new state("TX", 7.50)
    this[3]=new state("WA", 8.01)
    this[4]=new state("NY", 0.54)
}

function calculateTax(stateField){
    index=0
    var result="not defined"
    while (taxGuide[index]) {
            if (stateField.value.toUperCase() ==
              taxGuide[index].state) {
                    result=taxGuide[index].tax
            }
            index++
    }
    alert("The tax for " + stateField.value.toUperCase() +
    " is " + result)
}

</SCRIPT>
</HEAD>
```

(continued)

(continued)

```
<BODY onLoad="taxGuide = new taxTable();
            document.taxForm.stateField.focus()">
<FORM NAME="taxForm">
<H1>Tax values are defined for AZ, CA, TX, WA, and NY.</H1>
<H2>Enter a two-digit state code and then click somewhere
            else on the page.</H2>
<INPUT TYPE="text" NAME="stateField" SIZE=4
onChange="calculateTax(this)">In which state are you located?

</FORM>
</BODY>
</HTML>
```

Notice that two objects appear in the script, one object nested inside of the other. The `taxTable` object has five entries, each of which are states. Each state contains two properties: the state's name and the state's tax rate. This example is of a fairly trivial database, but I think that you can see the potential here!

The database example given is just one teensy-tiny example of what you can do with JavaScript. Any rules or static data that you'd like to incorporate into your objects can be kept in a similar JavaScript mini-database by using the same approach as shown in the database example.

Chapter 9

Hey! Can I Get Some Service Around Here?

· ·

In This Chapter

▶ Calling CGI programs

▶ Interacting with Java applets

▶ Interacting with plug-ins

▶ Exploring server-side JavaScript

· ·

*A*lmost all of the examples of scripts in this book have concentrated on *client-side JavaScript scripts:* scripts that are loaded onto viewers' machines and are interpreted there. But you may want to do some things that you just plain can't (or don't want to) do on the client. For that matter, you may want to do some things that JavaScript just can't handle itself — for example, you may want to inherit objects from other objects. (See Chapter 4 for a discussion of inheritance and why the fact that JavaScript doesn't have it is no reason to jump off a bridge).

Fortunately, JavaScript is flexible. If you're running client-side JavaScript (and my guess is that you are, because client-side JavaScript is the focus of this book), you've got several choices if you want more power. For more power, you can integrate your scripts with the following:

✔ CGI programs

✔ Java applets

✔ Netscape plug-ins

All of these programs hang out on a Web server and only execute when they're told to by a statement in your script.

As far as server-side JavaScript support goes, right now your choices are the following:

✔ **Livewire:** A set of visual Web site-management tools from Netscape, which includes Netscape Navigator Gold and a JavaScript compiler

✔ **Netscape Enterprise Server:** An industrial-strength server-in-a-box that also supports JavaScript

This book doesn't dwell on server-side JavaScript; after all, if you're keen to learn all about either Livewire or Enterprise, you're probably a Webmaster or something, in which case there's a better-than-average chance that you either (a) already know everything about server-side JavaScript (in which case a section here wouldn't help you) or (b) don't know much at all about it (in which case you can use another whole book on the subject).

Instead, this chapter concentrates on services that you can call from client-side JavaScript — Java applets, CGI programs, and plug-ins — and just briefly discusses JavaScript server implementations.

Client-Side JavaScript Is JavaScript

When you think client-side JavaScript, think Netscape Navigator and Internet Explorer. You can take advantage of all of the services in this section — CGI, Java, and plug-ins — by inserting statements (specifics are detailed in each of the following sections) into the same HTML documents you use with Navigator and Internet Explorer (and with the 3.0 release of Navigator, by inserting them directly into your JavaScript scripts!).

CGI programs: services that execute on the server

All of the services in this section live on the server; the difference is that one (CGI programs) actually executes on the server, and the other two (plug-ins and Java applets) are downloaded to the client and execute there, on the client. This distinction is quite important, when you think about it. For one thing, CGI programs have to conform to the runtime requirements of the server, not the client — which means that CGI programs must have authorization to run on the server and access server resources (something only the Web server administrator can grant).

CGI is often referred to as *server-side scripting,* and it's all anyone had in the way of Web scripting until JavaScript came along. This is how CGI works: You create a script in Perl or a full-blown program in C. (These two languages are commonly used because they're not only powerful but are also fairly standard on many platforms; technically, though, you can use whatever language you want.) You install your CGI script/program on a Web server. Then, in your HTML document, you call your CGI program. The program executes on the server, does whatever it was coded to do (often CGI programs are used to verify passwords, access databases, and that sort of thing), and passes back any results (often in the form of another Web page) to the client browser, which then displays the results.

Pay attention while you're surfing the Web, and you can tell when the page that you're accessing is invoking a CGI program. In Navigator's Location field (it's the Address field if you're running Internet Explorer), you see a regular URL followed by `/cgi-bin/programName`. Often the name of the program has a cgi extension; the program is almost always located in a special cgi directory — that's how the Web server knows that it's a CGI program. Sometimes the URL and CGI program name are followed by a question mark and some data. The question mark means that any data that follows is input data being sent to the CGI program.

Here's what you need to do in order to integrate a CGI program with a Web page:

1. **Set up values for the** `ACTION` **and** `METHOD` **properties of the form. The value for** `ACTION` **needs to be the complete URL of the CGI program you want to execute. For example**

```
<FORM
ACTION="http://altavista.digital.com/cgi-bin/
query?pg=q&what=web&fmt=.&q=JavaScript">
```

The `METHOD` property of the `<FORM>...</FORM>` tag also affects CGI program execution. The `METHOD` property's value can either be `GET` (meaning that the user's input data is tacked on to the end of the URL and sent to the server that way; the CGI program then retrieves it via the environment variable `QUERY_STRING`) or `POST` (meaning that the user's input data is sent to the server in a stream of bytes and is retrieved on the other side via something called *stdin,* which is computer shorthand for "standard input" and is explained in more detail in Chapter 19). `GET` is the default value, so if you don't specify a value for `METHOD`, it's the same thing as specifying `GET`.

```
<FORM
ACTION="http://altavista.digital.com/cgi-bin/
query?pg=q&what=web&fmt=.&q=JavaScript" METHOD="POST">
```

2. **Along with setting up the** `ACTION` **and** `METHOD` **properties of the form, you also need to provide a mechanism to kick off the actual call to the CGI program. In this example, the user triggers form submission by clicking the Submit button (as explained in Chapter 10, submit buttons are hard-wired to submit the form automatically when they're clicked).**

```
<INPUT TYPE="submit" VALUE="Submit">
```

Now I've explained how to set up a form to trigger a CGI program, take a look at the order in which things happen from the time a user clicks on the Submit button clear through until the data (if any) is received back from the server:

- ✔ First, the user clicks on the Submit button, which causes the browser to send a request to the server to invoke the CGI program.

- ✔ Second, the server receives the request, picks out the URL that was passed (the value for the ACTION property), and executes the correct CGI program.

- ✔ Third, the CGI program executes and returns any data to the server (often formatted as another Web page).

- ✔ Fourth, the server accepts the return data and sends it back to the client browser.

- ✔ Fifth, the browser displays the returned data to the user.

Listing 9-1 (found later in this chapter) shows how a CGI program is called from an HTML document; Listing 9-2 (also found later in this chapter) is the other side of the coin — the source listing for a CGI program.

Remember that CGI programs run on Web servers, not clients. That means (in part) that CGI programs must execute on a machine that has the HTTP daemon (a fancy term for *Web server software*), called *httpd* for short, running. Your machine probably doesn't have httpd running, and so your machine isn't a Web server; therefore, you can't run a CGI program on your machine. You can invoke one *from* your machine, but the CGI program itself must reside on a Web server.

When you're testing your ability to call CGI programs, you need to look for ones that you can readily access. (Some folks, for a variety of very good reasons, restrict who can run programs on their servers; so just finding a CGI program doesn't necessarily mean you have authority to run it.) Search engines often fall into the category of freely usable programs, as the example in Listing 9-1 shows.

Take a look at the HTML file list0901.htm, located on the companion CD, to see the code in Listing 9-1 in action (without having to type any of it in!).

Listing 9-1: Example of Invoking a CGI Program from an HTML Document

```
<HTML>
<HEAD>
<TITLE>Example of Calling a CGI Program</TITLE>
</HEAD>
<BODY>
<H1>Press the button to search Alta Vista automatically for
all documents including the word 'JavaScript'
<FORM NAME="myForm" METHOD="POST" ACTION="http://
          altavista.digital.com/cgi-bin/
```

```
                    query?pg=q&what=web&fmt=.&q=JavaScript">
<INPUT TYPE="submit" VALUE="Submit">
</FORM>
</BODY>
</HTML>
```

Notice that the CGI program file is named `query` and is located in the `http://altavista.digital.com/cgi-bin` directory.

Also, do you see the `METHOD="POST"` in the `<FORM>`...`</FORM>` declaration? This bit of code means that you already have data that you want to throw at the CGI program so the CGI program can take a look at the data right away. (The data follows the question mark in the value for the `ACTION` property.) If the value for `METHOD` were `GET`, running this script would send the data, all right, but the CGI program wouldn't know to start the search immediately (which is what you want to do in this case). Whether or not you should use `GET` or `POST` always depends on how the CGI program wants to receive data — and that's something that's best figured out either by asking the CGI program's author directly, or by studying examples of how other JavaScripters have done it.

Remember that you can send anything you like to a CGI program. That potential material includes not only values that users type in, but values calculated by JavaScript functions, too.

Listing 9-2:   Example of CGI Program (Written in Perl) that Generates a Random Number

```
#*****************************************************************
#** This Perl example is provided "as is".  This code is    **
#** not supported, but I will try to answer questions as    **
#** time allows.  Email: wizjd@panix.com                    **
#** Visit: <URL:http://www.panix.com/~wizjd/> for updated,  **
#** and new examples.                                       **
#*****************************************************************
#!/usr/local/bin/perl

$number = $fields{'number'};

print("Content-Type: text/html\n\n");
print("<HEAD><TITLE>Random Number Page</TITLE></HEAD>\n");
print("<BODY>\n");

srand;
$number = rand(100);
$number = substr($number,0,2);
```

(continued)

(continued)

```
print "<H3>The random number is <B>", $number, "</B></H3>";
print "<HR>";
print "<A href=\x22/~wizjd/random.cgi/number=", $number,
"\x22>";
print "<B>Get another Random number</A>\n";
print "<HR>";
print "<BR>See the Perl";
print "<A href=random_src.html> Source Code</A>";
print "(random.cgi) for this page";
print "<HR><A href=\x22/~wizjd/test.html\x22>Back to Examples
         Page</A>\n";

print("</BODY>");
print("</HTML>");
```

If you think that the Perl script in Listing 9-2 looks a little more complicated than plain-vanilla JavaScript, I'd have to agree with you. Perl programmers are a fairly rare breed; so even though Perl is less extensive (and, therefore, ostensibly easier to learn) than full-blown programming languages, some folks opt to write their CGI programs in C instead, just because those folks are more familiar with that language (and because more examples are lying around on the Web to steal — er, I mean *borrow*).

In diplomacy, a *protocol* is a set of procedures that need to be followed in a given situation. In computer science, it's the same thing (only in this case, the parties involved in the situation are made out of silicon instead of carbon). The *protocol* that's used to transfer a request from a Web client to a Web server is called *hyper text transfer protocol (HTTP),* and the communications method for interaction between the Web server and a CGI program is called CGI. That statement means that not just any old machine can be a Web server; in order to *call* itself a Web server, the machine must support HTTP and CGI.

Services that serve on the client

Some services aren't actually executed on the server where they're stored. Instead, some are downloaded into the client browser's memory or even hard drive, and run there. Services that fall into this category include Java applets and Netscape plug-ins. With HTML alone, you can integrate both applets and plug-ins into Web pages. With Navigator 3.0, you can integrate them directly into JavaScript scripts. (A fine distinction, but one I'm sure that you'll appreciate after you glance through this section.)

JavaScript and Java, together at last

Java *applets* are special programs that can be loaded into Java-supportive Web browsers (such as Navigator 3.0 and Internet Explorer 3.0) and executed with the HTML <APPLET>...</APPLET> tag. An example of an HTML document invoking a Java applet is coming up in Listing 9-3.

The code in Listing 9-3 can be found in its entirety in the HTML file list0903.htm (located on the companion CD). Check it out!

Listing 9-3:   Example of HTML Document Invoking a Java Applet

```
<HTML>
<HEAD><TITLE>Java Applet Example</TITLE></HEAD>
<BODY>

<APPLET CODE=Animator.class CODEBASE="http://java.sun.com/
books/Series/Tutorial/" WIDTH=55 HEIGHT=68>
<PARAM NAME="imagesource"
VALUE="http://java.sun.com/books/Series/Tutorial/images/
duke">
        <PARAM NAME=endimage value=10>
        <PARAM NAME=pause VALUE=100>
        <PARAM NAME=pauses
            VALUE=2500|100|100|100|100|100|100|100|100|100>
<APP CLASS="Animator" IMG="http://java.sun.com/tutorial/
images/duke" WIDTH=55 HEIGHT=68
ORDER=1:2500|2:100|3:100|4:100|5:100|6:100|7:100|8:100|9:100
            |10:100>
</APPLET>

</BODY>
</HTML>
```

You may recognize this source from a listing in Chapter 8. This time around, though, take a close look at the point in the document when the applet is loaded. The applet is loaded automatically. If only a way to invoke an applet from JavaScript was available — well, then life would be complete, wouldn't it? You could invoke applets when you wanted to, not automatically — in response to user events, perhaps, or based on whatever conditions you decided to set up. Wouldn't having that capability be *great*? Well, that's exactly what Navigator 3.0, via LiveConnect, enables you to do! (*LiveConnect,* available in Netscape Navigator Version 3.0, is the software responsible for enabling Java applets, JavaScript scripts, and Netscape plug-ins to communicate directly with each other. Internet Explorer 3.0 also supports applets, Javascript scripts, and plugin integration.) The following code fragment shows you how.

```
...
<APPLET

...
NAME="SomeApplet">
</APPLET>

<FORM NAME="myForm">
<INPUT TYPE="button" VALUE="Start" NAME="startButton"
onClick="document.SomeApplet.start()">
</FORM>
...
```

Note the addition of the NAME property. You refer to the NAME property in your JavaScript statements so you can identify a particular applet.

Also, take a look at the statement that calls the applet (it's assigned to the onClick event handler of the Start button): onClick="document. SomeApplet.start()" The start() method is a method of the Java applet called SomeApplet. How would you know this if you hadn't actually coded SomeApplet? You wouldn't — unless whoever *did* told you.

Fortunately, it's common practice in object-oriented languages like Java for programmers to *publish* what are known as *public* methods. (*Publishing* in this context just means making something known somehow; sometimes it's as down-to-earth as one person calling another person on the phone and saying, "Hey, George, what public methods did you code for SomeApplet, anyway?") A *public* method is a special kind of method that the applet programmer makes available to the programming public on purpose, so they can call it. The start() method of SomeApplet is such a public method, and that's why it can be called from a JavaScript script. JavaScript in Navigator 3.0 can call any public method of any Java applet (or access any of the applet's public variables or properties, for that matter).

JavaScript & Netscape plug-in cohabitation

Plug-ins are special programs written in C++ and optimized for Netscape Navigator, and are loaded into HTML files via the <EMBED> tag. The syntax is much like that needed to call a Java applet:

```
<EMBED SRC=myPlug.exe WIDTH=420 HEIGHT=200>
```

In addition to providing JavaScript/Java interoperability, Navigator 3.0's LiveConnect technology also provides the capability to create JavaScript scripts that can pass information directly to plug-ins and vice versa. As with applets, the capability to trigger a plug-in based on a user event is mighty useful. Here's how you can go about triggering a plug-in in Navigator:

```
var result = ""
if (document.embeds.length > 0) {
    for (var i=0; i<document.embeds.length; i++) {
        result += document.embeds[i]
    }
}
return result
```

The `embeds` array is organized in source code order, which means that `embeds[0]` is the first plug-in defined, `embeds[1]` is the second plug-in defined, and so on.

Version 3.0 of Microsoft's Internet Explorer is expected to support JavaScript/plug-in integration when it becomes generally available. For more information, visit

```
http://www.microsoft.com/ie/ie3/nsplugin.htm
```

Server-Side JavaScript: Almost Ready for Prime Time

This section describes JavaScript implementations designed for Web servers (as opposed to Web clients, which are the focus of this book). In general, server-side JavaScript is a little newer than client-side; another difference is that server-side JavaScript is *compiled* instead of *interpreted*. (Check out Chapter 1 if you're interested in the difference between compiled and interpreted languages). Read on for further details. . . .

Livewire (not to be confused with LiveConnect!)

Livewire, from Netscape, is a suite of visual tools designed to make creating and managing Web content, Web sites, and Web applications easy enough for regular people. Livewire includes Netscape Navigator Gold, site managing software, a JavaScript compiler, and a database connectivity library. This is heavy-duty server software and, at the time of this writing, it's only available for Windows 95, Windows NT, and UNIX. For more information on Livewire, you can check out

```
http://home.netscape.com/comprod/products/tools/
              livewire_datasheet.html
```

Enter Enterprise

Slated for availability in the second half of 1996, the Enterprise server from Netscape is a full-blown, high-performance World Wide Web platform for creating and managing *distributed information* (information that's distributed to, and stored on, multiple machines) and online applications. The Enterprise server includes JavaScript support as well as a whole bunch of Web page creation, site management, communications, and security tools. The Enterprise server is the whole ball of wax when it comes to Web software, and it's far beyond the scope of this book. The Enterprise server is just mentioned here because it provides JavaScript support, and you'll probably be hearing a great deal about it in the future. Remember, you heard it here first!

Information about the Enterprise server from Netscape is available at

```
http://home.netscape.com/comprod/server_central/product/
                 enterprise/index.html
```

Part III
JavaScript
Language Reference

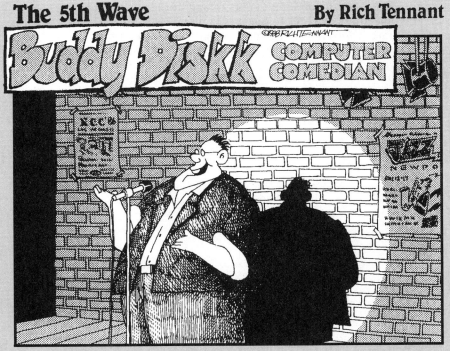

"SO I SAID, 'WAITER! WAITER! THERE'S A BUG IN MY SOUP!' AND HE SAYS, 'SORRY, SIR, THE CHEF USED TO PROGRAM COMPUTERS.' AHH HAHA HAHA THANK YOU! THANK YOU!"

In this part . . .

*I*f Parts I and II were the appetizer and cocktail, Part III is the main course. Every object, method, property, function, and event handler available to you in JavaScript is dissected, categorized, organized, flambéed, and cross-referenced. If you want to understand the intrinsic objectness of a built-in object, Chapter 10 is the place to start. If you know the name of a method but aren't sure which objects support it, check out Chapter 12. No matter what your dining style is (I'm a grazer, myself), Part III provides an easy way to get at the information you may be most interested in — and get at it quickly. What's more, actual code examples clarify the definitions every step of the way.

Chapter 10

Fun with Objects

● ●

In This Chapter

▶ Using built-in objects

▶ Accessing object properties

▶ Invoking object methods

● ●

*T*he quick-and-dirty definition of an *object*, as you may recall, is "a software representation of some useful thing." JavaScript objects are no exception: Each of them are representations of the things you need to build Web pages — push buttons, input fields, dates, and so on. This chapter contains an exhaustive list of all of the JavaScript objects, grouped according to how they're used (notice that most of them fall into the *form* category). This list isn't just a plain, ordinary old list, though; it also includes examples of how each object is created and accessed along with hints on why you should use the object in the first place!

Each of the objects mentioned has a corresponding .htm file on the companion CD-ROM. For example, the `applet` object can be found in the applet.htm file.

Fill In the Form, Please

The objects in this category are all elements of an HTML form, so you must always define them between the `<FORM>`...`</FORM>` tags (except the *form* element, which *is* the `<FORM>`...`<FORM>` tag — but you probably could have figured that out without my telling you!). Forms provide a way for users to interact with your Web pages, so most of the elements (although not all) are visible.

For each element, you'll find four separate sections:

> ✔ **Tag syntax**
>
> This section contains the generic syntax that you need to follow if you want to include a form in your Web page.

▶ **Real-life code example**

Because generic syntax can be a little vague until you've seen a couple of examples, this section provides a code fragment that actually defines a form element, just the way you would in your own page.

▶ **Accessing properties**

One of the neatest things about JavaScript is that it lets you examine and change a form element's property values. This sections shows you real-life code examples of exactly how you can go about doing just that. For even more in-depth explanation of each property, feel free to flip to Chapter 11.

▶ **Invoking methods**

Because form elements are objects, they can have methods associated with them (take a look at Chapter 4 if you're a little shaky on exactly what a method is). This section shows you a working example of how to *invoke,* or *call,* each method of an element. Check out Chapter 12 if you'd like more detailed information on a specific method.

Remember that you work with objects' data in JavaScript, not HTML; so all of the code fragments in these the "Accessing properties" and "Invoking methods" sections should be placed between <SCRIPT>...</SCRIPT> tags.

Applet

The applet object corresponds to a Java applet on an HTML form.

Tag syntax:

<APPLET	beginning <APPLET> tag
CODE="classFileName"	file name of the applet to load (*.class)
HEIGHT=height	height of the applet in pixels
WIDTH=width	width of the applet in pixels
[MAYSCRIPT]	if specified, this permits the applet to access JavaScript values (optional)
[NAME="appletName"]	name of applet for internal coding purposes (optional but recommended)
[CODEBASE="classFileDirectory"]	directory where classFileName is located (optional but recommended)
[ALT="alternateText"]	text to display in place of applet (for browsers that don't support the <APPLET> tag; optional)

`[ALIGN="`*position*`"]`	specifies alignment of applet on HTML page (optional)
`[HSPACE=`*numberOfPixels*`]`	horizontal margin of applet, in pixels (optional)
`[VSPACE=`*numberOfPixels*`]`	vertical margin for applet, in pixels (optional)
`[<PARAM>...</PARAM>]`	*below, can be repeated as many times as necessary*
`[<PARAM`	opening `<PARAM>` tag (optional)
`NAME="`*parameterName*`"`	name of parameter to pass to applet (optional)
`VALUE="`*parameterValue*`">]`	value to pass to applet (optional)
`[</PARAM>]`	closing `<PARAM>` tag (optional)
`</APPLET>`	ending `</APPLET>` tag

The value for `ALIGN` can be any of the following string values: `"left"`, `"right"`, `"top"`, `"absmiddle"`, `"absbottom"`, `"texttop"`, `"middle"`, `"baseline"`, or `"bottom"`.

Real-life code example:

```
<APPLET NAME="NervousApplet" CODE="NervousText.class"
         width=400 height=50>
<PARAM NAME="text" VALUE="Enter your text here.">
</APPLET>
```

Accessing applet properties:

The properties available to you depend on the specific Java applet you're working with. There is, however, one property that's available for *all* Java applets, and that's the `name` property:

```
document.applets[0].name
```

Invoking applet methods:

The `applet` methods available to you depend on the specific Java applet you're working with. Ask the person who developed the Java applet you're including in your Web page for a list of public methods that you can invoke on it.

Area

The area object is used to make an area of an embedded image responsive to user events. (Think of it as a big, fat, invisible link sitting on top of an image). You can make an area respond to a click event or to mouse pointer movement events.

Three separate HTML entities need to be defined as part of an area: an area (of course!), an HTML <MAP>, and an image. A complete example awaits you below.

Tag syntax:

<MAP NAME="*mapName*">	opening <MAP> tag (you need to define a map to define an area)
<AREA	opening <AREA> tag
NAME="*areaName*"	name of area for internal coding purposes
COORDS="*x1, y1, x2, y2*"	coordinates of the image map, in integers
HREF="*location*"	URL of document to load when area is clicked or "javascript:*functionName()*"
[SHAPE="*shape*"]	shape of the map (see tip below)
[TARGET="*windowName*"]	window to load link into when area is clicked
[onMouseOut="*handlerText*"]	code to execute when mouse pointer moves out of area
[onMouseOver="*handlerText*"]	code to execute when mouse pointer is dragged across area
</MAP>	closing </MAP> tag

The value for SHAPE can be any of the following strings: "rect", "poly", "circle", or "default". If you don't define any value for the SHAPE attribute, it will default to "rect".

Real-life code example:

```
<MAP NAME="thistleMap">
<AREA NAME="topThistle" COORDS="0,0,228,318"
          HREF="javascript:displayMessage()"
onMouseOver="self.status='When you see this message, click
          your left mouse button'; return true"
onMouseOut="self.status=''; return true">
</MAP>
<IMG NAME="currentImage"
SRC="images/thistle.gif" ALIGN="MIDDLE" ALT="[Scottish
          thistles]"
USEMAP="#thistleMap">
```

Accessing area properties:

No, this isn't a typo — areas are stored in the links array, right along with the regular, "skinny" links.

```
document.links.length
document.links[index].hash
document.links[index].host
document.links[index].hostname
document.links[index].href
document.links[index].pathname
document.links[index].port
document.links[index].protocol
document.links[index].query
document.links[index].target
```

Invoking area methods:

There are no methods associated with the area object.

Button

A *button* is a push button on an HTML form.

Tag syntax:

`<INPUT`	single `<INPUT>` tag
`TYPE="button"`	specifies the kind of input control (button)
`NAME="buttonName"`	internal name of button (for coding purposes)
`VALUE="buttonText"`	text to display on face of button
`[onClick="handlerText"]>`	code to invoke when button is clicked (optional)

Real-life code example:

```
<FORM NAME="myForm">
<INPUT TYPE="button" NAME="inStateButton" VALUE="In State"
            onClick="display(this)">
```

In this example, the name of the button is inStateButton (you see how the name is used to access the button's property values in the next section) and the text displayed on the face of the button is "In State". When a user clicks on this button, the JavaScript interpreter will call the display() function and pass it one argument: the entire inStateButton object (denoted by this).

In the preceding example code, the function display() is called when a user clicks the inStateButton, but you can specify any function or method you like in response to the onClick event handler.

Accessing button properties:

```
document.myForm.inStateButton.name
document.myForm.inStateButton.type
document.myForm.inStateButton.value
```

The JavaScript code fragments above represent the button's name (inStateButton), type ("button"), and value ("In State"), respectively.

Invoking button methods:

```
document.myForm.inStateButton.click()
// used to click button programmatically
```

Checkbox

A *checkbox* is — well, a checkbox. A checkbox is like a toggle switch, and its value is always either off or on.

Tag syntax:

`<INPUT`	single <INPUT> tag
`TYPE="checkbox"`	specifies the type of control (checkbox)
`NAME="checkboxName"`	internal name of checkbox (for coding purposes)
`VALUE="checkboxValue"`	value returned to the server when form is submitted
`[CHECKED]`	specifies initial display marked as checked (optional)
`[onClick="handlerText"]>`	code to invoke when checkbox is clicked (optional)
`textToDisplay`	descriptive text to display next to checkbox

Real-life code example:

```
<INPUT TYPE="checkbox" NAME="jazzCheckbox"VALUE="checkedJazz"
CHECKED onClick="display(this)"> Click here if you like jazz.
```

In this example, the name of the checkbox is `jazzCheckbox` (you'll see how the name is used to access the checkbox's property values in the next section) and the value is "`checkedJazz`" (this is the value that will be submitted to the CGI program if the checkbox is checked). The checkbox will automatically be checked the first time it appears to the user, and the text displayed next to the checkbox is `"Click here if you like jazz."`

Accessing checkbox properties:

```
document.myForm.jazzCheckbox.checked
document.myForm.jazzCheckbox.defaultChecked
document.myForm.jazzCheckbox.name
document.myForm.jazzCheckbox.type
document.myForm.jazzCheckbox.value
```

The JavaScript code fragments above represent, respectively,

- ✔ Whether or not the checkbox is checked (true or false)
- ✔ Whether or not the checkbox was defaulted to "`checked`" initially (true)
- ✔ The name of the checkbox ("`jazzCheckbox`")
- ✔ The type of the checkbox object ("`checkbox`")
- ✔ The value of the checkbox ("`checkedJazz`")

Invoking checkbox methods:

```
document.myForm.jazzCheckbox.click()
// used to set checkbox programmatically
```

Elements array

The *elements array* is an array of all the form elements resident in a form, in the order in which they were defined in the source code.

Tag syntax:

None — the `elements` array is automatically defined for you by the HTML interpreter when you define a form (that is, when you use the `<FORM>...</FORM>` tags).

Real-life code example:

This one's a freebie; you don't have to write a lick of code to define the elements array!

Accessing elements array properties:

```
document.myForm.elements[0]
document.myForm.elements[1].value
document.myForm.elements[2].name
...
document.myForm.elements.length
```

The preceding code fragments represent, respectively,

- ✔ The first element defined for myForm
- ✔ The value of the second element defined
- ✔ The name of the third element defined
- ✔ The total number of elements defined for the form

Invoking elements array methods:

The elements array has no associated methods.

You can use the length of the array (the value of elements.length) to loop through each of the array elements with a statement like the following:

```
for (var i=0; i<document.myForm.elements.length; i++) {
    document.write("Here's an element: " +
        document.myForm.elements[i].name)
}
```

The preceding code fragment steps through the elements array one element at a time and displays the name of each (as you see when you load the HTML file elements.htm located on the companion CD).

FileUpload

A fileUpload object consists of a Browse button and a text field. To specify a file name, users can either click the Browse button and choose from the displayed list of files, or enter a filename directly into the text field.

Tag syntax:

<INPUT	single <INPUT> tag
TYPE="file"	specifies the type of element (file)
NAME="*fileUploadName*">	specifies the name of the element

Real-life code example:

```
<INPUT TYPE="file" NAME="myFileName">
```

Accessing fileUpload properties:

```
document.myForm.myFileName.name
document.myForm.myFileName.type
document.myForm.myFileName.value
```

Invoking fileUpload methods:

The fileUpload object has no associated methods.

Form

A *form* is used to gather input from users and to post data (including, but not limited to, user input) to a server for additional processing.

Tag syntax:

`<FORM`	opening `<FORM>` tag
`NAME="formName"`	internal name of form (for coding purposes)
`[TARGET="windowName"]`	window to display server response (optional; default is current window)
`[ACTION="serverURL"]`	URL where form data is sent on submit (optional)
`[METHOD=GET	POST]`	data send method; GET is default (optional)
`[ENCTYPE="encodingType"]`	special data encoding scheme, if any (optional)
`[onReset="handlerText"]`	code to invoke when the form is reset (optional)
`[onSubmit="handlerText"]>`	code to invoke when form is submitted (optional)

form elements defined here

`</FORM>`	closing `<FORM>` tag

Real-life code example:

```
<FORM NAME="myForm" METHOD="POST" TARGET="_parent"
ACTION="http://altavista.digital.com/cgi-bin/
            query?pg=q&what=web&fmt=.&q=JavaScript"
ENCTYPE="multipart/form-data"
onSubmit="return verifyComplete()">
</FORM>
```

Accessing form properties:

```
document.myForm.action
document.myForm.elements
document.myForm.encoding
document.myForm.length
document.myForm.method
document.myForm.target
document.forms[0]// first form defined in the document
document.forms.length   // total number of forms defined in
                            the document
```

Invoking form methods:

```
document.myForm.reset()
document.myForm.submit()
```

Remember that you need to place all the definitions for form elements between the <FORM>...</FORM> tags; otherwise, the interpreter doesn't recognize them.

Hidden

A *hidden* element is an input text field that doesn't display. Hidden elements are usually used to store programmer-calculated values to be sent to the server when the form is submitted.

Tag syntax:

<INPUT	single <INPUT> tag
TYPE="hidden"	specifies the type of element (hidden)
NAME="*hiddenName*"	internal name of hidden element (used in coding)
[VALUE="*textValue*"]>	initial value of hidden object (optional)

Real-life code example:

```
<INPUT TYPE="hidden" NAME="markupPercent" VALUE=80>
```

Pretty straightforward, isn't it? The preceding line of code defines a hidden element named `markupPercent` and stuffs it with the initial value of 80.

Accessing hidden properties:

```
document.myForm.markupPercent.name
document.myForm.markupPercent.type
document.myForm.markupPercent.value
```

As you'd expect, the statements above represent `markupPercent`, `"hidden"`, and 80, respectively.

Invoking hidden methods:

The `hidden` object has no associated methods.

Image

The `image` object in JavaScript corresponds to the HTML `<IMG>` element. It represents an image embedded into a document.

JavaScript provides an Image constructor that you can use to create and load an image behind the scenes, before it's needed for display. You might want to do this if you have a large image (or series of images, if you're thinking about do-it-yourself animation) that you want to load secretly, while your user is doing something else; that way, when it's time to display the image, it is already loaded into memory, so it displays right away. Here's how it works:

```
// To load the image, do this:
// first, create an image variable
var myImage = new Image()

// then, load the image into memory
myImage.src = "images/thistle.gif"

// Finally, to display the image, do this:
document.images[0].src = myImage.src
```

Tag syntax:

`<IMG`	opening `<IMG>` tag
`NAME="imageName"`	name of image for internal coding purposes
`SRC="location"`	URL of image to load
`[LOWSRC="location"]`	URL of alternative low-resolution version of the image
`[HEIGHT="pixels" | "value"%]`	height of the image, in pixels or as a percentage of the window height
`[WIDTH="pixels" | "value"%]`	width of the image, in pixels or as a percentage of the window height
`[HSPACE="pixels"]`	space between left-hand side and right-hand side of the image, and the edge of the window, in pixels
`[VSPACE="pixels"]`	space between top and bottom of image and the edge of the window, in pixels
`[BORDER="pixels"]`	width of the image's border in pixels
`[ALIGN="position"]`	specifies alignment of image (see following tip)
`[ISMAP]`	whether or not the image is a server-side map
`[USEMAP="location#mapName"]`	whether or not the image is a client-side map
`[onAbort="handlerText"]`	code to execute when image load is aborted
`[onError="handlerText"]`	code to execute when an error occurs on image load
`[onLoad="handlerText"]>`	code to execute on image load

Real-life code example:

```
<IMG NAME="currentImage"
SRC="images/jazzman.gif" ALIGN="MIDDLE" ALT="[Jazz
          guitarist]"
USEMAP="#jazzMap">
```

Accessing image properties:

```
document.myForm.currentImage.border
document.myForm.currentImage.complete
document.myForm.currentImage.height
```

```
document.myForm.currentImage.hspace
document.myForm.currentImage.lowsrc
document.myForm.currentImage.name
document.myForm.currentImage.prototypeName
document.myForm.currentImage.src
document.myForm.currentImage.vspace
document.myForm.currentImage.width
```

Invoking image methods:

There are no methods associated with the image object.

Password

A *password* object is a special text input field that displays asterisks on the screen in place of the characters actually typed.

Tag syntax:

`<INPUT`	single `<INPUT>` tag
`TYPE="password"`	specifies the type of element (password)
`NAME="passwordName"`	internal name of password (for coding purposes)
`SIZE=integer`	number of display characters before scrolling
`[VALUE="textValue"]>`	initial value of password (optional)

Real-life code example:

```
<INPUT TYPE="password" NAME="userPassword" SIZE=15
VALUE="secret!">
```

Accessing password properties:

```
document.myForm.userPassword.defaultValue
document.myForm.userPassword.name
document.myForm.userPassword.type
document.myForm.userPassword.value
```

Invoking password methods:

```
document.myForm.userPassword.focus()
document.myForm.userPassword.blur()
document.myForm.userPassword.select()
```

Plugin

Think of the plugin object as the space on an HTML form where the output of a plug-in will appear. The plugin object has no associated properties or methods. To get information about plugins, you must access the navigator property called plugins.

Tag syntax:

<EMBED	opening <EMBED> tag
SRC="*source*"	URL containing the source of the plug-in
NAME="*embedName*"	name of embedded plug-in object (for internal coding purposes)
HEIGHT=*height*	height of the embedded plug-in, in pixels
WIDTH=*width*	width of the embedded plug-in, in pixels
(<PARAM>...</PARAM>),	*below, can be repeated as many times as necessary*
[<PARAM	opening <PARAM> tag (optional)
NAME="*parameterName*"	name of parameter to pass to plug-in (optional)
VALUE="*parameterValue*">]	value to pass to plug-in (optional)
[</PARAM>]	closing </PARAM> tag (optional)
</EMBED>	closing </EMBED> tag

Real-life code example:

```
<EMBED NAME="myEmbed" SRC="http://www.adobe.com/acrobat/
         3beta/PDFS/Times.pdf" WIDTH=450 HEIGHT=450>
</EMBED>
```

Accessing plugin properties:

There are no properties associated with the plugin object. Use the navigator.plugins array to access plugin properties.

Invoking plugin methods:

There are no methods associated with the plugin object.

Radio

A *radio* button is a toggle switch, like a checkbox; unlike a checkbox, though, radio buttons are most often grouped in sets to allow users to select a *single* option from a list.

Tag syntax:

`<INPUT`	single `<INPUT>` tag
`TYPE="radio"`	specifies the kind of element (radio)
`NAME="radioName"`	internal name of radio button (for coding purposes)
`VALUE="buttonValue"`	specifies a value to be returned to the server
`[CHECKED]`	specifies that button is initially selected (optional)
`[onClick="handlerText"]>`	code to invoke when radio is clicked (optional)
`textToDisplay`	descriptive text

Real-life code example:

```
What's your favorite time of day?
<INPUT TYPE="radio" NAME="timeChoice" VALUE="morningSelected"
          CHECKED
onClick="showValues(0)"> Morning
<INPUT TYPE="radio" NAME="timeChoice"
          VALUE="afternoonSelected"
onClick="showValues(1)"> Afternoon
<INPUT TYPE="radio" NAME="timeChoice" VALUE="eveningSelected"
onClick="showValues(2)"> Evening
```

Accessing radio properties:

```
document.myForm.timeChoice[index].checked
document.myForm.timeChoice[index].defaultChecked
document.myForm.timeChoice.length  // number of radio buttons
document.myForm.timeChoice[index].name
document.myForm.timeChoice[index].type
document.myForm.timeChoice[index].value
```

Invoking radio methods:

```
document.myForm.timeChoice[index].click()
```

Reset

A *reset* object is a special kind of button. When a reset button is clicked, it clears out all the user-input values in a form and resets each field to its default value.

Tag syntax:

`<INPUT`	single `<INPUT>` tag
`TYPE="reset"`	specifies type of control (reset)
`NAME="resetName"`	internal name of control (for coding purposes)
`VALUE="buttonText"`	text to display on face of reset button
`[onClick="handlerText"]>`	code to invoke when button is clicked (optional)

Real-life code example:

```
<INPUT TYPE="reset" NAME="resetButton" VALUE="Reset"
onClick="reinitializeFormulas()">
```

Accessing reset properties:

```
document.myForm.resetButton.name
document.myForm.resetButton.type
document.myForm.resetButton.value
```

Invoking reset methods:

```
document.myForm.resetButton.click()
```

Select

The *select* element is used to display both a single-selection list and a scrolling multiple-selection list.

Tag syntax:

`<SELECT`	Opening `<SELECT>` tag
`NAME="selectName"`	internal name of control (for coding purposes)
`[SIZE=integer]`	number of options visible (optional; default is 1)
`[MULTIPLE]`	specifies multiple selection scrolling box (optional)

[onBlur="*handlerText*"]	code to invoke when focus is lost
[onChange="*handlerText*"]	code to invoke when value changes and focus is lost
[onFocus="*handlerText*"]>	code to invoke when focus is received
<OPTION	specifies a selection item
[VALUE="*optionValue*"]	value returned to server when form is submitted
[SELECTED]>	specifies that this option is selected by default
textToDisplay	descriptive text to display next to option

(repeat OPTION tag as many times as necessary)

</SELECT>	closing </SELECT> tag

Real-life code example:

```
<SELECT NAME="fave" SIZE=3 MULTIPLE
          onBlur="displayResult(this)">
<OPTION VALUE="popChosen" SELECTED> pop
<OPTION VALUE="rockChosen" > rock
<OPTION VALUE="dogsChosen" > dogs barking Jingle Bells
<OPTION VALUE="rapChosen" > rap
<OPTION VALUE="showChosen" > show tunes
<OPTION VALUE="africanChosen" > African classical
</SELECT>
```

Accessing select properties:

```
document.myForm.fave.length
document.myForm.fave.name
document.myForm.fave.options
document.myForm.fave.selectedIndex
document.myForm.fave.options[index].defaultSelected
document.myForm.fave.options[index].index
document.myForm.fave.options.length
document.myForm.fave.options[index].selected
document.myForm.fave.options[index].text
document.myForm.fave.options[index].type
document.myForm.fave.options[index].value
```

Invoking select methods:

```
document.myForm.fave.blur()
document.myForm.fave.focus()
```

Submit

A *submit* object is a special kind of button that, when clicked, submits the form values to the server.

Tag syntax:

`<INPUT`	single `<INPUT>` tag
`TYPE="submit"`	specifies kind of control (submit)
`NAME="submitName"`	internal name of submit button (for coding purposes)
`VALUE="buttonText"`	text to display on face of submit button
`[onClick="handlerText"]>`	code to invoke when submit button is clicked

Real-life code example:

```
<INPUT TYPE="submit" NAME="submitButton"
VALUE="Submit Form" onClick="verifyInput()">
```

Accessing submit properties:

```
document.myForm.submitButton.name
document.myForm.submitButton.type
document.myForm.submitButton.value
```

Invoking submit methods:

```
document.myForm.submitButton.click()
```

Clicking on the submit button sends a form to the URL value specified in the form's `ACTION` property. The data is sent as a series of attribute-value pairs, and each pair is separated by an ampersand (&).

Text

The *text* object is a single-line input field.

Tag syntax:

`<INPUT`	single `<INPUT>` tag
`TYPE="text"`	specifies the kind of control (text)

NAME=" *textName* "	internal name of the text field (for coding purposes)
VALUE=" *textValue* "	specifies the initial value of the text field
SIZE=*integer*	number of characters to display before scrolling
[onBlur=" *handlerText* "]	code to invoke when focus is lost (optional)
[onChange=" *handlerText* "]	code to invoke when value changes and focus is lost (optional)
[onFocus=" *handlerText* "]	code to invoke when focus is received (optional)
[onSelect=" *handlerText* "]>	code to invoke when text in the field is highlighted (optional)

Real-life code example:

```
<INPUT TYPE="text" NAME="lastName" VALUE="your name here"
SIZE=30 onBlur="validate()" onChange="validate()">
```

Accessing text properties:

```
document.myForm.lastName.defaultValue
document.myForm.lastName.name
document.myForm.lastName.type
document.myForm.lastName.value
```

Invoking text methods:

```
document.myForm.lastName.focus()
document.myForm.lastName.blur()
document.myForm.lastName.select()
```

Textarea

A *textarea* object is just like a text object, except that instead of defining one scrolling input line, the textarea object defines a multi-line scroll box.

Tag syntax:

<TEXTAREA	opening <TEXTAREA> tag
NAME=" *textareaName* "	internal name of textarea object (for coding)
ROWS=*integer*	number of rows to display
COLS=*integer*	number of columns to display

`[onBlur="handlerText"]`	code to invoke when focus is lost (optional)
`[onChange="handlerText"]`	code to invoke when value changes and focus is lost (optional)
`[onFocus="handlerText"]`	code to invoke when focus is received (optional)
`[onSelect="handlerText"]>`	code to invoke when text is highlighted (optional)
textToDisplay	initial text to display inside scroll box
`</TEXTAREA>`	closing `</TEXTAREA>` tag

Real-life code example:

```
<TEXTAREA NAME="directions" ROWS=4 COLS=60
onBlur="validate()" onChange="display()"
onFocus="welcome()" onSelect="changeMode()">
This is default text. You can type right over it,
add to it, cut it, paste it, or copy it.
</TEXTAREA>
```

Accessing textarea properties:

```
document.myForm.directions.defaultValue
document.myForm.directions.name
document.myForm.directions.type
document.myForm.directions.value
```

Invoking textarea methods:

```
document.myForm.directions.focus()
document.myForm.directions.blur()
document.myForm.directions.select()
```

Data Types

Some kinds of objects, specifically *dates* and *strings,* are really basic; they're so basic, in fact, that almost every script you'll ever write will probably contain a reference to one or both of them. Because they're so common, JavaScript thoughtfully provides them for you as built-in objects — but because JavaScript is loosely based on C, these really basic objects are still referred to by the conventional name of *data types.*

There's another difference between JavaScript objects like the ones earlier in this chapter, which were all defined in HTML, and JavaScript data types, though. The difference is that you don't define them in HTML with tags. Instead, you declare them inside the <SCRIPT>...</SCRIPT> tags, with JavaScript statements, as you see below.

Array

An *array* object is an indexed list of things called *elements*. Element values can be whatever you want them to be; numbers, strings, even other objects. You can fill an array with elements when you create it by passing values to the Array constructor, or you can create an empty array and fill it with elements later.

Generic JavaScript syntax:

```
arrayName = new Array([element1, element2, … elementN
|arraySize])
```

Real-life code example:

```
var listOfPets = new Array("dog", "cat", "gerbil")
listOfPets[3]="bird"

// signals 2 initial elements are expected, but
// the interpreter won't complain if you assign more
var favoriteFoods = new Array(2)
favoriteFoods[0]="frozen yogurt"
favoriteFoods[1]="barbecued beef"
favoriteFoods[2]="stir-fry" // 3 elements is okay
var toDoList = new Array()
```

Accessing array properties:

```
favoriteFoods.length
favoriteFoods.prototypeName
```

Invoking array methods:

```
favoriteFoods.join()
favoriteFoods.reverse()
favoriteFoods.sort()
```

Date

A *date* object in JavaScript is just what it is in real life — a specific time including second, minute, hour, day, month, and year information. You can create new date objects based on the current time or on values you provide. Once you've created a date object, you can modify and manipulate it to your heart's content, as you see below.

Generic JavaScript syntax:

```
dateName = new Date()
// if no parameters passed, result is current date/time

dateName = new Date("month day, year  hours:minutes:seconds")

dateName = new Date(year, month, day)

dateName = new Date(year, month, day, hours, minutes,
            seconds)
```

Real-life code example:

```
today = new Date()
birthday = new Date("October 21, 1973 01:40:00")
graduation = new Date(1990, 8, 6)
wedding = new Date(92, 07, 12, 10, 30, 21)
```

Netscape Navigator 3.0 for Windows 95 reports all date fields correctly except for the month, which it underreports by one (getMonth() will try to tell you that October is month 9; perhaps if you think of January as month 0...) Earlier versions of Navigator — especially the beta releases, but version 2.0 as well — are known for varying calculations involving getMonth() and getDay(), so to be on the safe side, always make sure that you very carefully test any calculations involving date fields.

Accessing Date properties:

You access the contents of a data type a little differently than you do the contents of, say, a form object. Accessing Date properties (all except one) is done by calling methods, as you see in the following example.

One property, called *prototype,* is different from all the rest. A prototype is used to create a new property for a Date object. The new property can be whatever you like.

```
// create a new date variable called "today"
var today = new Date()

// create a new property for date objects called
// "description"
Date.prototype.description=null

// assign a value to the new date object property
today.description="Today I lost my first tooth!"
```

Invoking Date methods:

If you think about it, there are basically only two things you can do with a property once it's defined: you can **get** the value of it to see what it is, and you can **set** the value. Data types have pre-defined properties; you never have to define them yourself. That means all you have to worry about is getting values (you do this with what's affectionately known as *getter* methods, or *getters* for short) and setting values (using *setter* methods, or *setters*).

Getters

```
birthday.getDate()
birthday.getDay()
birthday.getHours()
birthday.getMinutes()
birthday.getMonth() // subtracts 1 from the correct value
birthday.getSeconds()
birthday.getTime()
birthday.getTimeZoneoffset() // undefined in Navigator 2.0
birthday.getYear()
birthday.toGMTString()
birthday.toLocaleString()
Date.UTC(1983, 6, 24, 2, 51, 8)
```

Setters

```
birthday.setTime(Date.parse("January 7, 1995"))
birthday.setDate(21)
birthday.setHours(3)
birthday.setMinutes(59)
birthday.setMonth(11)
birthday.setSeconds(50)
birthday.setTime(identicalTwinsBirthday.getTime())
birthday.setYear(82)
```

Specifying a date before 1970 causes Navigator versions earlier than 3.0 to *crash* (so unless you're a young whippersnapper, don't try to set a date object equal to your birthday unless you're running Navigator 3.0 or later!)

Option

An *option* object can be used to represent one of the options assigned to a single- or multiple-selection list box (a `select` element). You create it first, and then insert it into the associated `select` element's `options` array.

The Option constructor accepts four optional arguments, as follows:

`optionText`	the text to display in the select list next to this option
`optionValue`	the value to be sent to the server when this option is selected
`defaultSelected`	whether or not this option should be selected by default (*true* or *false*)
`selected`	whether or not this option is currently selected (*true* or *false*)

Generic JavaScript syntax:

```
optionName = new Option([optionText, optionValue,
            defaultSelected, selected])
selectName.options[index] = optionName
```

Real-life code example:

```
var blues = new Option("Blues music", "blues", true, true)
document.myForm.musicSelection[0] = blues
```

You can delete an option from the `options` array of a `select` element like this:

```
document.myForm.musicSelection[0] = null
```

Deleting an element in an array causes the array to be compressed together, so if you delete the second element of an array containing three elements, the array would then hold two elements — the first and the third.

Accessing option properties:

```
blues.defaultSelected
blues.index
blues.prototypeName
```

```
blues.selected
blues.text
blues.value
```

Invoking option methods:

There are no methods associated with the `option` object.

String

A *string* object is nothing more or less than a series of characters, usually surrounded by quotes, like this: `"Ralph"`, `"Henrietta and Bugsy"`, `"123,456,789.00"`, `"1600 Pennsylvania Avenue"`. Strings are used for passing pieces of text around inside JavaScript. Unless you're expecting to do some arithmetic operations on a value, you probably want to work with it in string form, which you see exactly how to do in the section below.

Generic JavaScript syntax:

There are two ways to create a string. One is to use the built-in `String` object; the other is simply to surround the string value with double quotes (`"like this"`). Strings can be stored in variables, but the don't have to be; when they're not stored in variables, they're called *string literals*.

Real-life code example:

```
var lastName = "Smith" // a string variable
var firstName = new String("Barney") // a string variable
alert("Millions, including the "  // a string literal
      + lastName +
      "'s, enjoy JavaScript daily with their morning
          pastry.")
```

Accessing String properties:

```
lastName.length
String.prototype.description = null
middleName = new String("T.J.")
middleName.description = " T.J. doesn't actually stand for
anything."
```

Invoking String methods:

```
lastName.anchor("tableOfContentsAnchor")
lastName.big()
```

(continued)

(continued)

```
lastName.blink()
lastName.bold()
lastName.charAt(3)
lastName.fixed()
lastName.fontcolor("springgreen")
lastName.fontsize(7)
lastName.indexOf("i")
"George".italics()
"George".lastIndexOf("r")
"George".link("http://www.netscape.com")
"George".small()
"George".strike()
"George".sub()
"George".substring(0, 3)
"George".sup()
"George".toLowerCase()
"George".toUpperCase()
```

Creating Links

Links enable folks to click on an area of your Web page and pop automatically to someone else's Web page. Each link has two pieces: the *anchor* (the piece of text that marks a spot on someone else's page that you want to link to) and the *link* (the spot on your page where you want to define a link to the other person's page).

Anchor

An *anchor* is a piece of text that uniquely identifies a spot on a Web page. Once you've defined an anchor — say, in the middle of a page — you (or anyone else for that matter) can set up a link so that when the link is clicked, the page loads right where the anchor is located.

Tag syntax:

`<A`	opening `<A>` tag
`NAME="`*anchorName*`"`	name of anchor that links will refer to
anchorText	text to display at the anchor site
`</A>`	closing `</A>` tag

Real-life code example:

```
<A NAME="TOC">Table of Contents</A>
```

Accessing anchor properties:

```
document.anchors.length
```

Invoking anchor methods:

The anchor object has no associated methods.

Link

A *link* is a piece of text (or an image) that, when clicked, loads another Web page. (A link often loads a specific spot, or *anchor,* on another Web page.)

Tag syntax:

`<A`	opening <A> tag
`HREF="`*locationOrURL*`"`	URL and (if appropriate) anchor to link to
`[TARGET="`*windowName*`"]`	window to load linked page into (optional)
`[onClick="`*handlerText*`"]`	code to invoke when link is clicked (optional)
`[onMouseOut="`*handlerText*`"]`	code to invoke when mouse moves off link (optional)
`[onMouseOver="`*handlerText*`"]>`	code to invoke when mouse moves across the link (optional)
linkText	text to display at link site
`</A>`	closing </A> tag

Real-life code example:

```
<A HREF="#TOC" onClick="verifyData()"
onMouseOver="displayScrollingText()" >Back to Table of
Contents</A>
```

Accessing link properties:

```
document.links.length
document.links[index].hash
document.links[index].host
document.links[index].hostname
document.links[index].href
document.links[index].pathname
document.links[index].port
document.links[index].protocol
document.links[index].query
document.links[index].target
```

Invoking link methods:

Neither the `link` object nor the `links` array has any associated methods.

JavaScript Objects

Some of the objects that you work with as a JavaScript author are yours courtesy of your Web browser's HTML implementation. Although in most cases you won't *set* values for these objects yourself — your Web browser does that for you — being able to look at the values these objects contain is mighty handy at times.

Document

A *document* defines characteristics of the overall body of a Web page and is declared by using the `<BODY>...</BODY>` tag.

Tag syntax:

`<BODY`	opening `<BODY>` tag
`[BACKGROUND="backgroundImage"]`	image file for background graphic (optional)
`[BGCOLOR="backgroundColor"]`	specifies background color (optional)
`[TEXT="foregroundColor"]`	specifies default text color (optional)
`[LINK="unfollowedLinkColor"]`	specifies color of unclicked link (optional)

`[ALINK="activatedLinkColor"]`	specifies color of link during click (optional)
`[VLINK="followedLinkColor"]`	specifies color of clicked link (optional)
`[onBlur="handlerText"]`	code to invoke when document is blurred (optional)
`[onFocus="handlerText"]`	code to invoke when document receives focus (optional)
`[onLoad="handlerText"]`	code to invoke when document is loaded (optional)
`[onUnload="handlerText"]>`	code to invoke when document is unloaded(optional)
`</BODY>`	closing `</BODY>` tag

Real-life code example:

```
<BODY BGCOLOR="lime" TEXT="maroon"
LINK="purple" ALINK="yellow" VLINK="blue" onLoad="welcome()"
onUnload="goodbye()"> </BODY>
```

Accessing document properties:

```
document.alinkColor
document.anchors[index] // array of anchors defined for
                        this document
document.bgColor
document.cookie
document.fgColor
document.forms[index] // array of forms defined for this
document
document.lastModified
document.linkColor
document.links[index] // array of links defined for this
document
document.location
document.referrer
document.title
document.vlinkColor
```

Invoking document methods:

```
document.clear()
document.close()
document.open("text/html")
document.write("Some text here")
document.writeln("Some more text here")
```

Frame

A *frame* is a special kind of window. Think of little portholes in the side of a ship; a frame is like that. You can have several frames per "regular" window, and each frame can be independently scrollable. Each frame can also be associated with a separate URL. What fun! What possibilities! (And, potentially, what confusion!)

Tag syntax:

`<FRAMESET`	opening `<FRAMESET>` tag (group of frames)
`ROWS="rowHeightList"`	comma-separated list of values for row height
`COLS="columnWidthList"`	comma-separated list of values for column width
`[onBlur="handlerText"]`	code to invoke when window is blurred (optional)
`[onFocus="handlerText"]`	code to invoke when window receives focus (optional)
`[onLoad="handlerText"]`	code to invoke when window is loaded (optional)
`[onUnload="handlerText"]>`	code to invoke when window is unloaded (optional)
`[<FRAME`	single `<FRAME>` tag (optional but recommended)
`SRC="locationOrURL"`	URL to be displayed in this frame
`NAME="frameName">]`	internal name of frame (for coding purposes)
`</FRAMESET>`	closing `</FRAMESET>` tag

Real-life code example:

```
<HTML>
<HEAD><TITLE>Frames Example</TITLE></HEAD>
<FRAMESET ROWS="50%,50%" COLS="40%,60%">
```

```
<FRAME SRC="framcon1.html" NAME="frame1">
<FRAME SRC="framcon2.html" NAME="frame2">
</FRAMESET>
</HTML>
```

Accessing frame properties:

```
frames.length
frames[index].name
frames[index].length
frames[index].parent
frames[index].self
frames[index].window
```

Invoking frame methods:

```
frames[index].blur()
frames[index].clearTimeout(timerID)
frames[index].focus()
timerID = frames[index].setTimeout("method(), 5000")
```

Frames declared inside a `<FRAMESET>...</FRAMESET>` tag are called *child* frames; the window that they're in, coincidentally, is called a *parent*. Other terms that refer to frames include *self* and *window* (which are synonyms for the current frame) and *top* (which refers to the topmost window that contains frames). All these properties are explained in more detail in Chapter 11.

History

The *history* object contains a linked list of all the URLs that a user has visited from within a particular window. Your Web browser uses this object (this object provides the list of URLs you see when you select the Go menu item in Navigator or Internet Explorer), and so can you.

Tag syntax:

None; the history object is defined for you by your Web browser, so you don't have to define it at all. Every time you load a new Web page, your browser adds that URL to the history object automatically.

Real-life code example:

This one's a freebie; you don't have to write a lick of code to define the history object!

Accessing history properties:

```
history.length
```

Invoking history methods:

```
history.back()
history.forward()
history.go(-3)
```

Location

Think of the *location* object as a mini-version of the `history` object. Instead of holding information on all the URLs visited, like the `history` object, the `location` object contains information about just one URL — the one that's currently loaded.

Tag syntax:

None; the `location` object is defined for you automatically by your Web browser the second you load a Web page.

Real-life code example:

This one's another freebie; just like the `history` object, you don't have to write so much as a line of code to define the `location` object — it's set up for you automatically by your Web browser.

Accessing location properties:

```
location.hash
location.host
location.hostname
location.href
location.pathname
location.port
location.protocol
location.search
location.target
```

Invoking location methods:

The `location` object has no associated methods.

Do the properties of location look familiar? They should — you've probably seen them before! A link object is also a location object.

Navigator

The *navigator* object contains information about the version of Navigator currently in use.

Tag syntax:

None; the navigator object is defined for you automatically when you bring up your Web browser.

Real-life code example:

You never define the navigator object yourself; it's done for you automatically. You can, however, access its properties, as shown below.

Accessing navigator properties:

```
navigator.appCodeName
navigator.appName
navigator.appVersion
navigator.complete

// The mimeTypes array elements must be accessed
// through the array, as shown
navigator.mimeTypes[0].description
navigator.mimeTypes[0].enabledPlugin
navigator.mimeTypes[0].suffixes
navigator.mimeTypes[0].type

// The plugins array elements must be accessed
// through the array, as shown
navigator.plugins[0].description
navigator.plugins[0].filename
navigator.plugins[0].length
navigator.plugins[0].name
navigator.userAgent
```

Invoking navigator methods:

```
navigator.javaEnabled()
```

Window

The *window* object is the top-level granddaddy object for all document objects.

Perhaps you remember when I said you can skip typing in **window** every time that you want to access a window's property because typing in **window** is a given. Well, that statement is true. (Hey, would I lie to you?) But if you have more than one window associated with a document, well, then you *do* have to specify which window you mean. To do this, just remember to store each new window that you open in a variable (see the example below for specifics). When you store each new window that you open in a variable, you can use the unique window variable as a reference later on if you need to, like this: myOtherWindow.document.myFrame.myButton.name.

Generic JavaScript syntax:

```
windowVar = open("URL", "windowName", ["windowFeatures"])
```

Real-life code example:

```
myOtherWindow = open("win2.html", "secondWindow",
"toolbar=yes, location=yes, directories=yes, status=yes,
menubar=yes, scrollbars=yes, resizable=yes, width=250,
height=400")
```

The example definition only needs to be coded if you want an *extra* window. You're given the first window gratis, complements of the <BODY>...</BODY> tag. If you do create your own extra window, remember to tack on the name (myOtherWindow, in the example above) in front of any window property or method you access (see the following sections of this chapter) so the interpreter knows which window you're referring to at all times.

Accessing window properties:

```
defaultStatus
frames
length
name
opener
parent
self
status
top
window
```

Invoking window methods:

```
alert("Form will be sent now…")
blur()
close()
confirm("Do you really want to quit?")
focus()
myOtherWindow = open("", "secondWindow", "toolbar=yes,
location=yes, directories=yes, status=yes, menubar=yes,
scrollbars=yes, resizable=yes, width=250, height=400")
prompt("Enter the file name:", "testfile.txt")
scroll(50, 100)
timeoutID=setTimeout("displayAlert()", 2500)
clearTimeout(timeoutID)
myOtherWindow.write("Here is myOtherWindow.")
```

Math Utility

The *Math* object is a built-in object that contains properties and methods for all kinds of mathematical constants and functions (like logarithms and square roots). Hey, why reinvent the wheel?

Tag syntax:

None; the Math object is defined for you. That means it's always there waiting for you whenever you need to include a mathematical function in your JavaScript script.

Real-life code example:

You never define the Math object yourself; it's done for you automatically. All you have to do is use it, as shown in the following examples.

Accessing Math properties:

```
Math.E
Math.LN2
Math.LN10
Math.LOG2E
Math.LOG10E
Math.PI
Math.SQR1_2
Math.SQRT2
```

The `with` keyword is useful when you want to access several of an object's properties or methods in one spot in your code. If you're to be using a great deal of `Math` constants or methods, for example, the following keeps you from typing a couple of extra "Maths":

```
with (Math) {
    a = PI * E
    y = r*sin(theta)
    x = r*cos(theta)
}
```

Invoking Math methods:

```
Math.abs(23)
Math.acos(123)
Math.asin(1)
Math.atan(1)
Math.atan2(1)
Math.ceil(25.85)
Math.cos(0)
Math.exp(1)
Math.floor(25.85)
Math.log(1)
Math.max(5,15)
Math.min(5,15)
Math.pow(8,3)
Math.random()
Math.round(15.58)
Math.sin(0)
Math.sqrt(49)
Math.tan(0)
```

Chapter 11

For Sale By Owner: Object Properties

In This Chapter

▶ What they're good for

▶ How to access them

L ooking for a few good properties of the JavaScript variety? Well, this is the chapter that can deliver!

This chapter is organized alphabetically, so it's really useful if you know the name of the property you're interested in. If you'd like to see all the properties for a particular object instead, flip to Chapter 10 where the properties are organized according to object.

The listing for each property also tells you whether you can change the value of a property. (In the case of a read-only property, the value is set automatically by your Web browser, and you can look at the value but not change it.)

If you'd like to see how to access any of these properties, you can find the corresponding HTML file on this book's companion CD. The properties are named so they correspond to each property's associated object. For example, you can find the `action` property in the file named form.htm.

Preview of Properties

Properties are used to define and describe objects. Each of the properties listed in this chapter is associated with, and describes, a particular JavaScript object. Along with the name and description of each property is the name of its associated object and an example of how you go about accessing it programmatically. For example, when you see a line of code like the following:

```
document.myForm.action
```

what it means is, that's how you get the value for the *action* property of the form object. What you do with this value is completely up to you, of course; you can display it, assign it to a variable, use it in some calculations, or whatever makes sense for your particular Web page.

When you see a reference to "myForm" or "myButton" or "myWhatever," realize that these are the names of real objects in real code samples (the ones on the companion CD). Your objects can have whatever names you choose for them, so in the examples, mentally substitute the name you gave to your form, or button, or whatever for the names you see.

Three properties — name, value, and length — are so ubiquitous that they're presented a little differently than the others. Just about every object contains these three properties; they're universally applicable. What's more, their values are very similar. form.name refers to the form's name, document.name refers to the document's name, and so on. So instead of listing each of these properties separately, I've listed them in their naked form, with no qualifiers. Under their headings, you can find a list of all the objects that support these three properties, how to use these properties, and other useful stuff that you're dying to know.

action

Use the action property of the form object to access the value of the ACTION attribute. This value represents the URL (usually a CGI program, a Livewire program, or a mailto URL) that the form is sent to when the submit button is clicked. You can change the value for this property.

```
document.myForm.action
```

Array primer

Quite a few properties are arrays. *Arrays* are nothing more than indexed lists of objects. Basically, arrays are another way of getting hold of an object; and after you've got the object, you can do whatever you want with it. For example, consider the links array: document.links. After you get the length of the array (document.links.length), you know how many links are in the array. For argument's sake, say there are three links. After you know that, you can get to information about each individual link by going through the links array, like this:

document.links[0].hash → the anchor name of the first link

document.links[1].href → the URL of the second link

document.links[2].target → the target of the third link

This technique works on *almost* all arrays. (A quirk exists with the anchors array; you find out about that quirk soon enough.) See Chapter 10 for information about the array object and how you can use it to create your own arrays.

alinkColor

Use the `alinkColor` property of the `document` object to access the value of the `ALINK` attribute. The value of `ALINK` represents the color that link text turns when a user *activates,* or clicks on, the link. Valid values for this property include hexadecimal RGB triplets (such as `"00FFFF"`) and predefined strings (such as `"red"`), and you can change them. (To get the lowdown on hexadecimal RGB triplets and predefined color strings, check out Chapter 16.)

```
document.alinkColor
```

appCodeName

Use the `appCodeName` property of the `navigator` object to access the code name of the version of Navigator currently in use. As you'd expect, this property is a read-only property.

```
navigator.appCodeName
```

applets

The `applets` array of the `document` object contains entries for each of the applets currently loaded in a page. This property is read-only.

```
document.applets[0]
document.applets.length
```

appName

Use the `appName` property of the `navigator` object to access the name of the browser currently in use. You can't change the value for this property.

```
navigator.appName
```

appVersion

Use the `appVersion` property of the `navigator` object to access the version of the browser currently in use. This property is a read-only property.

```
navigator.appVersion
```

arguments

The arguments array is a property of the function object. The elements of the arguments array correspond to all of the arguments defined for a particular function object. This is a read-only property.

```
myFunctionName.arguments[0]
```

bgColor

Use the bgColor property of the document object to access the value of the BGCOLOR attribute defined with the <BODY>...</BODY> tag. The value of bgColor represents the color of the entire document background, and it can be changed.

```
document.bgColor
```

border

Use the border property of the image object to assess the border size of an image (in pixels). This property is read-only.

```
document.myImage.border
```

checked (checkbox)

Use the checked property of the checkbox object to assess whether or not your user has checked a checkbox (clicked it on) or not (clicked it off). The value for the checked property always returns either *true* (for checked) or *false* (meaning unchecked). You can change the value of this property.

```
document.myForm.myCheckbox.checked
```

checked (radio)

Use the checked property of the radio object to assess whether your user has set a radio button (clicked it on) or not (clicked it off). The value for the checked property always returns either *true* (for set) or *false* (not set). You can change the value of this property.

```
document.myForm.myRadioButton[0].checked
```

complete

Use the read-only `complete` property of the `image` object to assess whether or not your Web browser has completed its attempt to load an image.

```
document.images[0].complete
```

cookie

A `cookie` is a property of the `document` object. A *cookie* is a piece of information about the client that is saved persistently by a server-resident CGI program for later retrieval. The value can be any string value (except no white space, semicolons, or commas are allowed). A JavaScript statement can change this property. (See the nearby sidebar to find out more about cookies.)

```
document.cookie
```

defaultChecked (checkbox)

Use the `defaultChecked` property of the `checkbox` object to assess whether a checkbox was initially defaulted to *selected*. The value for the `defaultChecked` property always returns either *true* (meaning that the defaultChecked property was initially defaulted to *on*) or *false* (meaning that it wasn't). You can change the value of this property to override future default behavior.

```
document.myForm.myCheckbox.defaultChecked
```

defaultChecked (radio)

Use the `defaultChecked` property of the `radio` object to assess whether or not a radio button was initially defaulted to *selected*. The value for the `defaultChecked` property always returns either *true* (meaning that the defaultChecked property was initially defaulted to *on*) or *false* (meaning that it wasn't). You can change the value of this property to override future default behavior.

```
document.myForm.myRadioButton[0].defaultChecked
```

Mmmm... cookies!

Unfortunately, if you're like me, you can't even *read* the word *cookie* without visions of fragrant oatmeal-raisin bars dancing in your head. (The term *cookie,* in this context, is actually derived from some obscure UNIX ritual involving goats, motor oil, and fudge brownies, I believe.) To clarify things, think of a cookie as a hand stamp. (You know, when you go to a bar and they stamp your hand with a vile-colored, smeary logo?) The guy who stamps your hand is the CGI program on the server; the stamp is the cookie; and you're the client browser.

✔ You get a hand stamp if they want you to have one. (The client browser gets a cookie if the CGI program that it's loading wants it to have one.)

✔ You have to show your stamp to the doorman when you leave. (The client browser returns the cookie to the URL that assigned it.)

✔ If you come back later, sometimes they've changed the stamp and you have to get another one. (CGI programs can give client browsers multiple values for cookies.)

✔ Sometimes it takes forever for the darn things to wear off, even if you use soap. (Cookies can be persistent across browser sessions.)

The concept of cookies opens up a brave new world of Web applications. Imagine a Web application that remembers a little bit about the last time you used it — for example, your password and the fact that you changed the Web page's background color to a soothing cerulean and its font to large-scale so that you could read it easier. The next time you load the URL for this application, it can remember the changes that you made and make them itself, so you don't have to!

The official geek term for this concept is *client-side persistence,* and it raised some eyebrows when it first hit the Web-monitoring press. Because cookies, if they're stored across browser sessions, need to be stored *somewhere* on the client, guess where they're stored? In a file on your client machine called cookie.txt. Egads! Not only do cookies *keep track of your preferences,* but they *write to your hard drive!* Some folks are worried about the potential for malicious mischief, and some aren't. Heck, the way I look at it, just plugging in a modem is like backpacking in the wilderness; you're taking a risk, but if you pay attention, you can reduce the risk to a manageable level — and the benefits can be enormous. For more cookie-related discussion, take a look at Chapter 19.

defaultSelected

Use the `defaultSelected` property of the `option` object (an `option` object is stored in the `options` array which belongs to the `select` element, remember?) to assess whether a selected option was selected by default (value will be *true*) or not (value will be *false*). You can change the value of this property.

```
document.myForm.selectMusic.options[0].defaultSelected
```

defaultStatus

Use the `defaultStatus` property of the `window` object to access the default message that appears in a window's status bar. The value for this property can be changed.

```
window.defaultStatus
```

defaultValue (password)

Use the `defaultValue` value of the `password` object to see the initially-defined default password value.

```
document.myForm.myPassword.defaultValue
```

defaultValue (text)

Use the `defaultValue` property of the `text` object to access the value of the `VALUE` attribute of a `text` object. You can change the value for this property.

```
document.myForm.myTextField.defaultValue
```

defaultValue (textarea)

Use the `defaultValue` property of the `textarea` object to access the contents of the `textToDisplay` textarea attribute. You can change the value for this property.

```
document.myForm.myTextareaField.defaultValue
```

description

The read-only `description` property is associated with both the `mimeTypes` object and the `plugins` object. When associated with the `mimeTypes` object, it represents a description of the corresponding MIME type. When associated with the `plugins` object, `description` represents a description of the corresponding plugin.

```
navigator.mimeTypes[0].description
navigator.plugins[0].description
```

E

The E property of the Math object represents Euler's mathematical constant and the base of natural logarithms (if you don't understand any of this, trust me, you'll never have to use it!). This property is read-only.

```
Math.E
```

elements

The elements array is associated with the form object, so the elements array enables you to access all the elements that have been defined for a form (button, checkbox, hidden, password, radio, reset, select, submit, text, and textarea). The array is in *source code order* (the first element defined is the element in the array, and so forth). Elements in the array are read-only.

```
document.myForm.elements[0]
document.myForm.elements.length
```

embeds

The embeds array associated with the document object enables you to access all the plug-ins loaded into your page. Each element in the embeds array corresponds to an element defined with the HTML tag <EMBED>.

```
document.embeds[0]
document.embeds.length
```

enabledPlugin

Use the enabledPlugin property of the mimeTypes object to access the plugins object that handles the corresponding MIME type (see navigator.mimeTypes.type).

```
navigator.mimeTypes[0].enabledPlugin
```

encoding

Use the encoding property of the form object to access the ENCTYPE form
attribute. (The value is one of the following two strings: application/x-www-
form-urlencoded, which is the default value, or multipart/form-data). You
can change the value for this property.

```
document.myForm.encoding
```

fgColor

The fgColor property of the document object describes the color of the text
displayed in a document. It corresponds to the TEXT attribute defined as part of
the <BODY>...</BODY> tag. The value for this property can be changed, but
values must be either hexadecimal RGB triplets or predefined strings (both of
which are explained in Chapter 16).

```
document.fgColor
```

filename

Use the filename property of the plugins object to access the name of the
plug-in executable file on disk.

```
navigator.plugins[0].filename
navigator.plugins["myPlugin"].filename
```

forms

The forms array associated with the document object enables you to access all
the forms that have been defined for a document. The forms array is in *source
code order* (the first form defined is the 0th element in the array, and so forth).
Elements of the forms array are read-only.

```
document.forms[0]
document.forms.length
```

frames

The frames array of the window object enables you to access all the frame objects associated with a window. The frames array of the window object contains an entry for each child frame (an object defined with the <FRAME> tag) declared within a <FRAMESET> tag, in the order they appear in the source code. Elements of the frames array are read-only.

```
frames[0]
frames.length
```

hash

The hash property is associated with the area, link, and location objects. In all of these objects, the hash property references one little piece of the overall href property belonging to each object. The href property contains an entire URL; the hash property contains the piece of that URL that represents an anchor name. (In case you're wondering why the hash property is named hash, it's because anchor names are always preceded by a hash symbol (#), like this:"#TOC").

You can change the value for this property (although because the hash property describes just one piece of a complete URL, changing the value implicitly by changing the href property instead is probably safer).

```
// syntax for link object as well as for area object
document.links[index].hash
location.hash
```

height

The height property of the image object lets you access the value of the HEIGHT attribute of the HTML <IMG> tag. A valid value for the height property can either be an integer (in pixels), or a percentage (expressing percent of total window height). The value for this property is read-only.

```
document.myImage.height
```

host

The host property is associated with the area, link, and location objects. Use the host property of each object to access the hostname:port portion of a URL. A valid value for the host property must be a string representing a hostname and a port, separated by a colon (:). (A *port,* or more correctly, a *port address,* tells your browser exactly what software process on a server machine it should talk to when it loads a URL.) In practice, ports are often predefined, so you may never have occasion to worry about specifying a port name.

The value for this property can be changed (although because the host property describes one piece of a complete URL, changing the value implictly by changing the href property instead may be safer).

```
// syntax for link object as well as area object
document.links[index].host
location.host
```

hostname

The hostname property is associated with the area, link, and location objects. The hostname property of each object refers to the host and domain name of a network host. A valid value for the hostname property is a string similar to the following: austin.ibm.com. You can change the value for the hostname property; but because the value represents one chunk of an entire URL, changing the hostname property implicitly by changing the href property instead may be safer.

```
// syntax for link object as well as for area object
document.links[index].hostname
location.hostname
```

href

The href property is associated with the area, link, and location objects. The href property of each object enables you to access a string that represents the entire URL for that object. You can change the value for this property. An example of a valid value is http://austin.ibm.com.

```
// syntax for link object as well as for area object
document.links[index].href
location.href
```

hspace

The hspace property of the image object enables you to access the value of the HSPACE attribute of the HTML <IMG> tag. This value specifies a margin (in pixels) between the left and right edges of an image and the surrounding screen real estate. (This property only applies to images that have "left" or "right" defined for the value of the ALIGN attribute of the <IMG> tag.)

```
document.myImage.hspace
```

images

The images array associated with the document object enables you to access all the images loaded into your page. Each element in the images array corresponds to an element defined with the HTML tag <IMG>.

```
document.images[0]
document.images.length
```

index

The index property of the option object enables you to access the position of an option in a select object. Values for the index property are integers, beginning with zero, and are read-only.

```
document.myForm.mySelectField.options[0].index
```

lastModified

Access the lastModified property of the document object to determine when a document was last modified. The value for this property is a string, and it's read-only.

```
document.lastModified
```

length

The length property is used on several different objects and arrays, and its value is always read-only. (See tables 11-1 and 11-2 for more information.)

Table 11-1   The Lengths One Goes To I: Objects that Contain a Length Property

Object	Usage	Value
array	`myArray.length`	Number of array elements
form	`document.myForm.length`	Number of elements for a form
frame	`myFrame.length`	Number of child frames within a frame
history	`history.length`	Number of entries in the history object
radio	`document.myForm.myRadio.length`	Number of radio buttons in a radio object
select	`document.myForm.mySelect.length`	Number of options in a select object
string	`document.myForm.myString.length`	Number of characters in a string
window	`length`	Number of frames within a window

Table 11-2   The Lengths One Goes To II: Arrays that Contain a Length Property

Array	Usage	Value
anchors	`document.anchors.length`	Number of anchors in a document
elements	`document.myForm.elements.length`	Number of elements defined for a form
forms	`document.forms.length`	Number of forms defined in a document
frames	`frames.length`	Number of frames in a frame/window
images	`document.images.length`	Number of images in a document
links	`document.links.length`	Number of links in a document

(continued)

Table 11-2 *(continued)*

Array	Usage	Value
options	document.*myForm*.*mySelect*. options.length	Number of options in a select object
embeds	document.embeds.length	Number of embedded elements

Surprise! Even though anchors is an array and its elements are purportedly in source code order (that is, the 0th element corresponds to the first anchor defined in a file, the 1st element to the second anchor defined, and so on), the value of document.anchors[index] is *always null* (*null* is geekspeak for "never existed"). What a sense of humor those JavaScript architects had, huh?

Actually, you can get around this situation, depending on what you want with the anchor names and values in the first place. If the names of all of the anchors in a document are consecutive numbers from 0 to whatever, you can use the document.anchors.length property to find out how many anchors are in the array and (by implication) what their names are. Of course, this only works if the naming convention is followed exactly (which implies that it only works on documents that *you* create, because getting other people to follow rules just because you want them to has a fairly high historical rate of failure).

linkColor

Use the linkColor property of the document object to access the value of the LINK attribute. This value represents the color of initially displayed link text. Valid values for this property include hexadecimal RGB triplets (such as "00FFFF") and predefined strings (such as "red"), and you can change them.

```
document.linkColor
```

links

The links array of the document object enables you to access all the links that have been defined for a document. The array is in source code order (the first link defined is the 0th element in the array, and so forth). Elements of the array are read-only.

```
document.links[0]
document.links.length
```

LN2

The LN2 property of the Math object represents the natural logarithm of two (approximately 0.693). Because the natural logarithm of two is a mathematical constant, this property is read-only. (Unless you're a heavy-duty math person, my guess is you'll never feel the urge to use LN2 in your own JavaScript calculations — but please feel free!)

```
Math.LN2
```

LN10

The LN10 property of the Math object represents the natural logarithm of ten (approximately 2.302). Because the natural logarithm of ten is a mathematical constant, this property is read-only.

```
Math.LN10
```

location

Use the location property of the document object to access a document's complete URL. The value for this property is read-only.

```
document.location
```

LOG2E

The LOG2E property of the Math object represents the base two logarithm (approximately 1.442). Because the base two logarithm is a mathematical constant, this property is read-only.

```
Math.LOG2E
```

LOG10E

The LOG10E property of the Math object represents the base ten logarithm (approximately 0.434). Because the base ten logarithm is a mathematical constant, this property is read-only.

```
Math.LOG10E
```

lowsrc

The `lowsrc` property of the `image` object reflects the value of the `LOWSRC` attribute defined as part of the HTML `<IMG>` tag. A valid value for this property is a URL for a low-resolution version of the image to be loaded.

```
document.myImage.lowsrc
```

method

The `method` property of the `form` object enables you to access the value for the `METHOD` attribute defined as part of the `<FORM>`...`</FORM>` tag. A valid value for this property is a string that specifies how form field input is sent to the server when the form is submitted (either `"GET"` or `"POST"`). Take a look at the entry for Form in Chapter 10 for a complete discussion of the difference between setting this property equal to `"GET"` and to `"POST"`.

```
document.myForm.method
```

mimeTypes

The `mimeTypes` array associated with the `navigator` object enables you to access all the MIME types supported by the client (whether they were defined internally, by helper applications, or by plug-ins). Each element in the `mimeTypes` array is a `mimeTypes` object.

```
navigator.mimeTypes[0]
```

name

The `name` property is available on many different objects, as shown in Table 11-3. Unless otherwise noted, the `name` property always represents the `NAME` attribute for an object.

Table 11-3	An Object by Any Other Name Would Smell as Sweet: The Name Property
Object	*Usage*
applet	`document.applets[0].name`
button	`document.myForm.myButton.name`

Object	Usage
checkbox	`document.`*`myForm.myCheckbox`*`.name`
fileUpload	`document.`*`myForm.myFileUpload`*`.name`
frame	*`myFrame`*`.name`
hidden	`document.`*`myForm.myHidden`*`.name`
image	`document.`*`myForm.myImage`*`.name`
password	`document.`*`myForm.myPassword`*`.name`
plugin	`document.embeds[0].name`
radio	`document.`*`myForm.myRadio`*`[0].name`
reset	`document.`*`myForm.myReset`*`.name`
select	`document.`*`myForm.mySelect`*`.name`
submit	`document.`*`myForm.mySubmit`*`.name`
text	`document.`*`myForm.myText`*`.name`
textarea	`document.`*`myForm.myTextarea`*`.name`
window	`window.name`
options array	`document.`*`myForm.mySelect`*`.options[0].name`

It's a fact that all radio buttons in a set have the same name. Nothing particularly special applies to the implementation of radio buttons, though. *Any* group of form objects to which you give the same name are automatically organized in an array! For example, if you wanted to keep an array consisting of a `text` element, a `textarea` element, and two `checkboxes`, you can give them all the same name (say, "chameleon"), and you'd automatically have an array called `document.myForm.chameleon`. To access the first element, you'd type `document.myForm.chameleon[0]`; the second element, `document.myForm.chameleon[1]`; and so on. Cool, huh?

opener

When a window is opened by the `open()` method, you can use the `opener` property of the `window` object to access the window of the calling document.

```
windowReference.opener
```

options

The `options` array, associated with the `select` object, enables you to access all the options that have been defined for a `select` object. The array is in source code order (the first option defined is the 0th element in the array, and so forth). Elements of the array are read-only.

```
document.myForm.selectFieldName.options[0]
document.myForm.selectFieldName.options.length
```

parent (frame)

The `parent` property of the `frame` object is a synonym for a frame whose frameset contains the current frame (the frame you're in when you're referencing the `parent` property). When the parent is a frame, the value for the `parent` property is the value of the `NAME` attribute defined as part of the `<FRAME>`... `</FRAME>` declaration. When the parent is a window, the value for the parent property is an internal reference. (That is, you can use the internal reference to refer to the properties of the window, but the internal reference is not much to look at.) The value for the `parent` property is read-only.

```
parent
```

parent (window)

The `parent` property of the `window` object is a synonym for a frame whose frameset contains the current window (the window you're in when you're referencing the `parent` property). When the parent is a frame, the value for the `parent` property is the value of the `NAME` attribute defined as part of the `<FRAME>`...`</FRAME>` declaration. When the parent is a window, the value for the parent property is an internal reference. (That is, you can use the internal reference to refer to the properties of the window, but the internal reference is not much to look at.) The value for the `parent` property is read-only.

```
parent
```

pathname

The `pathname` property is associated with the `area`, `link`, and `location` objects. Use the `pathname` property of each object to access the path portion of that object's URL. Although you can set the string value for the `pathname` property directly, setting the `href` property instead may be safer. (The `href` property represents the entire URL for an object, and setting it implicitly sets the `pathname` property.)

```
// syntax for both the link object and the area object
document.links[index].pathname
document.location.pathname
```

PI

PI, a property of the Math object, refers to the mathematical constant for the ratio of the circumference of a circle to its diameter (approximately 3.1415). The value for PI is read-only.

```
Math.PI
```

plugins

The read-only plugins array associated with the navigator object enables you to access all the plug-ins currently installed on the client. Each element in the plugins array is a plugins object.

```
navigator.plugins[0]
```

port

The port property is associated with the area, link, and location objects. The port property of each object is a *substring,* or piece, of that object's host property (which is itself a substring of that object's href property!). (The port property is the piece of the host after the colon.) You can change the port property's value, but because it represents one chunk of an entire URL, changing the port property implicitly by changing the href property instead may be safer.

```
// syntax is for link object as well as for area object
document.links[0].port
location.port
```

For a given href, if no value appears for port and the value of protocol is http://, the server assumes a default port value of 80. Why 80? Why not? Computer folks figured 80 was a nice round number, so they decided to make it the default port for all Web-type communications.

protocol

The protocol property is associated with the area, link, and location objects. Use the protocol property of each object to access a substring of that object's URL, beginning with the first character and ending with the first colon. (A common value for protocol is http://.) You can change the protocol property's value; but like port, host, and hostname, the protocol property's value represents just part of an entire URL, so changing the value of protocol implicitly by changing the value of href instead may be safer.

```
// syntax is for both link and area objects
document.links[0].protocol
location.protocol
```

prototype

The prototype property is available for any object that's created with the new operator, as shown in the table below. Use the prototype property to add your own custom properties to whole types of objects:

```
// custom property called "description" is defined
// for all date objects
Date.prototype.description = null

// a new date variable is created, called "today"
today = new Date()

// the new description property is assigned a value
today.description="Today is my birthday!"
```

Data type	Usage
array	Array.prototype.*newPropertyName* = null
date	Date.prototype.*newPropertyName* = null
function	Function.prototype.*newPropertyName* = null
image	Image.prototype.*newPropertyName* = null
option	Option.prototype.*newPropertyName* = null
string	String.prototype.*newPropertyName* = null
Any user-defined object	Animal.prototype.*newPropertyName* = null

referrer

When a user loads a linked document, the `referrer` property of that document holds the value for the URL of the calling document. The value for referrer is read-only (which makes sense, doesn't it?).

```
document.referrer
```

search (link)

The `search` property of the `link` object is used to access the portion of the link URL that contains query information. (That is, form input fields sent to a CGI program to be used for a document-based database search.) A valid `search` value is a string that begins with a question mark (?) followed by any number of attribute-value pairs, each separated by an ampersand (&). You can change the value for `search`; but because `search` represents just part of an entire URL, changing the `search` value implicitly by changing the value of `href` instead may be safer.

```
document.links[0].search
```

search (location)

The `search` property of the `location` object is used to access the portion of the location URL that contains query information. (That is, form input fields sent to a CGI program to be used for a document-based search of a database.) A valid `search` value is a string that begins with a question mark (?) followed by any number of attribute-value pairs, each separated by an ampersand (&). You can change the value for `search`; but because `search` represents just part of an entire URL, changing the `search` value implicitly by changing the value of `href` instead may be safer.

```
document.location.search
```

Try out any of the popular Web search engines, such as Yahoo!, AltaVista, or Excite, and you can see the value of the `search` property being sent to the respective CGI programs — right there in either Navigator's Location window or Internet Explorer's Address window.

selected

Use the `selected` property of the `option` object to access a Boolean (true or false) value that describes whether an option in a selection has been selected. You can change the value of the `selected` property programmatically.

```
document.myForm.mySelectField.options[0].selected
```

selectedIndex (options)

Use the `selectedIndex` property of the `options` array to access the index of a selected `option` (an integer from 0 to however many options exist). If multiple options have been selected, the value of `selectedIndex` contains a reference only to the index of the very first `option` selected. The value for `options.selectedIndex` is the same as for `select.selectedIndex`, and you can change it.

```
document.myForm.mySelectField.options.selectedIndex
```

selectedIndex (select)

Use the `selectedIndex` value to access the index of a `select` object. If multiple options have been selected, the value of `selectedIndex` contains a reference only to the index of the very first option selected. The value for `select.selectedIndex` is the same as for `options.selectedIndex`, and you can change it.

```
document.myForm.mySelectField.selectedIndex
```

self (frame)

The `self` property of the `frame` object is a synonym for the current frame. (Gee, and all those philosophers spent so much time searching for the meaning of *self!* If only they had coded JavaScript!) The value for `self` is read-only.

```
self
```

self (window)

The self property of the window object is a synonym for the current window. The value for self is read-only.

```
self
```

SQRT1_2

The SQRT1_2 property of the Math object represents the mathematical constant for the square root of one-half (approximately .707). Its value can't be changed.

```
Math.SQRT1_2
```

SQRT2

The SQRT2 property of the Math object represents the mathematical constant for the square root of two (approximately 1.414). Its value can't be changed.

```
Math.SQRT2
```

src

The src property of the image object reflects the value of the SRC attribute defined as part of the HTML <IMG> tag. A valid value for this property is a URL for the image to be loaded.

```
document.myImage.src
```

status

The status property of the window object contains a text value to be displayed in the window's status bar. You can change the status property's value.

```
status
```

The status property is different from the defaultStatus property. The value of the defaultStatus property is displayed in the status bar when nothing else is going on; in contrast, the value of the status property is displayed for a specific reason — for example, in response to a onMouseOver event.

suffixes

The value for the `suffixes` property of the `mimeTypes` array represents a string listing, separated by commas, of all possible file suffixes (file suffixes are sometimes called file extensions) available for each corresponding MIME type (see `navigator.mimeTypes[0].type`).

```
navigator.mimeTypes[0].suffixes
```

target (form)

Use the `target` property of a `form` to access a string that specifies the window in which you want to receive responses back from the server. The value for `form.target` is initially defined by the `TARGET` attribute as part of the `<FORM>...</FORM>` tag, but you can change it.

```
document.myForm.target
```

target (link, area)

Use the `target` property of a `link` or `area` object to access a string that identifies the name of the window a linked (or area mapped) document should be loaded into. The string value for `link.target` is initially defined by the `TARGET` attribute of the `<A>...</A>` tag, and the string value for `area.target` is initially defined by the `TARGET` attribute of the `<AREA>` tag; you can change the values for both programmatically.

```
// same syntax for both link and area objects

document.links[0].target
```

text

Use the `text` property of the `option` object to access the text that follows an `<OPTION>` tag that is defined as part of a `select` object. You can change the value for this object.

```
document.myForm.mySelectField.options[0].text
```

title

The `title` property of the `document` object enables you to access the title of a document (the text that was defined between the `<TITLE>...</TITLE>` tags). The `title` property's value is read-only.

```
document.title
```

top

The `top` property of the `window` object refers to the topmost window that contains frames or nested framesets. Its value is read-only.

```
top
```

type

The read-only `type` property is available on many different objects, as shown in Table 11-4. The `type` property represents the HTML `TYPE` attribute for an object.

Table 11-4   What Type of Property Ya Got There?

Object	*Usage*	*Return value*
button	`document.`*myForm*`.`*myButton*`.type`	`"button"`
checkbox	`document.`*myForm*`.`*myCheckbox*`.type`	`"checkbox"`
fileUpload	`document.`*myForm*`.`*myFile*`.type`	`"file"`
hidden	`document.`*myForm*`.`*myHidden*`.type`	`"hidden"`
password	`document.`*myForm*`.`*myPassword*`.type`	`"password"`
radio	`document.`*myForm*`.`*myRadio*`[0].type`	`"radio"`
reset	`document.`*myForm*`.`*myReset*`.type`	`"reset"`
select	`document.`*myForm*`.`*mySelect*`.type`	`"select-one"`, `"select-multiple"` (MULTIPLE)
submit	`document.`*myForm*`.`*mySubmit*`.type`	`"submit"`
text	`document.`*myForm*`.`*myText*`.type`	`"text"`
textarea	`document.`*myForm*`.`*myTextarea*`.type`	`"textarea"`

userAgent

The `userAgent` property of the `navigator` object enables you to access a string value that represents the user-agent header that Navigator automatically sends every time a form is submitted from a client browser to a server. Servers use this value to identify the client that's making a request of them, so it makes sense that it's read-only.

```
navigator.userAgent
```

value

The `value` property represents a string that's associated with the value of whatever object you're trying to access, as you can see in Table 11-5.

Table 11-5	Good Value for the Money: The Value Property	
Object	*Usage*	*Comments*
button	`document.`*myForm.* *myButton.*`value`	read-only value is displayed on button face.
checkbox	`document.`*myForm.* *myCheckbox.*`value`	value is sent to server when checkbox is clicked (default is "on")
fileUpload	`document.`*myForm.* *myFileUpload.*`value`	reflects the value selected by a user (currently unimplemented)
hidden	`document.`*myForm.* *myHidden.*`value`	initially reflects the VALUE attribute
option	`document.`*myForm.* *mySelect.*`options[0].` `value`	value is sent to server when option is selected
password	`document.`*myForm.* *myPassword.*`value`	initially reflects the VALUE attribute
radio	`document.`*myForm.* *myRadio[0].*`value`	value is sent to server when checkbox is clicked (default is "on")
reset	`document.`*myForm.* *myReset.*`value`	read-only value is displayed on button face; default is "Reset"
submit	`document.`*myForm.* *mySubmit.*`value`	read-only value is displayed on button face; default is "Submit Query"

Object	Usage	Comments
text	document.*myForm.* *myText*.value	initially reflects the VALUE attribute
textarea	document.*myForm.* *myTextarea*.value	initially reflects the VALUE attribute
options array	document.*myForm.* *mySelect*.options[*0*]. value	value is sent to server when option is selected

vlinkColor

The vlinkColor property enables you to access the value defined by the VLINK attribute declared as part of the <BODY>...</BODY> tag. The vlinkColor property defines the color of a clicked-on, or followed, link. You can change the value for the VLINK attribute to a hexadecimal RGB triplet or to a predefined color string that corresponds to such a triplet (see Chapter 16 for examples of triplets and color strings).

```
document.vlinkColor
```

vspace

The vspace property of the image object enables you to access the value of the VSPACE attribute of the HTML <IMG> tag. This value specifies a margin (in pixels) between the top and bottom edges of an image and the surrounding screen real estate. (This property only applies to images that have "left" or "right" defined for the value of the ALIGN attribute of the <IMG> tag.)

```
document.myImage.vspace
```

width

The width property of the image object lets you access the value of the WIDTH attribute of the HTML <IMG> tag. A valid value for the width property can either be an integer (in pixels), or a percentage (expressing percent of total window width). The value for this property is read-only.

```
document.myImage.width
```

window

The `window` property is a synonym for the current window (or current frame, because frames *are* windows). The value for this property is read-only, and it's also the same as the `self` property of the `window` object.

```
window
```

Synonyms — aren't they for weenie writers?

Why bother with synonyms? After all, you're writing JavaScript code, not a *New York Times* bestseller. Well, there *is* a good reason: In some examples, using synonyms (like *parent, window, top,* and *self*) makes your code easier to read. For example, if you have a form named *status* and you want to change the value of the current window's `status`, typing **status** by itself may be confusing (even though technically it would refer to the status of the current window). Instead, you can type **window.status ="blah blah"** and what you were trying to do would be clearly obvious. Don't forget: More than 75 percent of the total cost and effort of *any* software development is maintenance, so make maintenance easy on yourself (or your successor).

Chapter 12

There's a Method to This Madness

*I*f you're looking for some methods to spice up your JavaScript objects, you've come to the right place. This chapter is chock-full of methods you'll find to be not only useful, but sometimes fun, too.

What Exactly Is This Method Stuff?

Methods are behaviors that are associated with specific objects. When you get down to it, methods are really just functions, with one difference: Unlike functions, which you can call all by themselves, methods work only if you invoke them with the fully qualified name of the object they belong to. This makes sense if you think about it. Take the method click(), for example. If you've got three buttons on a form — buttonOne, buttonTwo, and buttonThree, all of which support the click() method — how would the JavaScript interpreter translate click() by itself? It couldn't! You have to specify *which* button you want to click, like this: document.myForm.buttonOne.click(). (The exception to this, as always, is the window object, which is a given and doesn't usually need to be specified explicitly.) This chapter lists every method available to you in JavaScript.

Remember, you can define your own methods when you define your own objects.

To take a look at each method in action, load the HTML file corresponding to that method's object. For example, the abs method is exercised in the file Math.htm.

abs

Use the abs() method of the Math object to return the absolute value of a number.

Generic Javascript syntax:

```
Math.abs(number)
```

Real-life code example:

```
var myResult = Math.abs(1)
```

 Just like functions (which are described in detail in Chapter 13), when a method takes a certain type of parameter, it can take a literal, a variable, or even an expression that resolves to that type. For example, valid *number* parameters include 3, 4.6, myAge, and (numberOrdered * 10).

acos

Use the acos() method of the Math object to return the arc cosine (in radians) of a number.

Generic JavaScript syntax:

```
Math.acos(number)
```

Real-life code example:

```
var myResult = Math.acos(1)
```

alert

Use the alert() method of the window object to display a pop-up dialog box that contains a message that you define and an OK button.

Generic JavaScript syntax:

```
alert("message")
```

Real-life code example:

```
alert("Your order total is " + getOrderTotal())
```

anchor

Use the anchor() method of a string object to identify the string as an HTML anchor that you can then use as a hypertext link target.

Generic JavaScript syntax:

```
string.anchor(anchorName)
```

Real-life code example:

```
"Table Of Contents".anchor("TOC_anchor")
```

The anchor() method is one way of defining an anchor; the <A>...</A> tag is another. For example, you could have replaced the example above with the following:

```
<A NAME="TOC_anchor">Table of Contents</A>
```

asin

Use the asin() method of the Math object to return the arc sine (in radians) of a number.

Generic JavaScript syntax:

```
Math.asin(number)
```

Real-life code example:

```
Math.asin(1)
```

atan

Use the atan() method of the Math object to return the arc tangent (in radians) of a number.

Generic JavaScript syntax:

```
Math.atan(number)
```

Real-life code example:

```
Math.atan(1)
```

atan2

Use the atan2() method of the Math object to return a numeric value for the angle (theta component) of the polar coordinate (r, theta) that corresponds to the specified cartesian coordinate (x, y).

Generic JavaScript syntax:

```
Math.atan2(number)
```

Real-life code example:

```
Math.atan2(90, 15)
```

back

Use the back() method of the history object to load the previous URL in the history list.

Generic JavaScript syntax:

```
history.back()
```

Real-life code example:

```
history.back()
```

Invoking the back() method of the history object produces the same result as history.go(-1) (or as selecting Go⇨Back from the Navigator or Internet Explorer menu, for that matter).

big

Using the big() method of the string object enables you to display a string in big font.

Generic JavaScript syntax:

```
string.big()
```

Real-life code example:

```
"This is gonna be big!".big()
```

blink

Using the `blink()` method of the `string` object enables you to display a blinking string.

Generic JavaScript syntax:

```
string.blink()
```

Real-life code example:

```
document.write("FREE".blink())
```

Using the `blink()` method of the `string` object produces the same result as surrounding text with the `<BLINK>`...`</BLINK>` HTML tag.

blur

Use the `blur()` method of the `frame`, `password`, `select`, `text`, `textarea`, or `window` objects to remove focus from them.

Generic JavaScript syntax:

```
frameReference.blur()
passwordName.blur()
selectName.blur()
textName.blur()
textareaName.blur()
windowReference.blur()
```

Real-life code example:

```
parent.myFrame.blur()
document.myForm.myPassword.blur()
document.myForm.mySelectField.blur()
document.myForm.myTextField.blur()
document.myForm.myTextareaField.blur()
mySecondWindow.blur()
```

bold

Using the `bold()` method of the `string` object enables you to display a string in bold font.

Generic JavaScript syntax:

```
string.bold()
```

Real-life code example:

```
document.write("IMPORTANT".bold())
```

ceil

Use the `ceil()` method of the `Math` object to return the smallest integer greater than or equal to a specified number.

Generic JavaScript syntax:

```
Math.ceil(number)
```

Real-life code example:

```
document.write("The ceil of 36.25 is " + Math.ceil(36.25))
```

charAt

Use the `charAt()` method of the `string` object to return the character of a string at the specified index.

Generic JavaScript syntax:

```
string.charAt(index)
```

Real-life code example:

```
var thirdLetter = "Netscape".charAt(2)
```

clearTimeout

Use the `clearTimeout()` method of the `frame` or `window` objects to clear a timeout that was set by using the corresponding `setTimeout()` method (see the `setTimeout()` method described later in this chapter for details).

Generic JavaScript syntax:

```
clearTimeout(timeoutID)
```

Real-life code example:

```
readyYetTimer=setTimeout("alert('5 seconds has elapsed. Are
            you ready yet?!'), 5000")
...
clearTimeout(readyYetTimer)
```

click

Use the click() method of the button, checkbox, radio, reset, and submit objects to simulate a mouse click programmatically. Clicking a radio button selects the radio button; clicking a checkbox checks the checkbox and sets its value to *on*.

Generic JavaScript syntax:

```
buttonName.click()
checkboxName.click()
radioName[index].click()
resetButtonName.click()
submitButtonName.click()
```

Real-life code example:

```
document.myForm.myButton.click()
document.myForm.myCheckbox.click()
document.myForm.myRadioGroup[0].click()
document.myForm.myReset.click()
document.myForm.mySubmit.click()
```

close (document)

Use the close() method of the document object to close an output stream that was opened with the document.open() method (see the section for the open() method defined later in this chapter) and to force any data already sent to the document to be displayed.

Generic JavaScript syntax:

```
document.close()
```

Real-life code example:

```
myMessageWindow=window.open('', 'messageWindow')
myMessageWindow.document.writeln('This is a message window.')
myMessageWindow.document.close()
```

close (window)

Use the close() method of the window object to close a window that was opened with the open() method of the window object.

As you'd expect, if you leave off a specific reference to a window, the interpreter assumes that you want to close the current window — with one exception. In an event handler, you must specify window.close() if you want to close the current *window*. (If you leave off the specific reference to a window, the current *document* closes. Go figure.)

Generic JavaScript syntax:

```
windowReference.close()
```

Real-life code example:

```
close() // closes the current window
window.close // closes the current window from inside an
           event handler
myMessageWindow.close() // closes the window called
           myMessageWindow
```

confirm

Use the confirm() method of the window object to display a pop-up dialog box that contains a message, an OK button, and a Cancel button. The confirm() method returns *true* if the user clicks on the OK button and *false* if the user clicks on the Cancel button.

Generic JavaScript syntax:

```
confirm("message")
```

Real-life code example:

```
var submitOk = confirm("Do you really want to submit the
           form?")
```

cos

Use the cos() method of the Math object to return the cosine of a number.

Generic JavaScript syntax:

```
Math.cos(number)
```

Real-life code example:
```
Math.cos(0)
```

exp

Use the exp() method of the Math object to return e^*number* where *e* is Euler's constant and *number* is the number argument provided to exp().

Generic JavaScript syntax:
```
Math.exp(number)
```

Real-life code example:
```
Math.exp(1)
```

fixed

Using the fixed() method of the string object enables you to display a string in fixed-pitch font. Fixed-pitch font looks like the font from an old typewriter.

Generic JavaScript syntax:
```
string.fixed()
```

Real-life code example:
```
document.write("E = MC2".fixed())
```

floor

Use the floor() method of the Math object to return the biggest integer less than or equal to a specified number.

Generic JavaScript syntax:
```
Math.floor(number)
```

Real-life code example:
```
var result = Math.floor(88.78)
```

focus

Use the focus() method of the frame, password, select, text, textarea, or window objects to give them focus.

Generic JavaScript syntax:

```
frameReference.focus()
passwordName.focus()
selectName.focus()
textName.focus()
textareaName.focus()
windowReference.focus()
```

Real-life code example:

```
self.frame1.focus()
document.myForm.myPassword.focus()
document.myForm.mySelectField.focus()
document.myForm.myTextField.focus()
document.myForm.myTextareaField.focus()
mySecondWindow.focus()
```

The focus() method is handy for helping users navigate through your form. For example, if you attempt to validate an input value and determine that it's incorrect, you can set focus back to the input field so the user can retype the value without first having to tab backward to it. Or, based on the value a user enters, you can skip several fields and set focus to the next relevant input field for that user.

fontcolor

Using the fontcolor() method of the string object enables you to display a string in any conceivable color. See Chapter 16 for a complete list of predefined colors in addition to a recipe for mixing your own colors.

Generic JavaScript syntax:

```
string.fontcolor(color)
```

Real-life code example:

```
// using a pre-defined color string
document.write("This is brown".fontcolor("brown"))

// using hexadecimal RGB triplet notation
document.write("This is fuchsia".fontcolor("FF00FF"))
```

fontsize

Using the fontsize() method of the string object enables you to display a string in one of seven font sizes (*size* must be an integer between one and seven).

Generic JavaScript syntax:

```
string.fontsize(size)
```

Real-life code example:

```
var smallSize=1
document.write("This is large".fontsize(7))
document.write("This is small".fontsize(smallSize))
```

forward

Use the forward() method of the history object to load the next URL in the history list.

Generic JavaScript syntax:

```
history.forward()
```

Real-life code example:

```
history.forward()
```

Invoking the forward() method of the history object produces the same result as using history.go(1) (or selecting Go⇨Forward from the Navigator or Internet Explorer menu).

getDate

Use the getDate() method of a Date object to access the day of the month associated with a specified date. For example, if the Date object represented the 26th of June, 1996, getDate() would return the value *26*.

Generic JavaScript syntax:

```
dateObjectName.getDate()
```

Real-life code example:

```
var today = new Date()
var dayOfMonth = today.getDate()
```

getDay

Use the `getDay()` method of a `Date` object to access the day of the week associated with a specified date (Monday being 1; Tuesday, 2; and so on, with Sunday being 7). For example, if the `Date` object represented Wednesday, the 26th of June, 1996, `getDay()` would return the value *3*.

Generic JavaScript syntax:

```
dateObjectName.getDay()
```

Real-life code example:

```
var today = new Date()
var dayOfWeek = today.getDay()
```

getHours

Use the `getHours()` method of a `Date` object to access the hour (in military time) associated with a specified date. For example, if the `Date` object represented Wednesday, the 26th of June, 1996 at 3:45 p.m., `getHours()` would return the value *15*.

Generic JavaScript syntax:

```
dateObjectName.getHours()
```

Real-life code example:

```
var today = new Date()
var hour = today.getHours()
```

getMinutes

Use the `getMinutes()` method of a `Date` object to access the minutes associated with a specified date. For example, if the `Date` object represented Wednesday, the 26th of June, 1996 at 3:45 p.m., `getMinutes()` would return the value *45*.

Generic JavaScript syntax:

```
dateObjectName.getMinutes()
```

Real-life code example:

```
var today = new Date()
var numberMinutesAfterTheHour = today.getMinutes()
```

getMonth

Use the getMonth() method of a Date object to access the month of the year associated with a specified date. For example, if the Date object represented Wednesday, the 26th of June, 1996 at 3:45 p.m., getMonth() would return the value *5*.

For a date of June, you'd think getMonth() would return *6*, wouldn't you? Well, unfortunately, it returns *5*. That's because JavaScript counts January as month 0, February as month 1, and so on.

Generic JavaScript syntax:

```
dateObjectName.getMonth()
```

Real-life code example:

```
var today = new Date()
var month = today.getMonth()
```

getSeconds

Use the getSeconds() method of a Date object to access the number of seconds in the specified date. For example, if the Date object represented Wednesday, the 26th of June, 1996 at 3:45:16 p.m., getSeconds() would return the value *16*.

Generic JavaScript syntax:

```
dateObjectName.getSeconds()
```

Real-life code example:

```
var today = new Date()
var seconds = today.getSeconds()
```

getTime

Use the getTime() method of a Date object to access the number of milliseconds that have elapsed since January 1, 1970 00:00:00 (no, I'm not kidding!). About the only use that regular folks are going to have for this method is to assign one time to another, like this: timeToLeave = today.getTime() (That way you never have to actually look at, and decipher, the darn thing).

Versions of Navigator earlier than 3.0 (and the beta version of Internet Explorer version 3.0) tend to — well — blow up if they encounter a date earlier than January 1, 1970. So avoid giving them one! If you're running anything other than Navigator 3.0 and want to work with dates older than 1970, try using a more recent date (say, 1980) and then doing subtraction by using regular variables (as opposed to Date objects).

Generic JavaScript syntax:

```
dateObjectName.getTime()
```

Real-life code example:

```
var startDay = new Date()
var startTime = today.getTime()
```

getTimezoneOffset

Use the getTimezoneOffset() method of the Date object to get the difference in minutes between the time of the Date object and Greenwich Mean Time (GMT).

Generic JavaScript syntax:

```
dateObjectName.getTimezoneOffset()
```

Real-life code example:

```
today = new Date()
currentTimezoneOffsetInHours = today.getTimezoneOffset()/60
```

getYear

Use the getYear() method of a Date object to access the year of the specified date (less 1900). For example, if the Date object represented Wednesday, the 26th of June, 1996 at 3:45:16 p.m., getYear() would return the value *96*.

Generic JavaScript syntax:

```
dateObjectName.getYear()
```

Real-life code example:

```
var today = new Date()
var currentYear = today.getYear()
```

go

Use the `go()` method of the `history` object to load a URL from the history list. You've got two choices for parameters. You can supply `go()` with one of the following:

- ✔ An integer, which the interpreter uses to count forward (positive integer) or backward (negative integer) from the current list position to find a URL to load.
- ✔ A string that contains a whole URL or just part of a URL; the interpreter finds the nearest matching URL and loads it.

Generic JavaScript syntax:

```
history.go(delta | "location")
```

Real-life code example:

```
history.go(3) // loads the third URL forward
history.go(-2) // loads the second URL back
history.go("www.austin") // loads the closest URL that
             contains the parameter string
```

indexOf

Use the `indexOf()` method of the `string` object to search a specified string for the occurrence of another specified string. The `indexOf()` method accepts two parameters:

- ✔ A search value that consists of a string to search for.
- ✔ An optional index value that tells the interpreter where in the original string to begin searching for the search string. (The default value is 0, which means the search begins — where else? — at the beginning.)

`indexOf()` returns the first index of the original string that matches the search string (see the real-life example below). If it can't find a match at all, it returns *-1*.

Generic JavaScript syntax:

```
string.indexOf(searchValue, [fromIndex])
```

Real-life code example:

```
var theResult = "chocolate-chip-coconut
            shortbread".indexOf("chip") // returns 10
```

c	h	o	c	o	l	a	t	e	-	**c**	h
0	1	2	3	4	5	6	7	8	9	**10**	11

italics

Using the italics() method of the string object enables you to display an italicized string.

Generic JavaScript syntax:

```
string.italics()
```

Real-life code example:

```
"IMPORTANT".italics()
```

javaEnabled

The javaEnabled() method of the navigator object returns *true* or *false*, depending on whether or not Java is enabled or disabled.

Generic JavaScript syntax:

```
navigator.javaEnabled()
```

Real-life code example:

```
if (navigator.javaEnabled()) {
    alert("Java is enabled in this Navigator session.")
}
```

join

The join() method of the array object joins the elements of an array into one long string. join() accepts an optional separator argument; if one is provided, it's placed between the elements inside the string. If no separator is provided, a comma is used to join the elements.

Generic JavaScript syntax:

```
string = arrayName.join([separator])
```

Real-life code example:

```
var animalArray = new Array("cat", "dog", "bat", "bear")
var aString = animalArray.join(" and ")
// aString is assigned "cat and dog and bat and bear"
```

lastIndexOf

The lastIndexOf() method is practically a mirror image of the indexOf() method. lastIndexOf() starts searching from the *end* of the original string, and indexOf() starts searching from the *beginning* of the original string.

Use the lastIndexOf() method of the string object to search a specified string backwards for the occurrence of another specified string. The lastIndexOf() method accepts two parameters:

- ✔ A search value that consists of a string to search for.
- ✔ An optional index value that tells the interpreter where in the original string to begin searching for the search string. (The default value is length of the string minus one, which means that the interpreter begins searching at the end of the string.)

lastIndexOf() returns the last index of the original string that matches the search string. If it can't find a match at all, it returns *-1*.

Generic JavaScript syntax:

```
string.lastIndexOf(searchValue, [fromIndex])
```

Real-life code example:

```
var theResult = "chocolate-chip-coconut
        shortbread".lastIndexOf("chip") // theResult is
        set to 10
```

link

Use the link() method of the string object to create an HTML hypertext link programmatically. Remember to use the write() or writeln() methods of the document object to display the link. (It doesn't do much good to define a link on-the-fly if no one can see it to click on it, now does it?)

Generic JavaScript syntax:

```
linkText.link(hrefAttribute)
```

Real-life code example:

```
document.write("My Friend Fred's Dyn-O-Mite Web Page". link
          ("http://www.fictitious.com/fred/home.html"))
```

log

Use the `log()` method of the `Math` object to return the natural logarithm (base *e*) of a number.

Generic JavaScript syntax:

```
Math.log(number)
```

Generic JavaScript syntax:

```
Math.log(10)
```

max

Use the `max()` method of the `Math` object to return the greater of two numbers.

Generic JavaScript syntax:

```
Math.max(number1, number2)
```

Real-life code example:

```
var taxedAmount = Math.max(amount.calcOneWay(), amount.
          calcAnotherWay()) // pay taxes on greatest amount
```

min

Use the `min()` method of the `Math` object to return the lesser of two numbers.

Generic JavaScript syntax:

```
Math.min(number1, number2)
```

Real-life code example:

```
var youngest = Math.min(myAge, georgesAge)
```

open (document)

Use the open() method of the document object to open a document for writing via the write() and writeln() methods. (Well, technically you're opening something called an output *stream,* but you can think of the stream as the document.) When you use the open() method, be sure to use the corresponding close() method as well.

The open() method accepts one parameter, and the use of a parameter is optional. A *parameter* is a string that specifies the format of the data that you're planning to stick into the document. Most of the time, you won't have to specify a value for this parameter. If you do, however, here are your choices:

✔ text/html	HTML statements (this is the default)
✔ text/plain	plain old ASCII text with end-of-line characters
✔ image/gif	an image in GIF format
✔ image/jpeg	an image in JPG format
✔ image/x-bitmap	an image in bitmap format
✔ plugIn	a Netscape plugin

Generic JavaScript syntax:

```
document.open(["mimeType"])
```

Real-life code example:

```
document.open()
document.open("image/gif")
```

open (window)

Use the open() method of the window object to open a new Web browser window.

Generic JavaScript syntax:

```
[windowVar = ] [window].open("URL", "windowName"
            [, "windowFeatures"])
```

Real-life code example:

```
secondWindow = open("", "statusWindow", "scrollbars=yes,
            width=200,height=200")
```

As for the last optional value shown in "Generic JavaScript syntax," windowFeatures, you have your choice of any or all of the following features. Just make sure that you surround the entire list that you create with quotes and separate each attribute-value pair with a comma (no spaces), as shown in the example (just like in the syntax section in Chapter 3, the items bounded by square brackets are optional and the pipe symbol means "or"):

```
toolbar[=yes|no]|[=1|0],
location[=yes|no]|[=1|0],
directories[=yes|no]|[=1|0],
status[=yes|no]|[=1|0],
menubar[=yes|no]|[=1|0],
scrollbars[=yes|no]|[=1|0],
resizable[=yes|no]|[=1|0],
width=pixels,
height=pixels
```

parse

Use the parse() method of the Date object to determine the number of milliseconds between January 1, 1970 00:00:00 and a specified date/time.

Generic JavaScript syntax:

```
Date.parse(dateString)
```

Real-life code example:

```
myBirthday.setTime(Date.parse("Jul 26, 1996"))
```

The reason you call the parse() method this way (Date.parse()) instead of this way (myBirthday.parse()) is that the parse() method is a static method. *Static methods* are methods that have to do with the concept of a thing (in this case, a date) rather than an individual example of a thing (a particular date object). The same can be said of any of the Math methods: They're static because math is math — mathematical functions don't change from situation to situation.

pow

Use the pow() method of the Math object to return a specified base to the specified exponent power.

Generic JavaScript syntax:

```
Math.pow(base, exponent)
```

Real-life code example:

```
document.write("7 squared is equal to " + Math.pow(7,7))
```

prompt

Use the prompt() method of the window object to display a pop-up dialog box that contains a message that you define, an input field, an OK button, and a Cancel button.

Generic JavaScript syntax:

```
prompt("message" [, inputDefault])
```

Real-life code example:

```
prompt("What size t-shirt do you want?", "Large")
```

random

Use the random() method of the Math object to return a pseudo-random number between 0 and 1.

Generic JavaScript syntax:

```
Math.random()
```

Real-life code example:

```
var aRandomNumber = Math.random()
```

You can create your own random function, if you like (or you can take a peek at the one that's provided on the *JavaScript For Dummies CD-ROM* that came with this book, called random.htm). One way to create your own random function is to use an algorithm that uses the current date and time in some way. (Because the use of the current date and time is pretty much guaranteed to be unique, it makes a good starting point.)

reload

The reload() method of the location object forces a reload of the document specified by the URL in the href property of the location object. The result of the reload() method is the same as clicking the Reload button in Navigator (or the Refresh button in Internet Explorer).

Generic JavaScript syntax:

```
windowReference.location.reload()
```

Real-life code example:

```
<INPUT TYPE="button" NAME="reloadButton"
VALUE="Reload Now"
onClick="self.location.reload()">
```

replace

The replace() method of the location object replaces the current history entry with the specified URL. The upshot is that after the replace() method is called, the new URL is loaded — and the user can no longer navigate to the previously loaded URL by clicking the Back button.

Generic JavaScript syntax:

```
windowReference.location.replace("URL")
```

Real-life code example:

```
self.location.replace("http://home.netscape.com")
```

reset

The reset() method of the form object simulates a user clicking on a reset button; that is, it causes all of a form's elements to be reset to their default values.

Generic JavaScript syntax:

```
document.formName.reset()
```

Real-life code example:

```
if (resetOkay) {
    document.myForm.reset()
}
```

reverse

The reverse() method of the array object transposes the elements of an array; that is, the order of the elements is reversed (the first element becomes the last and the last element becomes the first).

Generic JavaScript syntax:

```
arrayName.reverse()
```

Real-life code example:

```
var listOfJobs = new Array("bookie", "writer", "nurse")
listOfJobs.reverse()
```

round

The round() method of the Math object returns the value of a specified number, rounded to the nearest integer.

Generic JavaScript syntax:

```
Math.round(number)
```

Real-life code example:

```
var closeEnough = Math.round(totalPrice)
```

scroll

The scroll() method of the window object lets you scroll a window to the coordinates you specify. scroll() accepts two arguments: an x-coordinate and a y-coordinate. Both values must be integers representing the number of pixels to scroll in each direction (x-coordinate is left-to-right and y-coordinate is up-and-down).

This method only executes if the page it's on contains enough displayed data to be scrollable (put another way, unless the page is so long that there are scroll bars visible, calling scroll() doesn't have a visible effect.

The coordinates for the upper left-hand corner of a document are 0,0.

Generic JavaScript syntax:

```
windowReference.scroll(x-coordinate, y-coordinate)
```

Real-life code example:

```
if(okayToScroll) {
    self.scroll(50, 100)
}
```

select

Use the select() method of the password, text, or textarea objects to select (highlight) their respective input areas programmatically.

Generic JavaScript syntax:

```
passwordName.select()
textName.select()
textareaName.select()
```

Real-life code example:

```
onBlur="document.myForm.myPasssword.select()"
onClick="document.myForm.myTextField.select()"
if (goBack()) {
    document.myForm.myTextareaField.select()
}
```

setDate

Use the setDate() method of the Date object to set the day of the month for a specified date. The required *dayValue* parameter can be any integer from 1 to 31.

Generic JavaScript syntax:

```
dateObjectName.setDate(dayValue)
```

Real-life code example:

```
myBirthday.setDate(26)
```

setHours

The setHours() method of the Date object enables you to set the hours for a specified date. The required *hoursValue* parameter can be any integer between 0 and 24.

JavaScript doesn't complain if you set the hours on a date to a value greater than 24 — it just wraps the date around. For example, if you pass 25 to the setHours() method, like this (aDate.setHours(25)) and then display the value with getHours(), you notice that JavaScript turns your 25 into 1 and adds 1 to the day.

Generic JavaScript syntax:

```
dateObjectName.setHours(hoursValue)
```

Real-life code example:

```
contractDate.setHours(12)
```

setMinutes

The setMinutes() method of the Date object enables you to set the minutes for a specified date. The required *minutesValue* parameter can be any integer between 0 and 60. (For anything over 60, the interpreter adds the excess onto the hours portion of the date.)

Generic JavaScript syntax:

```
dateObjectName.setMinutes(minutesValue)
```

Real-life code example:

```
firstHeeHawEpisode.setMinutes(30)
```

setMonth

The setMonth() method of the Date object enables you to set the month for a specified date. The required *monthValue* parameter can be any integer between 0 and 11, where 0 corresponds to January and 11 corresponds to December.

Generic JavaScript syntax:

```
dateObjectName.setMonth(monthValue)
```

Real-life code example:

```
christmas.setMonth(11)
```

setSeconds

The setSeconds() method of the Date object enables you to set the seconds for a specified date. The required *secondsValue* parameter can be any integer between 0 and 59. (For anything over 59, the interpreter adds the excess onto the minutes portion of the date — and that situation can get confusing quickly!)

Generic JavaScript syntax:

```
dateObjectName.setSeconds(secondsValue)
```

Real-life code example:

```
pickyDate.setSeconds(12)
```

setTime

The setTime() method of the Date object enables you to set the date and time for a specified date. The required *timeValue* parameter reflects the number of milliseconds since January 1, 1970 00:00:00. (That fact should give you a tip-off that this method is mainly used to assign one date to another, like this: oneDate.setTime(anotherDate.getTime().)

Generic JavaScript syntax:

```
dateObjectName.setTime(timeValue)
```

Real-life code example:

```
husbandAnniversary.setTime(wifeAnniversary.getTime())
```

setTimeout

Use the setTimeout() method of the frame or window objects to evaluate an expression after a specified time has elapsed. Using the setTimeout() method is just like setting a timer and then doing something when the timer goes off! (An obvious application for this method is a Web game: you can start the clock ticking when a user begins the game, and then pop up a message saying "Game Over" if the user hasn't completed the game in a certain amount of time.)

This method takes the following two parameters:

- ✔ An expression to evaluate.
- ✔ A number that represents the number of milliseconds to wait before evaluating the expression.

Although not strictly necessary, saving the return value from the `setTimeout()` method in a variable is a really good idea. That's because you need to use this variable if you ever want to cancel the timer. To cancel a timer, you need to pass the variable you saved to the `clearTimeout()` method of the `frame` or `window` object (see the example of `clearTimeout()` in the following example for clarification).

Generic JavaScript syntax:

```
timeoutID=setTimeout(expression, number)
```

Real-life code example:

```
readyYetTimer=setTimeout("alert('5 seconds has elapsed. Are
          you ready yet?!'), 5000")
...
clearTimeout(readyYetTimer)
```

setYear

The `setYear()` method of the `Date` object enables you set the year for a specified date. The required *yearValue* parameter must reflect a year between 1970 and 1999. (And because the range is so narrow, you don't have to specify the 20th century; for example, 1985 and 85 are both perfectly acceptable entries.)

Passing a *bogus* (out-of-range) value for the *yearValue* parameter may not cause an immediately obvious error. Because the interpreter assumes that every date falls in the 1900s, any value not between 70 (1970) and 99 (1999) has the effect of setting the date to the last day of 1969. No fireworks, no pop-up warnings — just really goofy date calculations.

Generic JavaScript syntax:

```
dateObjectName.setYear(yearValue)
```

Real-life code example:

```
nephewGraduation.setYear(98)
```

sin

Use the `sin()` method of the `Math` object to return the sine of a number (*not* the number of sins committed!).

Generic JavaScript syntax:

```
Math.sin(number)
```

Real-life code example:

```
document.write("Here is the sine of PI: " + Math.sin(Math.PI))
```

small

Using the small() method of the string object enables you display a string in small font.

Generic JavaScript syntax:

```
string.small()
```

Real-life code example:

```
"This is gonna be really teensy.".small()
```

sort

Use the sort() method of the array object to sort the elements in an array. The sort() method accepts an optional argument that specifies a function name to use for the sorting algorithm. If a function name isn't supplied, sort() converts the elements in the array to strings (if they're not already strings) and compares them in *lexicographic,* or alphabetic, order.

Unless your array elements contain numbers, the default sorting algorithm may be sufficient for your needs. But look what happens if your array *does* contain numeric values: 60, 9, and 100 will be sorted like this — "100," "60," "9" — which is probably not what you expected! The example below contains code for a numeric sorting algorithm that, when passed to the sort() method, causes numbers to be sorted correctly.

Generic JavaScript syntax:

```
arrayName.sort([compareFunction])
```

Real-life code example:

```
// this sort works just fine for string elements
anArray.sort()

// This function returns the lesser of two values.
// JavaScript automatically calls this function
```

```
// as many times as necessary, comparing two
// values at a time, until the entire array
// of elements is sorted.
function compareNumbers(a, b) {
    return a - b
}
...
anArrayOfNumbers.sort(compareNumbers)
```

split

Use the split() method of the String object to split a string into an array of smaller strings. split() accepts an optional separator. If a separator is provided, it is used to determine where the string is divided. If no separator is provided, the resulting array will consist of one element containing the entire original string.

Generic JavaScript syntax:

```
string.split([separator])
```

Real-life code example:

```
arrayOfWords="There once was a man from Nantucket".split(" ")
```

sqrt

Use the sqrt() method of the Math object to return the square root of a number. If the *number* parameter is negative, the return value is *always 0.*

Generic JavaScript syntax:

```
Math.sqrt(number)
```

Real-life code example:

```
document.write(The square root of 36 is " + Math.sqrt(36))
```

strike

Using the strike() method of the string object enables you display a string with strikeovers so the text looks like it's been crossed out.

Generic JavaScript syntax:

```
string.strike()
```

Real-life code example:

```
"Was $49.99".strike()
```

sub

Use the sub() method of the string object to display text as a subscript.

Generic JavaScript syntax:

```
string.sub()
```

Real-life code example:

```
document.write("H" + "2".sub() + "O = water")
```

submit

Use the submit() method of the form object to submit a form (that is, to send it for processing to the server program specified in the ACTION attribute defined as part of the <FORM>...</FORM> tag).

Generic JavaScript syntax:

```
formName.submit()
```

Real-life code example:

```
document.myForm.submit()
```

substring

Use the substring() method of the string object to return a *substring*, or portion, of a specified string. Remember that the first character of a string has index 0, not 1, so when you supply an index range of (2, 4) you're actually asking for the third and fourth characters of the string to be returned to you. Why not the third through the fifth characters? Because substring() stops one character before the second index you give it.

Generic JavaScript syntax:

```
string.substring(indexA, indexB)
```

Real-life code example:

The following example displays the string "Woman":

```
document.write("Wonder Woman".substring(7, 12))
```

W	o	n	d	e	r		W	o	m	a	n
0	1	2	3	4	5	6	7	8	9	10	11

Hey, so it's not intuitive. It works! If you do a great deal of text manipulation, you can get the hang of it in no time.

sup

Use the sup() method of the string object to display text as a superscript.

Generic JavaScript syntax:

```
string.sup()
```

Real-life code example:

```
document.write("Beezus' Crisp-Fried tater chips" +
          "TM".sup())
```

tan

Use the tan() method of the Math object to return the tangent of a number.

Generic JavaScript syntax:

```
Math.tan(number)
```

Real-life code example:

```
var myTangent = Math.tan(1)
```

toGMTString

Use the toGMTString() method of the Date object to convert a date to a string. This method uses the Internet GMT conventions (which means that the time is returned in Greenwich Mean Time), and the format of the result returned is slightly platform-dependent. Using Windows 95, you get a string similar to the following:

```
Thu, 27 Jun 1996 16:51:24 GMT
```

Generic JavaScript syntax:

```
dateObjectName.toGMTString()
```

Real-life code example:

```
var today = new Date()
var myDateString = today.toGMTString()
```

toLocaleString

Use the `toLocaleString()` method of the `Date` object to convert a date to a string that is based on local time. This method returns the correct local time, but the result is platform-dependent. Using Windows 95, you get a string similar to the following:

```
06/27/96 10:51:24
```

Generic JavaScript syntax:

```
dateObjectName.toLocaleString()
```

Real-life code example:

```
var today = new Date()
var myDateString = today.toLocaleString()
```

Every time that you hear the words *platform dependent,* your skin should begin to crawl and your limbs should start to twitch uncontrollably. Platform dependence is to be avoided whenever possible because it means that you either have to redo work (yuck!) or limit your audience to people running the same platform as you (double yuck!). Sometimes you have no way around platform dependence; but for dates, you can try to use the `getMonth()`, `getYear()`, and other such methods before you resort to the `toGMTString()` and `toLocaleString()` methods.

toLowerCase

Use the `toLowerCase()` method of the `string` object to convert a specified string to lowercase.

Generic JavaScript syntax:

```
string.toLowerCase()
```

Real-life code example:

```
document.write("DON\'T SHOUT, I CAN HEAR YOU JUST
            FINE".toLowerCase())
```

toString

Every JavaScript object supports the toString() method. Use it to represent any object as a string. If the object doesn't have a string value, toString() will return a string containing the type of the object. (For example, window.toString() returns the string "[object Window]".

Generic JavaScript syntax:

```
object.toString()
```

Real-life code example:

```
document.write(document.lastModified.toString())
document.write(myFunction.toString())
documet.write(myAge.toString())
document.write(Array.toString())
```

toUpperCase

Use the toUpperCase() method of the string object to convert a specified string to all uppercase.

Generic JavaScript syntax:

```
string.toUpperCase()
```

Real-life code example:

```
document.write("could you please speak up?".toUpperCase())
```

UTC

Use the UTC() method of the Date object to return the number of milliseconds between a specified date and January 1, 1970 00:00:00. (*UTC* stands for Universal Coordinated Time, and it's basically the same thing as Greenwich Mean Time.) Remember that because this is GMT, any difference between your local time and GMT is reflected in the return value. For example, if 6 hours are between your local time and GMT and you put in a value of hours as *0,* the return value has hours set to *6.*

Generic JavaScript syntax:

```
Date.UTC(year, month, day [, hours] [, minutes] [, seconds])
```

Real-life code example:

```
GMTDate = new Date(Date.UTC(96, 7, 24, 0, 0, 0))
```

write

Use the write() method of the document object to write expressions to the specified document.

Generic JavaScript syntax:

```
write(expression1 [, expression2] … [, expressionN])
```

Real-life code example:

```
document.write("Here is the monthly sales total: " +
            monthlyTotal)
```

writeln

Use the writeln() method of the document object to write any number of expressions to the specified document. Although writeln() appends a newline character (the HTML equivalent of a carriage return) to the end of the displayed expressions, unless you use the newline character within an HTML tag that cares (like <PRE>…</PRE>, which preformats text), the display is identical to that of write().

Generic JavaScript syntax:

```
writeln(expression1 [, expression2] … [, expressionN])
```

Real-life code example:

```
document.writeln("<PRE>")
document.writeln("moogoo")
document.writeln("gaipan")
document.writeln("</PRE>")
```

Chapter 13

Fully Functioning

● ●

In This Chapter

▶ Using built-in JavaScript functions

▶ Creating your own custom functions

● ●

*J*avaScript doesn't have a lot of built-in functions, so this chapter is short and sweet. It contains a list of all of the built-in functions JavaScript does provide, complete with instructions on how and when to use them. Of course, you're not limited to the functions in this list — you also have the ability to create your own functions whenever you need to. The last section of this chapter explains when, why, and how to create custom functions. It also contains some handy clip-and-save examples.

All of the functions that are listed in this chapter are on this book's companion CD, and are appropriately named. For example, you can find the escape() function at escape.htm.

Built-In Functions

Unlike methods (which are always associated with a particular object's data), functions don't "belong" to any particular object. (Not only does this make functions more flexible, but it also makes them easier to use — you don't have to specify a fully qualified object to call them.) Instead, functions work with the values (called *arguments*) that you pass to them when you invoke them. Read on for all the exciting details.

escape

Use the escape() function to encode "special" characters — characters such as spaces, tabs, dollar signs, hash marks, exclamation points, and so on — so those characters can be sent safely from one program (your Web page) to another (a CGI program on a server). You can use unescape() on the other side, inside the CGI program, to decode the characters.

The string that's returned from escape() is in the form *%xx*, where *xx* is the ASCII encoding of each character in the argument. The *string* argument must be a non-alphanumeric string in the *ISO Latin-1 character set* (which, translated into English, means any character that's not a punctuation mark or a number). If you pass escape() a string that contains numbers and punctuation marks by mistake, like this:

```
escape("123@$*") // Oops!
```

escape() doesn't even attempt to encode the string — it just returns the same string that you sent it.

Generic JavaScript syntax:

```
escape(string)
```

Real-life code example:

```
encodedStringToPass = escape("& ") // returns "%26%20"
```

eval

Use the eval() function to evaluate a string that contains a JavaScript phrase (as opposed to a regular old JavaScript phrase) and return the value. This function gives you the capability of constructing a string that describes a JavaScript statement or expression and then evaluating, or performing, the string just as you'd evaluate it if it *weren't* a string.

An example of where eval() may come in handy is if you integrate your JavaScript script with an external program (perhaps a Java applet) that generates a string containing a JavaScript statement. After you get hold of the string (check out Chapter 17 for tips on how to access properties and methods of Java applets), you can evaluate it just as if you'd called the statement directly from JavaScript. (Okay, file this one mentally under "advanced features that I may never actually have occasion to use.")

Generic JavaScript syntax:

```
eval(string)
```

TECHNICAL STUFF

So what?!

You're probably saying to yourself right now, "What?! What the heck is this *ISO* thing and why in the world would I ever care?!" Well, most of the time you won't. The only time you may care is when you need to pass a weird character (such as a space or a carriage return) to some external program (such as a CGI script) from JavaScript. (Hey, don't laugh; it could happen.) Then you need to do some kind of standard encoding, because special characters (such as tabs and spaces and dollar signs) don't translate very well when they're sent from one system to another in their human-readable form. That's where the escape() and unescape() functions come in: escape() encodes the special characters so they can be sent safely, and unescape() decodes them when they get to their destination.

If a situation ever arises where you need to pass special characters from your JavaScript-enabled Web page to some other program, grab the nearest digithead and respectfully request to borrow a copy of his ASCII Numerical Conversion Chart (or better yet, get your own — it makes wonderful bedtime reading when you're stressed and can't get to sleep).

Real-life code example:

```
var totalPrice = "((numberOrdered * price) * tax)"
if (noTaxRequired) {
    totalPrice = "(numberOrdered * price)"
}
...
...
document.write(eval(totalPrice))
```

isNaN

The isNaN() function enables you to determine whether a value is Not a Number (get it — isNaN?). This function returns *true,* or *1,* if the specified *testValue is not* a number. It returns *false,* or *0,* if the *testValue is* a number. (Your fifth-grade English teacher was right — double negatives are confusing! Unfortunately, many programming languages make liberal use of them.)

Generic JavaScript syntax:

```
isNaN(testValue)
```

Real-life code example:

```
if (isNaN(ageInputValue)) {
    alert("Please enter a number for the age field.")
}
```

parseFloat

The `parseFloat()` function turns a string argument into a floating-point number. Okay, you probably have two questions right off the bat: 1.) What's a floating-point number? 2.) Why would anyone in their right mind want to convert a string to one?

Well, a *floating-point number* is any number that has a decimal in it — 19.95, for example. And surprisingly enough, it turns out that it's handy at times to be able to turn a string into a number. For example: what if you have the value `"135.66"` in one of your input fields and you want to use it in some calculations? As it stands, you can't; it's a string (you know it's a string because it's got quotes around it), and you can't do much in the way of mathematical calculations on strings. The solution is to convert it to a floating-point value with the `parseFloat()` function, and then perform your calculations — and an example of how to do just that is coming right up.

If the string argument you give `parseFloat()` can't be converted completely, the `parseFloat()` function behaves in one of two ways:

- ✔ If the very first character can't be converted, `parseFloat()` returns "*NaN*" (Not a Number).
- ✔ If the first character can be converted but a subsequent character can't, `parseFloat()` returns the floating-point value of everything it could convert up until it encounters the invalid character.

Valid characters for the string argument include the numbers 0 through 9, plus (+), minus (-), decimal (.), and exponent (E).

Generic JavaScript syntax:

```
parseFloat(string)
```

Real-life code example:

```
function isANumber(inputValue){
    answer=true
    for (var i=0; i<inputValue.length; i++) {
        if ((inputValue.charAt(i) != "0") &&
            !parseFloat(inputValue.charAt(i))) {
                answer=false
            break
            }
        }
    return answer
}
```

The function in this example returns *false* if the argument sent to it is not a number, and *true* if it is a number. All the action is happening inside of the `if` statement (which is itself buried inside of a `for` loop). The `if` statement looks through the input value one character at a time and stops when it encounters a character that it can't convert.

parseInt

Use the `parseInt()` function to turn specified *string* and *radix* arguments into an integer. (A *radix* is a representation of a numbering system — it sounds much harder than it really is, and besides, there's a real-life example coming up to boot!) If the string argument you give `parseInt()` can't be converted completely, the function behaves in one of two ways:

- ✔ If the very first character can't be converted, `parseInt()` returns "*NaN*" (Not a Number).

- ✔ If the first character can be converted but a subsequent character can't, `parseInt()` returns the integer value of everything that it could convert up until it encountered the invalid character.

The *radix* argument tells `parseInt()` which base you want the string converted to; for example, decimal (radix = 10), octal (radix = 8), hexadecimal (radix = 16), binary (radix = 2), and so on. Fortunately for the non-geeks among us, decimal is the default; if you don't specify a radix, it returns an integer in good old base 10 (for most numbers; see the upcoming sidebar for exceptions) — the very same numbering system human beings use to communicate. Imagine that!

When you assume . . .

If you leave off the radix argument (and you can, because it's optional), JavaScript has to make some assumptions. If the radix is not specified or is specified as 0, JavaScript assumes the following:

✔ The radix is 16 (hexadecimal) if the input string begins with 0x.

✔ The radix is 8 (octal) if the input string begins with 0 but the second character isn't an x.

✔ The radix is 10 (decimal) if the input string begins with anything else.

Valid characters for the *string* argument include the numbers 0 through 9 plus any other characters that are allowed by the radix you choose. (For example, *F* is a valid character for the string argument if you've chosen 16 for your radix — but not if you've chosen 10 for your radix. If you're in a situation where you need to specify a radix, I promise you you'll already know what characters are allowed.) parseInt() truncates floating point values to integers.

Generic JavaScript syntax:

```
parseInt(string [, radix])
```

Real-life code example:

```
parseInt("F", 16)        // base 16; returns 15
parseInt("17", 8)        // base 8;  returns 15
parseInt("15", 10)       // base 10; returns 15
parseInt("15.99", 10)    // base 10; returns 15
parseInt("123")          // base 10; returns 123
parseInt("1111", 2)      // base 2;  returns 15
```

unescape

As you can probably guess, unescape() is the opposite of escape(). In other words, escape() encodes (or "escapes") a string, and unescape() decodes (or "unescapes") a string. The *string* argument can be in either of two forms:

✔ %*xx*, where *xx* is an integer between 0 and 255

✔ A hexadecimal number between 0X0 and 0XFF

The returned string will be a series of characters in the ISO Latin-1 character set (better known as the "non-numeric, non-punctuation-mark character set").

Generic JavaScript syntax:

```
unescape("string")
```

Both the escape() and unescape() examples from this chapter are located in the HTML file escape.htm on the companion CD. Check it out!

Real-life code example:

```
decodedString = unescape("%26%20") // returns "& "
```

Roll-Your-Own Functions

For all but the most trivial Web pages, you may want to code your own functions — in fact, you may well use your own functions on the order of about ten times more than you use the built-in ones.

Custom functions enable you to organize JavaScript statements into neat little packages. This capability not only improves the readability of your scripts, but it also helps when the time comes to debug your scripts. After all, testing a ten-line function thoroughly is much more straightforward than testing the same ten lines of code scattered throughout a file.

Probably the most powerful aspect of functions, though, is their reusability. After you define a function, you can call that function as many times as you need to, from anywhere in your script — even from within another function. In JavaScript as in life, the more you can recycle, the less energy you have to spend!

Some things to keep in mind when you're creating your own functions:

- ✔ **Keep functions small.** Moving half of your script into one huge function doesn't improve readability, reuse, or testing. (And remember, improved readability, reuse, and testing make up the whole reason for creating functions in the first place.) A good rule of thumb is, if you can't fit your entire function on a single screen of your favorite editor, break the function into two parts. Rinse and repeat as necessary.

- ✔ **Keep functions specific.** Ideally, functions are specialists: they should do one thing and do it well. The number of functions you can have is unlimited, so combining functions gains you nothing. One of the biggest payoffs you get by creating functions is being able to reuse them, and reusing functions that do a bunch of things is much harder than reusing ones that perform a single conceptual task.

✔ **Name functions properly.** Functions do things; they're active. In a word, they're *verbs*. Naming functions appropriately helps you remember what they do, which in turn encourages reuse. For example, `validateExistence()` is probably a better name choice than just plain `validate()` (or, heaven forbid, `val()`).

✔ **Define functions early.** Because the JavaScript interpreter reads your file from the top down, it doesn't recognize a function unless it's already encountered the definition of that function. If you get into the habit of defining all your functions in the head of a file (between the `<HEAD>`... `</HEAD>` tags), you never have to worry about your function call preceding your function definition.

Remember that the parentheses after a function name really are part of that function's name. For example, say you create a function called `display()`. You can't call the function like this:

```
<BODY onLoad="display">
```

It's magic!

From the point of view of the code doing the calling, functions are magic boxes. You can put things in (these things are called *arguments*, which are covered in the next section) and you can get things back out (*return values*). Anything you do inside a function (for example, declaring variables and setting their values, executing logical comparisons, and so forth) is invisible to the rest of your program.

Don't argue with me

Functions can (but don't have to) accept arguments. *Arguments* are values that are passed into a function, and the use of arguments is a great way to design reusable code. For example, if you have a function called `verifyPositiveNumber()`, you can set it up to accept a number argument. Then, every time that you need to make sure that an input field contains a positive number, you can call your `verifyPositiveNumber()` function and pass in the specific number that you want it to verify. Take a look:

```
function verifyPositiveNumber(aNumber) {
    if (aNumber <= 0) {
        alert("Please enter a positive number.")
    }
}
```

Here's how you might call `verifyPositiveNumber()`:

```
<INPUT TYPE="text" NAME="age" SIZE=3
        onChange="verifyPositiveNumber(this.value)">
```

The argument that you're passing in is `this.value`, which is the input value of the `document.myForm.age` element (29, in my case!). The value is received, all right, but it gets a new, generic name as it comes into the function: `aNumber`. That's the name it goes by inside the `verifyPositiveNumber()` function.

Giving function arguments (or *parameters*) generic names to remind you that any value could be passed in is a good idea.

Returns (but no refunds)

Not only can functions accept values, but they can also return them. As a matter of fact, returning values is one of the more useful properties of functions. After all, you're probably doing some calculations in the body of your function, and by the end of your function code, you've no doubt come to some stunning conclusion. But unless you pass that conclusion back to the statement that called your function in the first place, who will know?

Here's how you set up a return value, and how you may want to use it:

```
function verifyPositiveNumber(aNumber) {
    var returnValue = false

    if (aNumber > 0) {
        returnValue = true
    }
    …
    …
    return returnValue
}
<FORM NAME="myForm" onSubmit="return
            verifyPositiveNumber(document.myForm.age.value)">
```

The preceding code looks a little funny until you get used to the syntax. What it means is that, when it comes time for the form to be submitted, `verifyPositiveNumber()` is called with the value of the `age` input field. If the value is a positive number, the `onSubmit` event handler receives a return value of *true*. That return value signals `onSubmit` to go ahead and submit the form. If the value of the age field isn't positive, though, *false* is returned to `onSubmit` — and the form isn't submitted.

Sometimes programmers use the number 0 instead of the keyword false and the number 1 in place of the keyword true. This convention is a holdover from a meaner, harsher time when programmers had no choice! Even though they mean the same thing, using true and false is generally preferable to using 1 and 0 because using the words instead of the numbers makes your code easier to read.

Chapter 14

How Do You Handle a Hungry Event? Event Handlers!

● ●

In This Chapter

▶ Discovering JavaScript-supported event handlers

▶ Deciding how, why, and when to use them

● ●

*1*f you're looking to add event handlers to your JavaScript code, you've come to the right place. This chapter not only gives you a list of the event handlers available in JavaScript; it also gives you examples of those event handlers. So dive in and discover the joys of eventhandling!

JavaScript's capability to handle events is at the heart of its usefulness in client applications. Think of *event handlers* as special methods that you define as part of an object but don't have to invoke explicitly. (They're automatically set up to run in response to the event they're named for.) For example, when you click on a button, the JavaScript interpreter automatically looks to see if an onClick event handler has been defined for that particular button. If it has, the interpreter immediately executes the event handler code that you specified, without your having to do anything else.

Technically, you can set the value of an event handler to a huge string of JavaScript statements, as long as you remember to separate the statements with semicolons. For the sake of readability and reuse, though, putting the statements in a function and setting the value equal to the function name is usually better. This approach not only makes your scripts easier to read, but it also helps in debugging, because it encourages you to create reusable (and, therefore, less) code. Take a look at the before-and-after examples before to get a feel for what I mean:

```
// Technically possible but uglier than original sin
<INPUT TYPE="button" NAME="orderNow" VALUE="Order Now!"
        onClick="var subTotal =
        document.myForm.numberOrdered *
        document.myForm.price; var total = subTotal *
        document.myForm.tax; if (confirm('Is this total
        correct?', total)) { document.form.submit()}"
```

```
// Much better! Now tallyOrder() contains all of the
// logic to tally up the order, leaving this section
// brief and easy to understand at a glance.
<INPUT TYPE="button" NAME="orderNow" VALUE="Order Now!"
onClick="tallyOrder()">
```

Because the things that you can do to initiate an event are fairly limited, you have only a handful of event handlers to deal with in JavaScript. You can click on form elements, move the mouse pointer, and enter and change text. These basic events are mapped to event handlers slightly differently, depending on the form element, but all are fairly similar (and easy) to implement.

onAbort

onAbort, an event handler associated with the Image object, can be used to trigger the execution of some JavaScript code every time users *abort*, or stop, loading an image in a Web page. Users can abort an image load by clicking on the Stop button on their Web browsers while the image is loading (which they typically do if the image is so large that they become impatient!).

Generic JavaScript syntax:

```
onAbort="event handling text"
```

Real-life code example:

The onReset event handler is only available on the Image object, as shown:

```
<IMG NAME="thistle" SRC="images/thistle.gif"
          onAbort="alert('You missed a great picture!')">
```

onBlur

onBlur is an event handler associated with the frame, select, text, textarea, and window objects. Although the name onBlur may sound a little funny at first, it actually makes sense: onBlur is invoked when an element *blurs,* or loses focus. For example, this situation occurs when a user has finished entering text (or selecting an item from a list box) and tabs to the next form element or clicks somewhere else on the form.

Generic JavaScript syntax:

```
onBlur="event handling text"
```

Real-life code example:

The `onBlur` event handler can be used with the `frame`, `select`, `text`, `textarea`, and `window` objects. The sections below contain examples of each.

`frame`:

The following code fragment is found in the file frame.htm on this book's companion CD:

```
<FRAMESET ROWS="50%,50%" COLS="40%,60%"
onLoad="display()">
<FRAME SRC="framcon1.htm" NAME="frame1">
<FRAME SRC="framcon2.htm" NAME="frame2">
</FRAMESET>
```

The following code fragment is found in the file framcon1.htm on this book's CD:

```
<BODY BGCOLOR="lightgrey" onBlur="document.bgColor='black'"
onFocus="document.bgColor='white'">
```

`select`:

```
<FORM>
Product: <SELECT NAME="productSelection" SIZE=1
onBlur="processSelection(this)">
<OPTION VALUE="shirt"> t-shirt
<OPTION VALUE="mug"> mug
<OPTION VALUE="rag"> monogrammed dishrag
</SELECT>
```

`text`:

```
Last name: <INPUT TYPE="text" VALUE="" NAME="lastName"
           SIZE=25 onBlur="verifyExistence(this.value)">
```

`textarea`:

```
<TEXTAREA NAME="commentField" ROWS=5 COLS=50
onBlur="if (!this.value) { confirm('Are you sure you don\'t
        want to comment?')}">
</TEXTAREA>
</FORM>
```

window:

```
<BODY BGCOLOR="lightgrey" onBlur="document.bgColor='black'"
onFocus="document.bgColor='white'">
```

When calling a function from an event handler, passing along a copy of the object that's involved is a great idea. You can do this by passing the this keyword, and that way you can keep your function code generic enough to reuse over and over again. You saw an example of this in the code fragment above:

```
Last name: <INPUT TYPE="text" VALUE="" NAME="lastName"
            SIZE=25 onBlur="verifyExistence(this.value)">
```

When a user blurs the lastName field, the JavaScript interpreter will call the verifyExistence() function and pass it this.value. Instead of having to know what form element value to access in verifyExistence() (Yecch, hard coding! The root of all evil!), all you have to do in verifyExistence() is work with the generic value passed in.

onChange

The onChange event handler is similar to onBlur, except that onChange is invoked only if some change has been made in the value of a select, text, or textarea element in addition to the loss of focus. Depending on your application, sometimes you may want to call the functions that do your field-level validation from an onChange event handler instead of from onBlur. That way, a value is verified only if it has changed, not just when a user moves to a different area of the form. (Why go to all the trouble of revalidating a value if you know that the value hasn't changed since the last time that you validated it?)

Generic JavaScript syntax:

```
onChange="event handling text"
```

Real-life code example:

The onChange event handler can be used with the select, text, and textarea form elements. The following sections contain examples of each.

select:

```
<FORM>
Product: <SELECT NAME="productSelection" SIZE=1
onChange="processSelection(this)">
<OPTION VALUE="shirt"> t-shirt
<OPTION VALUE="sweat"> sweatshirt
<OPTION VALUE="horn"> monogrammed shoehorn
</SELECT>
```

text:

```
Last name: <INPUT TYPE="text" VALUE="" NAME="lastName"
           SIZE=25 onChange="verifyExistence(this.value)">
```

textarea:

```
<TEXTAREA NAME="commentField" ROWS=5 COLS=50
onChange="if (!this.value) { confirm('Are you sure you don\'t
          want to comment?')}">
</TEXTAREA>
</FORM>
```

onClick

Like onBlur and onChange, the onClick event presents you with a nice opportunity to execute any field-level validation code that makes sense for your particular application. (*Field-level validation* is a fancy name for examining the contents of your form fields one at a time and validating them to see if they meet your criteria.)

Generic JavaScript syntax:

```
onClick="event handling text"
```

Real-life code example:

The onClick event handler can be used with all of the following form elements: button, checkbox, link, radio, reset, and submit. The sections below contain examples of each.

button:

```
<INPUT TYPE="button" NAME="orderNow" VALUE="order"
onClick="tallyOrder()">
```

checkbox:

```
<INPUT TYPE="checkbox" NAME="firstBook" VALUE="firstBook"
onClick="if (this.checked) { sendThankYouLetter() }">
Is this your first ...For Dummies book purchase?
```

link:

```
<A HREF=""
             onClick="this.href=pickURLBasedOnUserPreferences()"
> You'll want to see this!
```

radio:

```
Which is your favorite vacation destination?
<INPUT TYPE="radio" NAME="vacationSelection" VALUE="beach"
onClick="displayPage('beachfront property')"> The beach
<INPUT TYPE="radio" NAME="vacationSelection" VALUE="mountain"
onClick="displayPage('mountain cabins')"> The mountains
<INPUT TYPE="radio" NAME="vacationSelection" VALUE="city"
onClick="displayPage('posh hotels')"> Anywhere I can get room
             service
```

reset:

```
<INPUT TYPE="reset" NAME="reset" VALUE="Clear form"
onClick="resetCalculatedTotals()">
```

submit:

```
<INPUT TYPE="submit" NAME="submit" VALUE="Submit form"
onClick="checkConsistency()">
```

onError

The onError event handler can be used to trigger the execution of some JavaScript code every time an error occurs while a user is attempting either to load an image (the Image object) or a document (the window object). A good use for the onError event handler is to have it invoke a custom function designed to examine the error and figure out what caused it, and then suggest solutions. The real-life example for the window object is an example of this approach.

The onError event handler is an important one. To see it in action, take a look at the HTML file onerror.htm, located on the companion CD.

Generic JavaScript syntax:

```
onError="event handler text"
```

Real-life code example:

The `onError` event handler can be used both with the `Image` and `window` objects. The sections below contain examples of each.

`Image`:
```
<IMG NAME="noSuchAnimal" SRC="dummy.gif"
onError="alert(document.myForm.noSuchAnimal.name + ' could
          not be loaded')">
```

`window`:
```
window.onerror=myOnErrorHandler
function myOnErrorHandler(message, url, lineNumber) {
    ...
    return true
}
```

You can suppress all errors that JavaScript generates for a page by setting the `onError` event handler equal to null, like this:

```
window.onerror = null
```

onFocus

`onFocus` is an event handler associated with the `frame`, `select`, `text`, `textarea`, and `window` objects. This event handler is the anti-`onBlur`; instead of responding when an object loses focus, `onFocus` is invoked when an object gains focus. Focus occurs when a user tabs to, or clicks on, a `frame`, `select`, `text`, `textarea`, or `window` object.

Guess what happens if you call a dialog box from `onFocus`? Well, after the element gets focus, the dialog box pops up. The user clicks OK or Cancel or whatever. Focus returns to the element. The dialog box pops up. The user clicks Okay or Cancel or whatever. Focus returns to the element. The dialog box pops up. . . . Can you say *endless loop?* Please, don't try this at home!

Generic JavaScript syntax:

```
onFocus="event handler text"Real-life code example
```

You can use the onFocus event handler with the frame, select, text, textarea, and window objects. The following sections contain examples of each.

frame:

The following code fragment is found in the file frame.htm on this book's companion CD:

```
<FRAMESET ROWS="50%,50%" COLS="40%,60%"
onLoad="display()">
<FRAME SRC="framcon1.htm" NAME="frame1">
<FRAME SRC="framcon2.htm" NAME="frame2">
</FRAMESET>
```

The following code fragment is found in the file framcon1.htm on this book's companion CD:

```
<BODY BGCOLOR="lightgrey" onBlur="document.bgColor='black'"
onFocus="document.bgColor='white'">
```

select:

```
<FORM>
Product: <SELECT NAME="productSelection" SIZE=1
onFocus="validateDependentFields()">
<OPTION VALUE="shirt"> t-shirt
<OPTION VALUE="mug"> mug
<OPTION VALUE="rag"> monogrammed dishrag
</SELECT>
```

text:

```
Last name: <INPUT TYPE="text" VALUE="" NAME="lastName"
            SIZE=25 onFocus="validateDependentFields()">
```

textarea:

```
<TEXTAREA NAME="commentField" ROWS=5 COLS=50
onFocus="validateDependentFields()">
</TEXTAREA>
</FORM>
```

window:

```
<BODY BGCOLOR="lightgrey" onBlur="document.bgColor='black'"
onFocus="document.bgColor='white'">
```

onLoad

The onLoad event handler is associated with both the window object and the Image object. You can use the onLoad event handler of the window object in two ways: to trigger some JavaScript code immediately after a window has been loaded, or to trigger some JavaScript code immediately after all frames in a frameset have been loaded. If you define an onLoad both for the window (in the <BODY>...</BODY> tag) and for a frameset (in the <FRAMESET>... </FRAMESET> tag), the onLoad associated with the window is executed first, and then the onLoad associated with the frameset is executed.

onLoad gives you the opportunity to do any initialization routines that are necessary for your application — things that need to be done before the user gets a crack at the page or the image. You might want to display the current date and time, for example, or play a little welcoming tune.

Generic JavaScript syntax:

```
onLoad="event handler text"
```

Real-life code example:

The onLoad event handler can be used either with the Image object or with the window object. The section below contains examples of both.

Image:
```
<IMG NAME="thistle" SRC="images/thistle.gif"
            onLoad="beginAnimation(this)">
```

window:
```
<BODY onLoad="displayCustomWelcome()">

<FRAMESET ROWS="50%,50%" COLS="40%,60%"
onLoad="initializeVariables()">
<FRAME SRC="frame1.htm" NAME="frame1">
<FRAME SRC="frame2.htm" NAME="frame2">
</FRAMESET>
```

onMouseOut

The onMouseOut event handler is associated with both the link and area objects. Use it to recognize when a user moves the mouse pointer off of a link or an area, respectively. One onMouseOut event is generated each time that a user moves a mouse from a link or area to someplace else on the form.

One way to use this event handler is to display a custom message in the status bar at the bottom of a document when a user drags a mouse pointer off of a link or an area.

Generic JavaScript syntax:

```
onMouseOut="event handler text"
```

Real-life code example:

onMouseOut is available for both the area and link objects, as shown below.

area:

```
<MAP NAME="thistleMap">
<AREA NAME="topThistle" COORDS="0,0,228,318"
        HREF="javascript:displayMessage()"
onMouseOver="self.status='When you see this message, click
        your left mouse button'; return true"
onMouseOut="self.status=''; return true">
</MAP>
```

link:

```
<A HREF="http://home.netscape.com/"
    onMouseOut="status='Thanks for visiting; return true">
Netscape</A>
```

You can do whatever you like in the onMouseOut event handler; however, if you want to set the value for the status bar, as in this example, you need to remember to return a value of true in the last JavaScript statement in the handler.

onMouseOver

Use the onMouseOver event handler of the link and area objects to recognize when a user moves the mouse pointer over a link (or over an area). One onMouseOver event is generated each time that a user moves a mouse to the link or area from someplace else on the form.

You can use this event handler to display a custom message in the status bar at the bottom of a document (instead of the default message) when a user drags a mouse pointer over a link or area. JavaScript automatically changes the user's mouse pointer from an arrow into a little hand when the pointer is dragged over a link or an area.

Generic JavaScript syntax:

```
onMouseOver="event handler text"
```

Real-life code example:

onMouseOver is an event handler of area and link. Examples of both are shown below.

area:

```
<MAP NAME="thistleMap">
<AREA NAME="topThistle" COORDS="0,0,228,318"
        HREF="javascript:displayMessage()"
onMouseOver="self.status='When you see this message, click
        your left mouse button'; return true"
onMouseOut="self.status=''; return true">
</MAP>
```

link:

```
<A HREF="http://home.netscape.com/"
   onMouseOver="status='Visit Netscape'; return true">
Mystery Link</A>
```

You can do whatever you like in the onMouseOver event handler; however, if you want to set the value for the status bar, as in this example, you need to remember to return a value of *true* in the last JavaScript statement in the handler. If you don't, the interpreter ignores you and the status bar displays the default value that it usually displays when a user moves a mouse over a link: the URL of the link.

onReset

Use the onReset event handler of the form object to trigger the execution of some JavaScript code every time a user clicks a reset button on a form.

Generic JavaScript syntax:

```
onReset="event handler text"
```

Real-life code example:

The onReset event handler is only available on the form object, as shown:

```
<FORM onReset="alert('The form values have been reset.')">
```

onSelect

Use the onSelect event handler of the text and textarea objects to trigger the execution of some JavaScript code every time that a user *selects* (highlights with the mouse) some part of the text displayed in either a text or textarea field.

Generic JavaScript syntax:

```
onSelect="event handler text"
```

Real-life code example:

The onSelect event handler can be used with either the text or textarea form elements. Below are examples of each.

text:

```
Last name: <INPUT TYPE="text" VALUE="" NAME="lastName"
           SIZE=25 onSelect="showHelp()">
```

textarea:

```
<TEXTAREA NAME="commentField" ROWS=5 COLS=50
onSelect="showHelp()"
</TEXTAREA>
</FORM>
```

In both of the preceding examples, the function showHelp() is supposed to be called when a user selects any text contained either in the lastName field or the commentField field. Unfortunately, it isn't! Version 3.0 Navigator (and earlier) as well as the beta 3.0 version of Internet Explorer ignore the onSelect event handler.

onSubmit

Use the onSubmit event handler of the form object to gain more control over the form-submission process. When you use a submit object (a button that automatically submits a form when a user clicks on it), you have no way to keep the form from being submitted after the button has been clicked. There is a way to bail out at the last minute when you use the onSubmit event handler instead. All you need to do is return a value of *false* if you don't want to go through with the submit, and a value of *true* if you do. Often the criterion you use to make your decision is the return value of a function whose job in life is to look at the input data in its entirety to see if it's complete enough to bother submitting to the server.

For example, say your Web application is an order form, and a user fills in a name—but no other order information—and then tries to submit the form. You can have the onSubmit event handler trigger a function that checks the completeness of the order form data and decide whether or not enough information exists to bother actually submitting the form. The sample code in the following section shows how you might go about coding this scenario.

The default return value for the onSubmit event handler is true, so if you forget to return a value explicitly, the form will always be sent.

Generic JavaScript syntax:

```
onSubmit="event handler text"
```

Real-life code example:

```
function verifyFormData(incomingForm)
{
    if ( // all the relevant values of incomingForm
  // are valid based on some criteria you
  // define) {
        return true
    }
    else {
        return false
    }
}
...
form.onSubmit="return verifyFormData(this)"
```

onUnload

Just like its counterpart, onLoad, you can use the onUnload event handler associated with the window object in two ways: to trigger some JavaScript code immediately after a window has been unloaded (exited) or to trigger some JavaScript code immediately after all frames in a frameset have been unloaded. If you define an onUnload both for the window (in the <BODY>...</BODY> tag) and for a frameset (in the <FRAMESET>...</FRAMESET> tag), the onUnload associated with the window is executed first, and *then* the onUnload associated with the frameset is executed.

Think of the onUnload event handler as a last-ditch opportunity to do something before a user leaves your page. If your Web application uses cookies (see Chapter 19 for a discussion of the persistent data cookie mechanism), you might want to take advantage of the onUnload event handler to write out some information to a cookie right before the user exits. Or, perhaps you'd just like to pop up a "Thank you for visiting" message. The choice is all yours.

Generic JavaScript syntax:

```
onUnload="event handler text"
```

Real-life code example:

```
<BODY onUnload="cleanUp()">

<FRAMESET ROWS="50%,50%" COLS="40%,60%"
onUnload="cleanUpFrameData()">
<FRAME SRC="frame1.htm" NAME="frame1">
<FRAME SRC="frame2.htm" NAME="frame2">
</FRAMESET>
```

Chapter 15

Reservations, Please: Reserved Words

- -

In This Chapter

▶ Discover the 53 words you can't say in JavaScript

- -

*M*ost of the words listed in this very short (my apologies) chapter are keywords that mean something special to the JavaScript interpreter. (You may have run into some of these words already.) JavaScript reserves other words for future incorporation, so even though some of these special words are not used for anything right now, you still can't use them indiscriminately. The upshot is that you get an error if you try to use any of these words to do anything other than what they were designed to do (for example, if you try to use these special words to name variables, functions, methods, or objects).

Check this list if you run into an unshakable bug. Your logic may be perfectly fine; the problem may just be that you chose a name that's off limits.

Figure 15-1 shows an example of the kind of error message that you can expect to see if you use a reserved word for an illegal purpose.

Figure 15-1:
An error
message
resulting
from an
incorrectly
used
reserved
word.

Netscape - [Alert]

JavaScript Error: file:///C|/JavaScript/reserve.html, **line 3:**

missing function name.

function double(aString) {

. . . .^

[OK]

Following is the list of words that are taboo unless you use them in the way that JavaScript wants you to. Steer clear of them in all other instances.

- abstract
- boolean
- break
- byte
- case
- catch
- char
- class
- const
- continue
- default
- do
- double
- else
- extends
- false
- final
- finally
- float
- for
- function
- goto
- if
- implements
- import
- in
- instanceof

- int
- interface
- long
- native
- new
- null
- package
- private
- protected
- public
- return
- short
- static
- super
- switch
- synchronized
- this
- throw
- throws
- transient
- true
- try
- var
- void
- while
- with

Chapter 16

Color Coded

● ●

In This Chapter

▶ Changing the colors of form elements

▶ Specifying predefined colors

▶ Creating your own custom colors

● ●

*Y*ou can change the color of any piece of text that's displayed on your Web page as well as change the color of the document background itself. Because colors are described numerically in JavaScript, the hues you can use are unlimited.

JavaScript requires that you describe color values in *hexadecimal RGB triplets* (whew, that was a mouthful!). Fortunately, somebody figured out that regular human beings have no clue what a hexadecimal RGB triplet *is* (much less how to specify one) and created a table that maps the required representation of just about any color you can imagine to *literal strings*. (Literal strings are nice, unmistakable words like "pink," "black," "purple," and so forth.)

The consequence is that you have a choice: You can use string values for any color you like in Table 16-2, *or* you can concatenate the red, green, and blue hexadecimal values together and pass the resulting six-digit string to JavaScript. If you're really feeling frisky, you can just toss Table 16-2 right out the window and create your very own color palette. This chapter shows you how.

How and When Can I Use a Color Value?

You can change the color of any of the items that appear in Table 16-1 to any of the color values (literal string or hexadecimal RGB triplet) shown in Table 16-2.

As you can see in Table 16-1, all of the items except the last one (the `fontcolor()` method of the `string` object) are properties of the document object. As such, you set the colors for these objects for the very first time at the same time you define the HTML document, which you do via the `<BODY>...</BODY>` tag. For example:

```
<BODY BGCOLOR="chartreuse" TEXT="blue" LINK="yellow"
            ALINK="white" VLINK="black">
```

Table 16-1	Things You Can Color	
Description	*How to Set the Color*	*How to Access the Color*
background color	`BGCOLOR="chartreuse"`	`document.bgColor`
foreground (text) color	`TEXT="blue"`	`document.fgColor`
unfollowed link color	`LINK="yellow"`	`document.linkColor`
activated link color	`ALINK="white"`	`document.alinkColor`
followed link color	`VLINK="black"`	`document.vlinkColor`
individual string color	`string.fontcolor("red")`	`string.fontcolor()`

I encourage you to load the HTML file list1601.htm, which contains a working copy of the source code in Listing 16-1, and play around with the colors. Keep in mind that contrast is very important. You'll notice, for instance, that a couple of the link colors are somewhat hard to read on top of the (ugly!) background color chosen. Try out some different colors and see if you can't come up with a few more palatable combinations!

Listing 16-1: Source for Color Example

```
<HTML>
<HEAD><TITLE>Color Example</TITLE></HEAD>
<SCRIPT LANGUAGE="JavaScript">
    document.write("This is cadetblue.".fontcolor("5F9EA0"))
</SCRIPT>
<BODY BGCOLOR="cyan" TEXT="crimson" LINK="burlywood"
          ALINK="FF4500"
VLINK="000000">
<FORM NAME="colorForm">
<BR><H2>Click on the links and watch the colors change:</
          H2><BR>
<A HREF="http://home.netscape.com/eng/mozilla/2.01/handbook/
          javascript/index.html">
JavaScript Handbook</A><BR>
<A HREF="http://www.idgbooks.com">IDG Books' Home Page</A><BR>
<A HREF="http://www.netscape.com">Netscape's home page</A><BR>
<A HREF="http://www.sun.com">Sun's home page</A><BR>
</FORM>
</BODY>
</HTML>
```

Notice the line `document.write("This is cadetblue.".fontcolor ("5F9EA0"))` in the preceding listing? This line is an example of the way to express a color (in this case, *cadetblue*) in hexadecimal RGB triplets. If you look up *cadetblue* in Table 16-2, you see that the hexadecimal number in the example matches the number sequence for cadetblue given in the table.

Of course, you can also take the easy way out and express the color using a literal string, as the line TEXT="crimson" shows (crimson was lifted straight from Table 16-2).

You can also express the triplet preceded by a hash symbol, like this: "#5F9EA0". You don't have to, but you can. (Okay, you probably won't, but some folks do — and I don't want you to be confused when you copy their code and see the hash symbol!)

Premixed Colors

Table 16-2 contains an alphabetical listing of all of the predefined colors available to you in JavaScript. As you look through the list, remember that setting a form element's color to the string "aliceblue" is equivalent to setting it equal to "F0F8FF" — the choice of format is yours.

Table 16-2	Predefined Color Values			
Color	*Red*	*Green*	*Blue*	*RGB Triplet*
aliceblue	F0	F8	FF	F0F8FF
antiquewhite	FA	EB	D7	FAEBD7
aqua	00	FF	FF	00FFFF
aquamarine	7F	FF	D4	7FFFD4
azure	F0	FF	FF	F0FFFF
beige	F5	F5	DC	F5F5DC
bisque	FF	E4	C4	FFE4C4
black	00	00	00	000000
blanchedalmond	FF	EB	CD	FFEBCD
blue	00	00	FF	0000FF
blueviolet	8A	2B	E2	8A2BE2
brown	A5	2A	2A	A52A2A
burlywood	DE	B8	87	DEB887
cadetblue	5F	9E	A0	5F9EA0
chartreuse	7F	FF	00	7FFF00
chocolate	D2	69	1E	D2691E
coral	FF	7F	50	FF7F50
cornflowerblue	64	95	ED	6495ED

(continued)

Table 16-2 *(continued)*

Color	Red	Green	Blue	RGB Triplet
cornsilk	FF	F8	DC	FFF8DC
crimson	DC	14	3C	DC143C
cyan	00	FF	FF	00FFFF
darkblue	00	00	8B	00008B
darkcyan	00	8B	8B	008B8B
darkgoldenrod	B8	86	0B	B8860B
darkgray	A9	A9	A9	A9A9A9
darkgreen	00	64	00	006400
darkkhaki	BD	B7	6B	BDB76B
darkmagenta	8B	00	8B	8B008B
darkolivegreen	55	6B	2F	556B2F
darkorange	FF	8C	00	FF8C00
darkorchid	99	32	CC	9932CC
darkred	8B	00	00	8B0000
darksalmon	E9	96	7A	E9967A
darkseagreen	8F	BC	8F	8FBC8F
darkslateblue	48	3D	8B	483D8B
darkslategray	2F	4F	4F	2F4F4F
darkturquoise	00	CE	D1	00CED1
darkviolet	94	00	D3	9400D3
deeppink	FF	14	93	FF1493
deepskyblue	00	BF	FF	00BFFF
dimgray	69	69	69	696969
dodgerblue	1E	90	FF	1E90FF
firebrick	B2	22	22	B22222
floralwhite	FF	FA	F0	FFFAF0
forestgreen	22	8B	22	228B22
fuchsia	FF	00	FF	FF00FF
gainsboro	DC	DC	DC	DCDCDC
ghostwhite	F8	F8	FF	F8F8FF
gold	FF	D7	00	FFD700

Color	Red	Green	Blue	RGB Triplet
goldenrod	DA	A5	20	DAA520
gray	80	80	80	808080
green	00	80	00	008000
greenyellow	AD	FF	2F	ADFF2F
honeydew	F0	FF	F0	F0FFF0
hotpink	FF	69	B4	FF69B4
indianred	CD	5C	5C	CD5C5C
indigo	4B	00	82	4B0082
ivory	FF	FF	F0	FFFFF0
khaki	F0	E6	8C	F0E68C
lavender	E6	E6	FA	E6E6FA
lavenderblush	FF	F0	F5	FFF0F5
lawngreen	7C	FC	00	7CFC00
lemonchiffon	FF	FA	CD	FFFACD
lightblue	AD	D8	E6	ADD8E6
lightcoral	F0	80	80	F08080
lightcyan	E0	FF	FF	E0FFFF
lightgoldenrodyellow	FA	FA	D2	FAFAD2
lightgreen	90	EE	90	90EE90
lightgrey	D3	D3	D3	D3D3D3
lightpink	FF	B6	C1	FFB6C1
lightsalmon	FF	A0	7A	FFA07A
lightseagreen	20	B2	AA	20B2AA
lightskyblue	87	CE	FA	87CEFA
lightslategray	77	88	99	778899
lightsteelblue	B0	C4	DE	B0C4DE
lightyellow	FF	FF	E0	FFFFE0
lime	00	FF	00	00FF00
limegreen	32	CD	32	32CD32
linen	FA	F0	E6	FAF0E6
magenta	FF	00	FF	FF00FF
maroon	80	00	00	800000

(continued)

Table 16-2 *(continued)*

Color	Red	Green	Blue	RGB Triplet
mediumaquamarine	66	CD	AA	66CDAA
mediumblue	00	00	CD	0000CD
mediumorchid	BA	55	D3	BA55D3
mediumpurple	93	70	DB	9370DB
mediumseagreen	3C	B3	71	3CB371
mediumslateblue	7B	68	EE	7B68EE
mediumspringgreen	00	FA	9A	00FA9A
mediumturquoise	48	D1	CC	48D1CC
mediumvioletred	C7	15	85	C71585
midnightblue	19	19	70	191970
mintcream	F5	FF	FA	F5FFFA
mistyrose	FF	E4	E1	FFE4E1
moccasin	FF	E4	B5	FFE4B5
navajowhite	FF	DE	AD	FFDEAD
navy	00	00	80	000080
oldlace	FD	F5	E6	FDF5E6
olive	80	80	00	808000
olivedrab	6B	8E	23	6B8E23
orange	FF	A5	00	FFA500
orangered	FF	45	00	FF4500
orchid	DA	70	D6	DA70D6
palegoldenrod	EE	E8	AA	EEE8AA
palegreen	98	FB	98	98FB98
paleturquoise	AF	EE	EE	AFEEEE
palevioletred	DB	70	93	DB7093
papayawhip	FF	EF	D5	FFEFD5
peachpuff	FF	DA	B9	FFDAB9
peru	CD	85	3F	CD853F
pink	FF	C0	CB	FFC0CB
plum	DD	A0	DD	DDA0DD
powderblue	B0	E0	E6	B0E0E6

Color	Red	Green	Blue	RGB Triplet
purple	80	00	80	800080
red	FF	00	00	FF0000
rosybrown	BC	8F	8F	BC8F8F
royalblue	41	69	E1	4169E1
saddlebrown	8B	45	13	8B4513
salmon	FA	80	72	FA8072
sandybrown	F4	A4	60	F4A460
seagreen	2E	8B	57	2E8B57
seashell	FF	F5	EE	FFF5EE
sienna	A0	52	2D	A0522D
silver	C0	C0	C0	C0C0C0
skyblue	87	CE	EB	87CEEB
slateblue	6A	5A	CD	6A5ACD
slategray	70	80	90	708090
snow	FF	FA	FA	FFFAFA
springgreen	00	FF	7F	00FF7F
steelblue	46	82	B4	4682B4
tan	D2	B4	8C	D2B48C
teal	00	80	80	008080
thistle	D8	BF	D8	D8BFD8
tomato	FF	63	47	FF6347
turquoise	40	E0	D0	40E0D0
violet	EE	82	EE	EE82EE
wheat	F5	DE	B3	F5DEB3
white	FF	FF	FF	FFFFFF
whitesmoke	F5	F5	F5	F5F5F5
yellow	FF	FF	00	FFFF00
yellowgreen	9A	CD	32	9ACD32

Custom-Made Colors

Perhaps you're not satisfied with any of the colors in listed Table 16-2. No problem. Create your own! You can go about this in a couple of ways (besides just making up numbers and seeing what the result looks like).

One way is to start with the hexadecimal representation of a color that's close to the shade you're after — like *salmon* — and for each of the contributing colors (red, green, and blue), try raising the color intensity by raising the numbers (and vice versa).

For example, the hexadecimal representation of salmon, from Table 16-2, is FA + 80 + 72. Hexadecimal digits are a little different than plain old ordinary numbers (hey, I'll bet you picked right up on that when you saw the "FA," right?). Table 16-3 helps you crack the code:

Table 16-3	**Decimal to Hexadecimal Digit Conversion Chart**
Decimal (base 10)	*Hexademical (base 16)*
0	0
1	1
2	2
3	3
4	4
5	5
6	6
7	7
8	8
9	9
10	A
11	B
12	C
13	D
14	E
15	F

In this scheme, the lowest two-digit number you can have is 00 (or 0 in decimal), and the highest is FF (or 255 in decimal). It's no coincidence that black is 000000 and white is FFFFFF! So if you're looking for something with a little more red in it, increase the red portion of the value (FA) to, say, FB. If you're looking for a shade that's just a touch less blue, reduce the blue portion of the value (72) to, say, 66. You probably get the idea, but if you'd like more examples, take a look at the sidebar Hexa-what?

The second way to devise your own hue involves using a visual tool. If you ever change the background color of your desktop, you probably use a tool that enable you to select (with your mouse pointer) just the shade you want from a spectrum of colors.

- ✔ In Windows 95, to get a color palette, you can select My Computer➪Control Panel➪Display➪Appearance➪Color➪Other.
- ✔ In Windows 3.*x*, select Main➪Control Panel➪Color➪Color Palette➪Define Custom Colors.
- ✔ On a Mac, do the following: From the Apple menu, select the Control Panels folder, double-click on the Color control panel, and select Other from the Highlight color drop-down list.

The percentages of red, green, and blue in the color you selected are displayed numerically as well as graphically — so you can use the color spectrum to find the precise color that you like and then copy down the number combination that's displayed. Then use the handy-dandy algorithm in the "Hexa-what?" sidebar to translate each decimal number in the triplet into a hexadecimal number to use in your JavaScript script. No muss, no fuss, no guesswork!

Hexa-what?

Here's a quick hexadecimal primer, should you ever need it. (Hey, it could happen!) *Hexadecimal* is a base-16 system (in contrast to the numbering system that we use every day, which is a base-10, or *decimal,* system). Computers really like *binary* (base-2) systems the best, but they're also partial to systems that are powers of 2, such as *octal* (base-8) and *hexadecimal* (like I said, base-16).

You're probably so familiar with base 10 that you don't even have to think about it, but base 10 works like this: You have 10 digits you can use, from 0 to 9. In a long number, you multiply the rightmost digit by 1(10^0), the second rightmost digit by 10 (10^1), the third rightmost digit by 100 (10^2), the fourth rightmost digit by 1000 (10^3), and so on (also known as using powers of 10).

327 (base 10) =

(**3** x 100) +

(**2** x 10) +

(**7** x 1) =

327 (base 10)

The same thing happens with base 16. You have 16 digits you can use, from 0 to 9 and A, B, C, D, E, and F. (See Table 16-3.)

To convert a base 16 number to base 10, you multiply the rightmost digit by 1 (16^0), the second rightmost digit by 16 (16^1), the third rightmost digit by 256 (16^2), and so on (also known as using powers of 16).

(continued)

(continued)

327 (base 16) =

(3 x 256) +

(2 x 16) +

(**7** x 1) =

807 (base 10)

The example above translates the base 16 number 327 into the base 10 number 807. In our color scheme, though, you're only going to be worried about the numbers from 0 to 255. Why? Glad you asked! (Bonus: when you finish reading this section, you'll know why, when computer folks brag about their monitors, they say "Yeah, it's a beauty. It can display *256* colors*!*").

You already know that it can only be two digits, and that the largest digit in hexadecimal notation is F (or 15), right? Well, given those two things, take a look at this:

FF (base 16) =

(**F** x 16) = (15 x 16)+

(**F** x 1) = (15 x 1)=

255 (base 10)

Now let's go the other way. Do this to translate decimal RGB triplet numbers that you get from a color palette tool into hexadecimal notation.

To go backwards, start with a decimal RGB triplet — say, 159. Now all you have to do is figure out two digits that equal 159 when the first one is multiplied by 16 (16^1) and the second is multiplied by 1 (16^0). Sound tough? Well, it's not if you have a calculator! Start by dividing 159 by 16 (forget about the remainder for now). The answer is 9, so that's what your first digit is. 9 x 16 = 144, and 159 - 144 is 15, and that right there is your second digit — the hex representation of 15 (which is F). That means the hex representation of 159 is 9F.

Here's the rule: just plug in your decimal number and crank!

first hex digit = (decimal number) / 16 (disregard the remainder)

second hex digit = (decimal number - (first hex digit * 16))

Here's another one: 245. Ready?

first hex digit = 245 / 16 = 15 (which is an **F**) (remember, discard the remainder)

second hex digit = (245 - (15 * 16)) = **5**

So the hexadecimal notation for the decimal number 245 is **F5**!

Part IV

Teaming Up JavaScript with Other Cool Stuff

The 5th Wave — By Rich Tennant

PC DESCENDING A STAIRCASE

"THE ARTIST WAS ALSO A PROGRAMMER AND EVIDENTLY PRODUCED SEVERAL VARIATIONS ON THIS THEME."

In this part . . .

One thing that makes JavaScript so cool is its capability to interact with other very diverse Web tools and languages. The chapters in Part IV focus on how Java applets, Netscape plug-ins, and CGI programs can all be added to JavaScript-enabled Web pages and invoked directly from JavaScript statements.

Each of these components is unique and useful in its own right. Java applets offer the power of platform-independent, active content; Netscape plug-ins, the ability of third-party applications to blend seamlessly into the Navigator environment; and CGI programs, raw server-side processing capability.

You can include any or all of these technologies in your Web pages. To help you make sense of it all, this part describes each component in detail with an emphasis on why you want to use each (and when). Tons of code samples have been included so you can see exactly how the components are integrated.

Chapter 17

Java: JavaScript's Big Sister

A great deal of confusion exists about Java and JavaScript. Java is often referred to as the big sister of JavaScript. Well, that may true; but like in regular families, just because you're sisters doesn't necessarily mean that you've got anything in common! As a matter of fact, Java and JavaScript aren't particularly similar at all, except that

▸ They share the same ancestor (the C language)

▸ They're both used to develop Web applications

▸ They're both promoted by the same companies

Java is worth knowing a little about, though, for a couple of reasons. One reason is that you can integrate Java applets into your JavaScript scripts to extend your scripts and make them more powerful. A second reason is that Java is really cool!

What Is Java?

Developed by Sun Microsystems, *Java* is an object-oriented programming language that was specifically designed to support the development of Internet applications. Effective Internet applications (unlike traditional mainframe- or personal-computer-based applications) need to be designed with the following considerations in mind:

✔ The applications need to work on all kinds of hardware and software platforms, because all kinds of systems are hooked up to the Internet.

✔ The applications need to be as small as possible in order to save space, time, and money — both when they're physically stored on servers and when they're being distributed (downloaded) all over the world.

✔ The applications need to be as reliable as possible; that is, the percentage of "Ratsitcrashedagains" needs to be reduced to the bare minimum.

✔ The applications need to be as mischief-proof as possible.

✔ The applications need to be as dynamic as possible so that folks can incorporate others' applications easily.

Java addresses each of these concerns in a C++−like syntax that's actually a synthesis of not only C++, but other object-oriented languages like Smalltalk, Eiffel, and Objective C.

You can't talk for long about Java without talking about the Java *virtual machine.* The virtual machine is what makes Java portable across multiple hardware configurations and operating systems. The Java *virtual machine* is an abstract machine, and it's identical on all of the Java-supported platforms. Java compilers generate something called *bytecode,* which is a type of code that the virtual machine can interpret. Bytecode is independent of hardware architectures, operating systems, and windowing (user interface) systems. The Java runtime, which *is* specific to each platform, is the software that translates the virtual machine interpretation into platform-specific instructions that actually make something happen.

The bottom line is this: All Java compilers produce code that can be interpreted and executed *without change* on any Java-supported platform. And when you're talking about Java, *without change* really means without change — you can literally copy the compiled programs from one platform to another and run them! (That's why you don't find separate sections for Windows Java applets, Macintosh Java Applets, and UNIX Java applets in your Web-surfing travels.)

If you've done any programming at all prior to your acquaintance with JavaScript, the hair is probably standing up on the back of your neck right now. Java does something that's practically unheard of: It gives programmers a simple, common ground. No more remaking the world because a header file was changed! No more re-implementing (or even recompiling) to take advantage of the markets on other platforms! No more !&^%$# bugs caused by faulty pointer arithmetic! (That last benefit alone is worth the price of admission, if you ask me.)

Throwing out the garbage

When Sun's designers created Java, they realized that (because they were after a language that would make the development of distributed systems easy) they should examine other successful object-oriented languages to start with. Sun's designers started there because the object-oriented model is a perfect parallel to complex systems like distributed networked applications. The designers looked at Smalltalk, Eiffel, C++, Objective C, and something called Cedar/Mesa (all object-oriented languages that have been around awhile), and they tried to keep all the good stuff while sifting out the troublesome, bug-prone, marginally useful stuff.

As a result, Java's "look and feel" is close to C++, but certain C++ conventions are gone. Java has no such thing as a pointer, for example, nor do typedefs, #defines, structures, functions, operator overloading, or multiple inheritance appear in Java. (If you've ever coded C++, you *know* why these constructs were tossed; they're hard, ugly, and error-prone, and you can do what you need to in much simpler ways.) There *is* garbage collection (automatic release of no-longer-in-use memory) and a complete object-oriented model, though, courtesy of Smalltalk; protocol definitions from Objective C; and built-in thread handling from Cedar/Mesa. You can think of Java as a distillation of other programming languages that was specifically targeted for Internet application development.

Because Java's goal is ambitious, the language itself is pretty extensive. C++ programmers often feel right at home with Java in almost no time at all. If you're not one of the anointed, though, looking at Java code may very well give you a blinding headache. Unlike client-side JavaScript, which gives you a couple dozen Navigator form elements, a couple of data types, and a Math utility, Java provides a comprehensive, everything-including-the-kitchen-sink object model. This object model is implemented through a suite of class libraries, including (but not limited to) the following:

- **java.lang**: A collection of basic objects and primitive data types
- **java.io**: A collection of objects that deal with input-output function
- **java.util**: A collection of utilities
- **java.awt**: A collection of cross-platform user interface objects

You may be wondering if Java is *compiled* or if it's *interpreted*, like JavaScript (there's a nice discussion of the differences between the two in Chapter 1). The answer is this: JavaScript is both compiled *and* interpreted. The Java *compiler* generates bytecode. This bytecode is then distributed to any Java-supported platform that requests it, where it's *interpreted*. Java-supported platforms (at the time of this writing) are SPARC/Solaris, x86/Solaris (both UNIX implementations), Windows 95 and Windows NT, and Macintosh.

Applets (Sorry, No Cotlets!)

A *Java applet* is a Java program specifically designed for inclusion in an HTML program. Compiled applet code is downloaded from a Web server to a browser and executes right there, in memory, on the client. All an HTML author needs to do is include a special tag called <APPLET>...</APPLET> that identifies values for attributes that specify the location of the applet code, the size of the initial display, and so on. The complete <APPLET>...</APPLET> tag specification is described in the next section, "Generic tag syntax."

Generic tag syntax:

`<APPLET`	Beginning <APPLET> tag
`CODE = "appletFile"`	Name of compiled applet file (*.class)
`WIDTH = pixels`	Width of initial applet display, in pixels
`HEIGHT = pixels`	Height of initial applet display, in pixels
`[CODEBASE = "codebaseURL"]`	URL where applet file defined in CODE is located (default is the same directory where the calling .html file is located)
`[ALT = "alternateText"]`	Alternate text to display (for non-Java browsers)
`[NAME = "appletInstanceName"]`	Internal name of applet (for coding purposes)
`[ALIGN = alignment]`	Specifies applet alignment (see the icon below for details)
`[VSPACE = pixels]`	Space (in pixels) to leave blank above/below applet
`[HSPACE = pixels]>`	Space (in pixels) to leave blank on each side of applet

(repeat the following PARAM tag as many times as necessary)

`[< PARAM`	Single <PARAM> tag (parameters are name/value pairs)
`NAME = "appletParameter1"`	Parameter name to be sent to applet
`VALUE = "value">]`	Parameter value to be sent to applet
`</APPLET>`	Closing </APPLET> tag

Notice that the only requirements for bare-bones, bargain-basement applet execution are the first three values—the values for CODE, HEIGHT, and WIDTH, which identify the applet .class file, display height, and display width respectively. (You can tell this because these properties are the only ones that aren't surrounded by the square brackets, which indicate optional code.)

Here's a behind-the-scenes look at what goes on when the HTML interpreter encounters an `<APPLET>`...`</APPLET>` tag. First, the interpreter reserves a display area according to the values set for the `HEIGHT` and `WIDTH` attributes. Then the interpreter loads the Java applet bytecode (specified by the `CODE` attribute) into memory. Finally, it creates an example of the class defined in the applet (which will always be a subclass of the Applet class, by the way) and calls the applet example's `init()` and `start()` methods.

Real-life code example:

Listing 17-1 shows an example of an HTML file that invokes a Java applet. To see the Java applet "Bubbles" in real life, load the HTML file list1701.htm (and wait for a few seconds; the bubbles run slowly). You can find it on the companion CD.

Listing 17-1: Example Source for Java Applet Execution

```
<HTML>
<HEAD><TITLE>Java Applet Example</TITLE></HEAD>
<BODY>
<APPLET CODE=Bubbles.class
CODEBASE="http://java.sun.com/applets/applets/Bubbles"
WIDTH=500 HEIGHT=500>
</APPLET>
</BODY>
</HTML>
```

The values for `CODE` and `CODEBASE` are combined to indicate that the fully-qualified filename of the compiled Java applet is `http://java.sun.com/applets/applets/Bubbles/Bubbles`. The easiest way to figure out what's wrong is to select Options⇨Show Java Console if you're running Navigator, and View⇨Options⇨Advanced⇨Enable Java Logging if you're running Internet Explorer. Up pops the Java console — a handy window that lets you know exactly what's on the Java interpreter's mind. Figure 17-1 shows an example of the kind of information that you can expect from this helpful tool. (In this case, the value for `CODEBASE` was missing the string `"/Bubbles"`, so the file couldn't be found.)

A good rule of thumb regarding "borrowed" applets: If you rely on them always being in the same place or being named the same thing (or even existing, for that matter), you may be in for a surprise! Web servers may not know or care what clients (or how many) are accessing their resources, and things staying the same from day to day is not guaranteed. Unless you control all of the applet files you access you can't count on them as far as you can throw a brood sow.

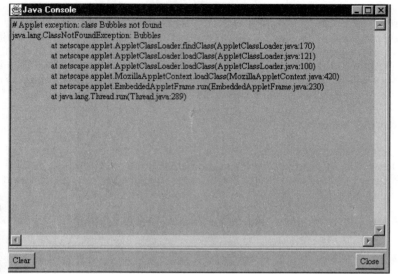

Security blanket

Security is a big issue for all Internet protocols and tools, not just the World Wide Web and Java. Keep in mind that the recent explosion of Internet traffic, protocols (including http and the World Wide Web), tools, and applications is just that — an explosion. Technology has advanced so rapidly that security measures haven't yet caught up.

Java applets pose a security threat because they're downloaded from heaven-knows-where and execute locally on client machines. Even though Java's implementation anticipates and deals with some of the most obvious security breaches, the implementation is not totally mischief-proof at the time of this writing. Already, malicious applets that hog resources and display unsettling messages have been reported. (There are always a few in every crowd, aren't there?). Security experts who make it their business to figure such things out claim to have found ways to

✓ Enter a browser undetected by fooling it into downloading their code instead of the applet that the browser requested

✓ Perform unauthorized file operations on the client machine (yikes!)

Sun Microsystems is aware of the potential for mischievous Java implementations and is working toward a solution that can enable *untrusted applets* (those applets that you download from heaven-knows-where) to run safely in an encapsulated, trusted environment (your browser). To keep up with the latest in this continuing saga, visit http://java.sun.com/sfaq/index.html.

What You Need to Get Started

If you're all fired up about Java, you probably want to jump right on in and get started. This section gives you all the specifics you need, whether you want to stick to using other peoples' applets, or whether you want to go hog-wild and become a Java jockey-for-hire your own bad self.

Invoking Java applets

If all you're interested in is calling Java applets from within your HTML files, you've probably got everything that you need to get started already. First off, of course, you need a Java-supportive Web browser (Internet Explorer 3.0 or Netscape Navigator 3.0), which presumably you have. Armed with the examples in this chapter, the only other thing that you need is an applet to call! The easiest way to locate an applet is to browse the Web. (Try typing the search string **Java +applet** in your favorite Web-searching utility.) Or you can check out the following URLs, which are already famous for having a ready supply of Java applets on tap:

```
http://java.sun.com/applets/applets.html
http://www.gamelan.com/
```

A good plan for scamming an applet follows:

1. **Check out the applet first.**

   That is, load a Web page that's already set up to invoke the applet that you're interested in.

2. **If the applet looks good, take note of the URL of the page that loaded it.**

   This URL (plus the `CODEBASE` value defined in the loading page, which you can get by selecting View⇨Document Source from Navigator or View⇨Source from Internet Exlporer) becomes the `CODEBASE` value in your HTML file.

3. **Fill out the rest of the** `<APPLET>...</APPLET>` **definition exactly the way that the loading page does.**

   You can always experiment with the values later.

Creating Java applets

Unfortunately, specifics for creating Java applets are well beyond the scope of this book — but if you're interested in developing in Java, my hat's off to you! *Java For Dummies* and *Java Programming For Dummies* provide a great starting point in terms of information and sample code.

To get started, you also need to get a copy of the Java developer's kit (JDK). You've got the Java runtime and interpreter (they come with all Java-enabled Web browsers), but you're missing the "meat" — specifically, the Java class libraries, a Java compiler, an applet viewer (good for testing your applets without having to go through a browser), and a debugger. You can download the JDK free of charge from the following URL:

```
http://java.sun.com/java.sun.com/products/JDK/CurrentRelease
```

For documentation, examples, and the latest Java specification, see this site:

```
http://java.sun.com/products/JDK
```

Integrating with JavaScript

The examples so far in this chapter have all been of HTML documents that invoke Java applets with the `<APPLET>...</APPLET>` tags. In versions of Navigator and Internet Explorer prior to 3.0, that's pretty much the extent of the Java story. With the 3.0 versions of these products, though, there's a twist: you can call Java applets directly from JavaScript statements!

If you're running a beta version of Navigator 3.0, in order to activate LiveConnect and run the example shown here, you also need to set an environment variable on your system. On UNIX and Windows, go to an MS-DOS window and type in **set NS_ENABLE_MOJA=1** at the command line prompt (or type the line into your autoexec.bat file and reboot your computer) to set the environment variable NS ENABLE MOJA=1. On Macintosh, edit the Navigator resources and add a resource of type 'MOJA' and ID 128.)

An *environment variable* is a system-wide variable. If you're running Windows, you can set the environment variable at a command line prompt — but if you do that, the next time you shut off your computer the value vanishes and you wonder why the heck your app doesn't run properly the next time you fire it up! The best way to set an environment variable is to put the set statement (`set NS_ENABLE_MOJA=1`, in this case) in your autoexec.bat file (again, assuming that you're running Windows) and then reboot your system. After that, every software application that knows the name of the environment variable can query its value.

To see a real, live demonstration of JavaScript/Java applet interaction, load the following URL and follow the instructions that you find there. Then check out Listing 17-2, which contains a scrap of the demo's behind-the-scenes source code for your viewing enjoyment.

```
http://home.netscape.com/comprod/products/navigator/
           version_3.0/developer/js-java-demo.html
```

Listing 17-2: Source Code Example of JavaScript Invoking Java Applet

```
<APPLET NAME="NervousApplet" CODE="NervousText.class"
           width=400 height=50>
<PARAM NAME="text" VALUE="Enter your text here.">
</APPLET>
<BR>
<FORM>
<INPUT NAME="InputText" TYPE=text SIZE=35 VALUE="Enter your
           text here.">
<BR>
<INPUT TYPE="button" NAME="appletButton" width=200
           value="Click here to change text."
           onClick="document.NervousApplet.changeText
           (form.InputText.value)">
```

Listing 17-2 highlights the pertinent snippet of a JavaScript statement (the onClick event handler, in this case) that changes the way that a running applet behaves. Notice that the applet is invoked when the interpreter encounters the <APPLET>...</APPLET> tag. Then, when the user clicks on appletButton, the applet's changeText() method is invoked. Take a look at Listing 17-3 to see how the changeText() method is implemented in the Java applet.

Listing 17-3: Java Applet Source Code

```
/*
        Test of text animation, LiveConnect version.
*/
import java.awt.Graphics;
import java.awt.Font;
import java.awt.Color;

public class NervousText extends java.applet.Applet
           implements Runnable
{
        char separated[];
        String s = null;
        Thread killme = null;
        int i;
        int x_coord = 0, y_coord = 0;
        String num;
        int speed=35;
        int counter =0;
```

(continued)

(continued)

```
public void init() {
        setFont(new Font("TimesRoman",Font.BOLD,36));

        s = getParameter("text");
        if (s == null)s = "Java is Hot";

        separated = new char [s.length()];
        s.getChars(0,s.length(),separated,0);
        setBackground(Color.white);
}
// This is the method that will be called by JavaScript
public void changeText(String text){
        stop();
        s = text;
        separated = new char [s.length()];
        s.getChars(0, s.length(), separated, 0);
        start();
}

public void start(){
        if(killme == null){
                killme = new Thread(this);
                killme.start();
        }
}...
}
```

When it encounters the <APPLET>...</APPLET> HTML tag shown in Listing 17-2, the interpreter loads the compiled version of the Java source file represented in Listing 17-3. Then the interpreter immediately creates an example of the NervousText class (the Java class that's defined by the Java statements in Listing 17-3) and invokes the example's init() and start() methods.

Notice that the changeText() function takes one parameter (which you probably expected, because that's all that was sent to it in Listing 17-2!). Notice also the public keyword in front of the changeText() method definition in Listing 17-3. As a JavaScript author, you can only access public methods and data of Java applets. If changeText() had been defined as a private method, you wouldn't have been able to call it. (This situation is on purpose, by the way. It's part of the object-oriented concept of *encapsulation* — that no program should be able to access the private concerns of any other. However, programmers often "publish" lists of public data and methods that they expect and encourage other programmers to access, usually by listing them in the online documentation that accompanies the programs. changeText() is such a method.)

Chapter 18

Putting in a Plug for Netscape Plug-Ins

● ●

In This Chapter

▶ Defining and finding Netscape plug-ins

▶ Using plug-ins stand-alone

▶ Embedding plug-ins in HTML documents

▶ Interacting with plug-ins by using JavaScript

● ●

*N*etscape plug-ins are software components that "plug in" to Netscape Navigator to extend its capabilities. Plug-ins are typically created by third-party vendors, but (by definition) they blend right into Navigator, and all that users notice when they use plug-ins is that their browsers appear to have gotten a little smarter. All of the main features of Navigator — the menus, the way the windows look, the icons — stay the same because plug-ins cooperate with the Navigator environment, providing their function in a way that closely matches Navigator's overall look and feel. Using plug-ins is almost like having an upgraded version of Navigator. (Except, unlike an upgraded version of Navigator, if you don't like a particular feature, you can just get rid of the offending plug-in and keep using your copy of Navigator and the plug-ins that you do like. Try *that* with a whole new upgraded version of anything!)

If you're running Microsoft's Internet Explorer instead of Netscape Navigator, you're probably wondering whether or not this chapter has anything in it for you. After all, Microsoft's top choice for providing active content in Web pages is ActiveX — and ActiveX modules are nothing at all like Netscape plug-ins. Well, the answer is yes — sort of. Microsoft has announced support for Netscape plug-ins in Internet Explorer 3.0, but has stopped short of announcing explicit support for scripting them. What that means is that you should be able to embed Netscape plug-ins in your Web pages inside Internet Explorer; you just won't be able to invoke them directly from JavaScript statements. At the time of this writing, though, basic plug-in support appears not to have been implemented. To keep up on the latest, check out the following URL:

```
http://www.microsoft.com/ie/most/howto/nsplugin.htm
```

What Exactly Is a Plug-in, and Why Should I Care?

Plug-ins are executable code modules generated from C++ source, and they all boast a dll file extension. When you start Navigator, it looks into its plugins directory and loads and registers any plug-ins that it finds there. (Actually, Netscape loads any file that it finds that starts with the letters *np* and ends with a dll extension in the plugins directory.) The pathname of the plug-ins directory may vary, depending on how wild you got when you installed Navigator; but if you accepted the defaults during the installation process, the pathname should be similar to the following pathname:

```
C:\Program Files\Netscape\Navigator\Program\plugins
```

The bottom line is, you need to have a plug-in physically resident on your machine, in the correct directory (something similar to C:\Program Files\Netscape\Navigator\Program\plugins), when you bring up Navigator in order for Navigator to recognize and load the plug-in.

The fact that you use plug-ins by downloading their executable files to your hard drive means that the plug-ins have to be compatible with your operating system. Unlike Java applets' one-size-fits-all approach (the same Java applet can be downloaded and run by users who are running Mac, Windows, or UNIX because of the Java virtual machine that is resident on each of these platforms), plug-ins are tailored for each environment. If you run Windows 95, for example, you have to make sure that any plug-ins you download are Windows 95 plug-ins, and so on.

Plug-ins *are* like Java applets in that they can do just about anything that a programmer codes them to do. (That is, plug-ins are not restricted to dealing with the JavaScript built-in objects you see listed in Chapter 10.) And, in one special case, plug-ins also are like Java applets in that you — JavaScript author extraordinaire — can invoke them directly and modify their behavior. See, plug-ins come in the following three basic flavors (okay, two basic flavors and one stealth flavor):

- Plug-ins that can be embedded in HTML files

- Plug-ins that can be invoked from Navigator and have nothing whatsoever to do with an HTML file

- Plug-ins that can be invisible (Don't worry about this type of plug-in, because it's not actually implemented yet.)

The first type of plug-in is the one most relevant to JavaScript programmers because typically the first type is the only kind of plug-in that you embed and interact with by using JavaScript statements. So naturally, that type of plug-in gets the most attention in the sections that follow. (You *can* embed full-page plug-ins, but the utility of doing so is less than inspiring, as you see later in this chapter.)

Where do I get plugged in?

Plug-ins that work with Navigator 2.*x* are available, but only Navigator 3.0 supports direct fraternization between JavaScript statements and plug-ins. If you install Navigator 3.0, you notice that it comes with a few plug-ins. You can verify this inclusion of plug-ins in one of two ways (the first way is easier if you already have Navigator running; otherwise, it's quicker to use the second way):

  ✔ From the Navigator menu, you can select Help⇨About Plug-ins. Take a look at Figure 18-1 to get an idea of the kind of information this helpful little menu item displays.

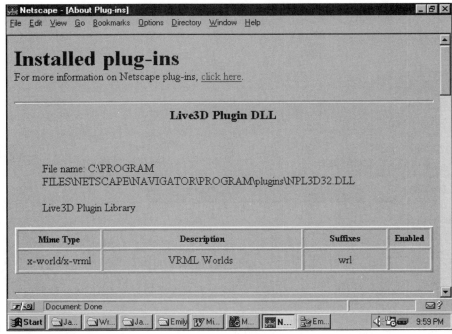

Figure 18-1: What's what: getting installed plug-in information via the About Plug-ins menu selection.

✔ You can look in the C:\Program Files\Netscape\Navigator\ Program\plugins directory and see if this directory has any files that start with the letters *np* and have a dll extension.

You can use either of the preceding methods to verify the successful installation of any plug-ins at the time that you find, download, and install them.

Of course, the whole point of plug-ins is that you can get them somewhere else than with Navigator itself! A ton of plug-ins are out there to choose from, and the following sites are good places to start looking.

```
http://home.netscape.com/comprod/products/navigator/
           version_2.0/plugins/index.html
http://browserwatch.iworld.com/plug-in.html
http://www.cnet.com/Content/Reviews/Compare/Plugin/index.html
```

Remember that, unlike Java applets that execute after they're loaded from a server into your client machine's memory (but that vanish when you close your browser session), plug-ins are tangible. That is, in order to use plug-ins, you have to download them and install them physically onto your machine.

Typically, when you try to do something that your current Navigator configuration (base Navigator and whatever plug-ins you've already collected) can't handle, you see a dialog box like the one shown in Figure 18-2.

Figure 18-2:
Help's on the way! Assisted Installation dialog box for downloading plug-ins.

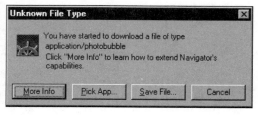

After you get the pop-up message in Figure 18-2, all you have to do is follow the instructions given for downloading the plug-in. There's even an information page (click on <u>M</u>ore Info) if you're squeamish about the whole process and need some reassurance.

Speaking of being squeamish, you have good reason for concern. Let's face it: You really can't be sure where that plug-in has been! It could have been distributed by a perfectly legitimate, respected third-party vendor, or it could have been the latest effort from Sam's Plug-Ins and Bait Shop (Tattoos While-U-Wait).

To be perfectly candid, you're exposing yourself to a risk that's even more hazardous than those you've encountered thus far in your JavaScript, CGI, and Java applet travels. The following section, "Security Matters," gives you the unvarnished facts on plug-in security.

Security matters

Remember the legend of the Trojan horse from your grade school days? Interestingly enough, the legendary Trojan horse has become a metaphor for a certain type of security risk — the type that's most likely to affect a user who takes advantage of Netscape plug-ins (or any other file that's physically downloaded from the Internet). The plug-in you download is like the wooden horse, and you're like the Trojans. "Hey," you say to yourself. "That's a nice-looking horse (plug-in). I could use that." So you download it, but in so doing, you leave yourself wide open to an enemy attack. An unscrupulous programmer can do pretty much anything he or she wants, because he or she has been invited into your system. The worst-case scenario, of course, involves damaging or erasing your data or system files.

The risk isn't limited to plug-ins by any matter of means; the Trojan horse scenario applies literally to any software that you install on your machine, whether you obtain the software electronically or purchase it shrink-wrapped at a local computer store and install it manually. Because distributing code on the Internet is easier (read: *cheaper*) than manufacturing software, though, potentially more suppliers of malicious software are around than ever before.

Conventional wisdom dictates that users be aware of the risks, back up important files frequently, and interact only with trusted servers and well-known companies. (Of course, that's like telling someone to date only *nice* people, isn't it? How the heck do you know whether a person is nice until after you've gone out with him or her?!) In addition, Netscape has built-in security features that you can take advantage of. (Click Options⇨Security Preferences or Help⇨On Security for a blow-by-blow description of these features.)

Security issues are enough to make your head hurt, aren't they? If you're concerned, make a habit of keeping up with Web sites that track security issues. The following are a few such Web sites:

```
http://www.tis.com/Home/NetworkSecurity/WWW/Article.html
http://www.auscert.org.au/Surfing_Between_the_Flags.html
http://home.netscape.com/newsref/ref/netscape-security.html
```

Integrating with JavaScript

If you've got Navigator up and running (and perhaps a nice strong cup of espresso at hand), you've got everything that you need to get started.

Finding and downloading a juicy plug-in

The first thing you want to do is pick a nice plug-in to work with. One of the first plug-ins on the market was the Adobe Acrobat Reader plug-in, which enables you to load documents with a pdf (portable document format) extension (and scroll through them, and magnify them, and other neat stuff). It's kind of like a word processor, only on steroids. This plug-in is a good choice because it's useful to have around, and because you can use this plug-in in its normal, full-page state or embed it into another document.

The URL you want to visit to download the Adobe Acrobat Reader plug-in is

```
http://www.adobe.com/acrobat/3beta/main.html#dl.
```

Follow the instructions that you find at this Web site in order to download the correct version of the Adobe Acrobat Reader plug-in for your operating system.

Did it work?

You downloaded the Adobe Acrobat Reader plug-in successfully, double-clicked on it (it's a self-extracting executable, so double-clicking on it extracts all the files necessary to start the install process and then starts the install process for you, automatically), and followed all the instructions carefully. Now what? How can you be sure that the plug-in downloaded properly? You can check in three ways (and an extra-added bonus is that becoming familiar with these three techniques also provides you with valuable information that you can use later for troubleshooting and debugging your scripts):

- You can look for a new dll extension in the C:\Program Files\Netscape\Navigator\Program\plugins directory.
- You can click Help⇨About Plug-ins from the Navigator menu.
- You can click Options⇨General Preferences⇨Helpers.

Take a look at Figures 18-3 and 18-4 for details on a couple of these ways of checking that your plug-in was downloaded successfully.

Figure 18-3 shows the type of file that this Adobe Acrobat Reader plug-in can display (that is, any filename with a pdf extension).

Figure 18-3:
Help⇨About
Plug-ins
display.

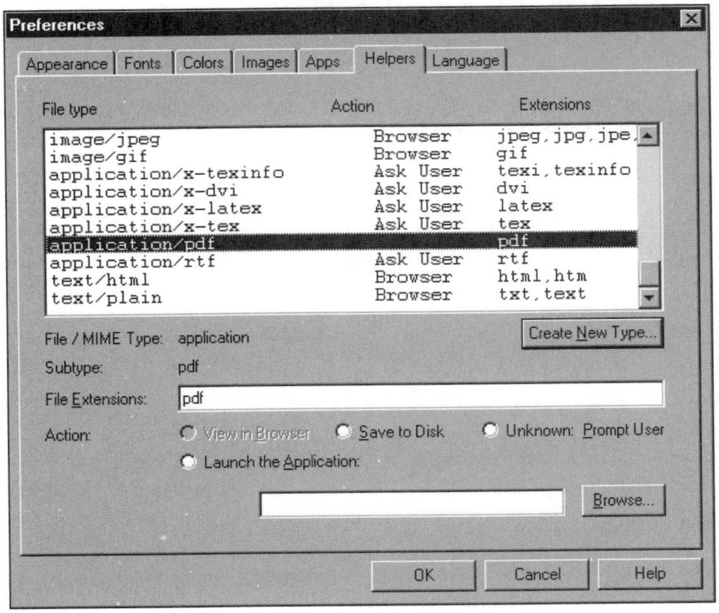

Figure 18-4:
Options⇨
General
Preferences⇨
Helpers
notebook
page.

Helper programs and plug-ins aren't quite the same thing, but they're similar. Helper programs also add function to Navigator; they just don't do it in the seamless, same-look-and-feel way that plug-ins do. The bottom line is, both helpers and plug-ins increase the number of file types that Navigator can understand and enable you to work with, which is why helper programs and plug-ins are displayed together on the *Helpers* notebook page (shown in Figure 18-4).

Fire it up!

The best way to make sure that you've got access to something is just to jump right in and try it. If you followed along earlier and installed a .pdf document viewer (Adobe Acrobat Reader), you should now have the ability to look at .pdf documents — so give it a shot! Choose a document that looks interesting from the following URL:

```
http://www.adobe.com/acrobat/3beta/amexamp.html
```

Acrobat is a *full-page plug-in,* so in a way, Acrobat *is* the document (as opposed to being part of, or embedded in, the document — which is what the following section, "Embedding a plug-in," is all about). You're still in Navigator, but you're also in Acrobat — with all of the functions that Acrobat provides.

Embedding a plug-in

You can use the `<EMBED>` tag to make a plug-in appear inside of an HTML document. Keep in mind that the `<EMBED>` tag is a Netscape extension to standard HTML; and as such, it's not set in stone (but hey, what is, right?). First, take a look at the generic tag syntax; then scope out a real-life example.

Generic tag syntax	Description
`<EMBED`	opening `<EMBED>` tag
`  SRC="pluginName"`	fully-qualified name of plug-in executable
`  HEIGHT=numberPixels`	height, in pixels, to display
`  WIDTH=numberPixels`	width, in pixels, to display
`  [attributeName="value"...]`	parameter name and value pair (optional; no limit to number of name/value pairs)
`</EMBED>`	closing `</EMBED>` tag

Load the file embed.htm, located on the companion CD, if you'd like to try out the code in the next example without actually having to type anything in!

Real-life code example:

The following example embeds the Adobe Acrobat Reader plug-in into a Web page and pre-loads it with a copy of the New York Times (stored in the Times.pdf file on Adobe's server).

```
<EMBED SRC="http://www.adobe.com/acrobat/3beta/PDFS/
          Times.pdf" WIDTH=450 HEIGHT=450>
```

Figure 18-5 shows the way that the plug-in is displayed when it's embedded into an HTML document. Embedding plug-ins is a great deal like embedding images (which I discuss how to do in Chapter 8), with an exciting difference: A plug-in is an application, not just a static display. Therefore, encapsulated in the Web page is a live version of Acrobat! When you click on the embedded plug-in, you notice that the plug-in expands (much as an image loads when you click on it) into its true nature; in this case, as a full-page application with its own toolbar and everything.

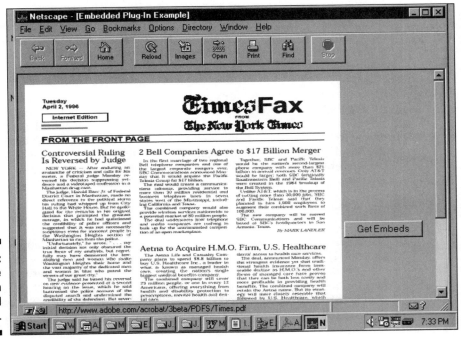

Figure 18-5:
Example
of an
embedded
plug-in.

Accessing a plug-in object with JavaScript

So far in this chapter all the code I've shown you that had to do with plug-ins was straight HTML code. Now comes the extra-special part: JavaScript interaction with plug-ins. Remember that *this* capability (JavaScript/plug-in communication) is only available with Netscape Navigator 3.0 (so don't even bother trying it if you have an earlier version).

First, you need to embed a plug-in that has defined some public methods for you to display (see Chapter 17 if you'd like to know more about public methods). Stand-alone plug-ins, such as the Acrobat plug-in, aren't really meant to be used as embedded elements, so they typically don't have public methods available for you to call. Others, though, such as the Envoy plug-in from Tumbleweed Software that I discuss soon, *are* meant to be embedded. (Envoy is a plug-in that allows you to distribute specially formatted documents electronically.)

You can find out whether a plug-in is embeddable in two ways. One is that the plug-in provider tells you. Usually, a Web page describes not only how to embed a plug-in but also how to call the plug-in after it's embedded. You may hear the term *API* used to describe the plug-in methods that you can call. (API stands for *application programming interface,* and for some reason, talking about an API is way cooler than talking about "a list of the public methods you can call," which is all an API is. Those wacky programmers!)

The other way is to look for examples of how other folks use the embeddable plug-in that you're interested in. (You may really come to love the View⇨Document Source menu option.) Open the following URL and then click on the sample Envoy documents link, followed by a click on the embedded in the HTML pages link. This Web page does both — it explains the Envoy embeddable plug-in API, and it also points you to several examples of how the Envoy embeddable plug-in API is invoked from HTML code.

```
http://www.tumbleweed.com/lc.htm
```

Listing 18-1 shows how to embed an "embeddable" plug-in and then access its innards. This example demonstrates a JavaScript statement that invokes a plug-in method and passes the plug-in method a value based on user input. The first part of this chapter notes that before you can embed a plug-in successfully, you have to have downloaded the plug-in dll and installed it in Navigator's Program/plugins directory on your hard drive. Here's where to find a copy of Envoy plug-in from Tumbleweed Software:

```
http://www.tumbleweed.com/download.htm
```

Take a look at the sample code in Listing 18-1 for yourself (in *real time,* as it were) by loading the HTML file list1801.htm off the companion CD. It's cool!

Listing 18-1: Example Code for Accessing a Netscape Plug-in Via JavaScript

```
<HTML><HEAD><TITLE>Embedded Plug-In Example</TITLE>
<SCRIPT LANGUAGE="JavaScript">

function displayFlag(flagToDisplay) {
    document.envoyPlugin.setCurrentPage(flagToDisplay)
    document.envoyPlugin.executeCommand(601)
}

</SCRIPT>
</HEAD>
<BODY>
<FORM NAME="myForm">

<EMBED NAME="envoyPlugin"
SRC="http://www.tumbleweed.com/evy/flags.evy" WIDTH=300
HEIGHT=250
BORDER=0 INTERFACE=STATIC ZOOM=fitwidth
PLUGINSPAGE="http://www.tumbleweed.com/plugin.htm">

<H2> Select a flag to display:</H2>
<INPUT TYPE="radio" NAME="flagToDisplay"
onClick="displayFlag(1)"> U.S.
<INPUT TYPE="radio" NAME="flagToDisplay"
onClick="displayFlag(4)"> Germany
<INPUT TYPE="radio" NAME="flagToDisplay"
onClick="displayFlag(8)"> Canada

<INPUT TYPE="button" NAME="test" VALUE="Get Number of Embeds"
onClick="alert('Number of embedded plug-ins in this document:
'
+ embeds.length)"

</FORM>
</BODY>
</HTML>
```

Notice the values that are being passed into the `displayFlag()` function? They mean something special to the plug-in. This vital information can be found either in example scripts or in official plug-in documentation (ditto the `setCurrentPage()` and `executeCommand()` syntax). Figure 18-6 shows you what the code in Listing 18-1 looks like when it's interpreted.

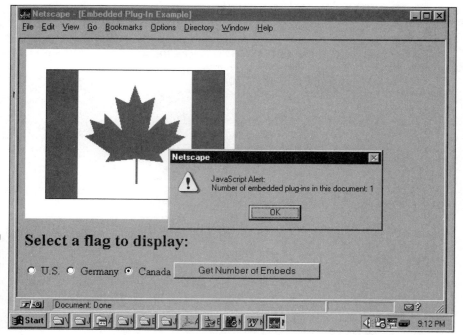

Figure 18-6:
JavaScript/
Netscape
plug-in
integration.

The LiveConnect-enabled Envoy plug-in that's referenced in Listing 18-1 is functional (at the time of this writing) for Windows 95 only. Plug-ins that exploit the LiveConnect JavaScript plug-in capability are just beginning to appear; so by the time that you read this, a good chance exists that the Envoy plug-in is available for more platforms and that other cool plug-ins are available as well. For another Windows 95 example, check out the following URL:

```
http://www.futurewave.com/livedemo/index.html
```

Chapter 19

The Common Gateway Interface: Emily Post for the Client/Server Set

● ●

In This Chapter

▶ Discovering CGI

▶ Relating to CGI and cookies

▶ Understanding CGI and Perl

▶ Coping with CGI security issues

▶ Using CGI programs

▶ Creating CGI programs

● ●

*U*ntil JavaScript came along, Common Gateway Interface (*CGI*) programs were the only way to add "intelligence" to Web pages. All HTML could do by itself was present a form to users, accept the users' input, and fire the input off in a bundle to a CGI program that was sitting on a Web server. The CGI program then processed the data, generated a reply (usually in the form of another HTML source file), and sent the reply back for the client browser to display. That method is still a really great way to get some things done; after all, if you have some heavy-duty program that needs to access a bunch of data-bases, you probably *don't* want to have it hanging around on the client side — that kind of accessing function is much more appropriate on a server.

Still, going to all the trouble of bundling up data and sending it to a server, which could be halfway around the world, just to figure out that a user forgot to enter a value for a required field does seem like somewhat of a waste! But that process is what you needed to do in the days B.J. (before JavaScript). Now that JavaScript is here, though, you can use it instead of Common Gateway Interface programs for such processes as validating or massaging user input.

Like my dad used to say, you've got to use the right tool for the job. (He used to say this quite frequently, usually after I'd managed to dent one of his good socket wrenches while trying to hammer in a ten-penny nail.) Although using JavaScript is a much more efficient way of validating user input than using a Common Gateway Interface program, CGI is a very powerful tool, and it can handle things that JavaScript just plain can't. This chapter explains exactly what CGI programs are, when you should use them, and how they can coexist with JavaScript-enabled Web pages.

The implication is that CGI programs are limited not by what's on the client, but by what's on the server. Typically servers are big, industrial-strength machines that run UNIX or Windows NT; they have a great deal of memory, huge amounts of disk space, fast processors, and scads of tools. Because servers have these advantages, CGI programs are a great choice if you want to connect your JavaScript-enabled Web page up to a full-blown program that has lots of bells and whistles, like the ability to store and retrieve data from a relational database or execute existing mainframe software.

What Exactly Is CGI, Anyway?

CGI is a protocol. A *protocol* in computer terms is pretty much the same thing it is in human terms: the combination of customs and regulations that govern formal relations between two parties. Instead of defining the proper behavior for representatives of two different countries or human cultures, though, *protocol* in this case refers to the required behavior of Web servers and clients (including Web browsers, such as Navigator) that want to do business with each other.

Because CGI is a protocol, not a programming language, you still need to pick a programming language to use *with* the CGI protocol. Technically, to implement a CGI program, you can use any programming language that your Web server supports. (Of course, technically you can make your own cloth out of plant fiber and weave your own clothes, too.) In practice, most programmers choose either C or Perl, as their CGI program implementation language of choice for a couple of reasons:

- ✔ C and Perl are powerful languages, and many people already know how to use them.
- ✔ C and Perl are supported on a wide variety of Web-server platforms.

Cookies Aren't Just for Breakfast Anymore

Before the advent of cookies, there was absolutely no concept of state or transactions between Web clients and Web servers. (Both of these terms, *state* and *transactions,* refer to an ongoing relationship between a client and a server. A *state* is a snapshot of the way a client or server looks at a specific time; a *transaction* is a complete conversation between a client and a server, from start to finish.)

Hi, I'm Daemon, and I'll be your server tonight

You can think of CGI as sitting square on top of another protocol, the hyper-text transfer protocol (HTTP). HTTP is what enables Web servers and Web clients to talk together at all. To implement HTTP, run the *httpd,* or HTTP daemon, on the server machine. The daemon has to be installed and running on the Web server before a Web client can make contact. (The word *daemon* — pronounced *demon* — is far less sinister than it sounds. All the word refers to is an executable server process that hangs around and waits for a client to call it up and ask it to do something.)

CGI defines how the two parties (client and server) can exchange data, and thus CGI enables the two parties to take their relationship a little further. It works like this: The Web page (on the client) defines how it intends to format the data that it will send to the CGI program, and the CGI program (on the server) defines the format of the data that it intends to return to the Web page. That way, both parties (client and server) know exactly what to expect from each other so they can handle the data that is to be transferred.

The client half of this definition can be found in the value for the form's METHOD attribute, which is used to enable the CGI program to know what data format to expect.

The server half is coded into the CGI program itself (in a line that sets the attribute Content-type to a description of the output that the CGI program intends to generate). This method is what the CGI program uses to tell the client browser what data format to expect in return.

After it threw a glob of data at a CGI program on a server, a client waited for the reply, received it, and that was that. If the client connected to the same server the next day, neither one of them acknowledged that they'd ever met (kind of like when you have a monumentally bad date and then run into the person at the grocery store later that week). With cookies, though, all that changes.

Cookies (in the Web world — I'm sure that you know what cookies are in the real world!) are mechanisms that enable CGI programs to store persistent data *about* clients *on* clients. (*Persistent data* is data that hangs around after you shut down your Web browser, and even after you turn off your machine.)

When you stop and think, this ability to store data is a tremendous advantage. For example: Say you're browsing the Web, looking for good jazz CDs. Say you load up a Web page that uses a CGI program — and cookies — to "remember" the CDs that you purchase (a Billie Holiday CD and one by Miles Davis). Then, a month later when the music-buying bug bites again, you load the same Web page. But — what's this? In place of the familiar list of CDs that was displayed the preceding time that you loaded the Web page, a page comes up that describes the new Miles Davis anthology and the just-released video (and CD soundtrack) of the late Billie Holiday's life. Coincidence? No! The CGI program that was invoked when you loaded the Web page the second time made notes about the kinds of music you purchased the preceding time and made some decisions, based on those notes, about what to show you first. Those notes are cookies. Cool, huh? Talk about an advertiser's dream! This process is what I call target marketing at its finest: the potential for a custom-built page for every single person who accesses your Web site!

Take a look at the following URL to see a really good example of the kind of application that cookies can help you implement. This URL is for the Netscape PowerStart application, an application that enables users to create their own custom Web pages. PowerStart uses a JavaScript-enabled Web page to display a menu that offers all kinds of choices regarding Web-page color, graphics, layout, and content. Users decide which of these features they want, and when the users are finished, they click on the Build button, which saves the users' preferences on their machines. (The saved files are named cookies.txt and are stored in the users' Navigator directories.) After that, every time a user selects the `MyPage` URL from the Netscape home page, the locally stored preferences in the file cookies.txt are extracted and are used to create a custom Web page dynamically. Check out Figure 19-1 to see what the Netscape Power-Start application looks like. Also check out Listing 19-1 (from the Netscape Power-Start Web page) to get a peek at how the JavaScript (client-side part) was coded.

```
http://personal.netscape.com/custom/modify.html
```

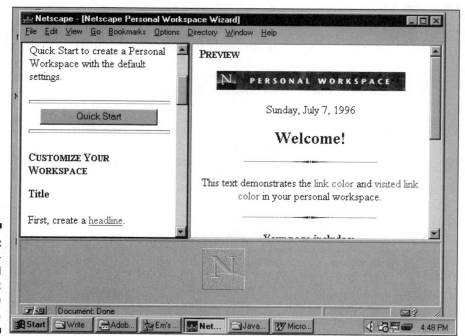

Figure 19-1:
A cookie-enabled application: Netscape PowerStart.

Listing 19-1: Code Snippet Taken from the Netscape PowerStart Web Page

```
<HTML>

<!------------------------------------------------------------->
<!-- Custom Page 'Lite' v1.5                                 ->
<!-- Written by Jonathan Feinstein and Alan Spar 2/26/96     ->
<!-- Copyright (C) 1996 Netscape Communications Corporation->
<!------------------------------------------------------------->

<SCRIPT LANGUAGE="JavaScript">
<!--
function resetall () {
    if (confirm('Are you sure you want to start over?
            You\nwill lose all the customizations you
            have\nalready made.')) {
        parent.SetCookie('custom',
            'n00FFFFFF000000CC0000006699y09yny10::Welcome!::blank::11111:
            :10001011100::000010::1111111::1100101110::');
        parent.SetCookie('pl', 'blank');
        parent.personalsize = 0;
        parent.SetCookie('note', 'Reminder: Add this page to
            your bookmarks list.');
        parent.examplewin.location = '/custom/example.html';
        parent.customwin.location = '/custom/blank.html';
    }
}
//-->
</SCRIPT>

...

...
<INPUT TYPE="button" NAME="reset" VALUE=" Start Over "
            onClick="resetall();">
</HTML>
```

The code shown in Listing 19-1 defines a JavaScript function called `resetall()` that reinitializes all of the user's cookie values in order to reset a user's preferences. `resetall()` is invoked when a user clicks the Start Over push button on the PowerStart display. Take a look at what's going on inside the `resetall()` function, near the top of the listing. First, a dialog box is displayed, asking if the user really wants to start over. Then the `SetCookie()` method is called several times to "blank out" the data that was stored in the cookie — so the user has a fresh, clean, display to start over with.

(To confirm that these things are really taking place, load PowerStart at `http://personal.netscape.com/custom/modify.html` and scroll to the very bottom of the left-hand frame, where you see the Start Over button. Click on it and see what happens!)

Perl(s) before Swine: A Popular CGI Implementation Language

The C language is sometimes used to implement CGI programs, but more and more, Perl is winning the coin toss. *Perl,* like JavaScript, is also known as a scripting language. (Therefore, you may hear CGI programs that are written in Perl referred to as CGI *scripts.*) I think that you may find, however, that Perl is a little more cryptic than JavaScript could ever hope to be, even on a bad day. Face it: All you need to know in order to write JavaScript scripts are a couple of logical constructs, such as if and for, and you need to know where to look up the JavaScript object model. If you know those items, you've got about 85 percent of JavaScript down cold.

Not so with Perl, unless you're one of those linguistically gifted folks who can learn entire programming languages in a weekend. (I met someone like that once. It was scary.) Still, the reason that you're using CGI in the first place is that you need the capability to do some heavy-duty data crunching; and if that capability is your criteria, Perl fills the bill. Take a look at Listing 19-2 (especially if you want to feel really good about coding JavaScript!). Listing 19-2 shows a small section of a Perl script that searches a plain old data file (that's *flat-file database* to you, pardner). If you like, you can visit the following URL and take a look at the entire Perl program:

```
http://anansi.panix.com/~wizjd/cgi-bin/phone.txt
```

Listing 19-2: Partial Example — Perl Program Designed to Search a Flat-File Database

```perl
#!/usr/local/bin/perl

#*********************************************************
#*************** Get Passed data from form *************
#*********************************************************
sub GET_STATE_INFO {
    read(STDIN, $save_string, $ENV{CONTENT_LENGTH});
        # Yes - Use it

    @prompts = split(/&/,$save_string);
    foreach (@prompts){
        ($tmp1, $tmp2) = split(/=/,$_);
        $tmp2 =~ s/\x2b/\x20/g;
        $tmp2 =~ s/%2C/\x2c/g;
        $tmp2 =~ s/%28/\x28/g;
        $tmp2 =~ s/%29/\x29/g;
        $fields{$tmp1}=$tmp2;
    }

    $keys = $fields{'keys'};
    $search_type = $fields{'search_type'};
```

```
}

#*************************************************************
#*********** Search file for lines with all search keys **
#*************************************************************
sub SEARCH_FOR_MATCH {
    @search_key = split(/\x20/,$keys);

    open(MYFILE,"phone_book.dat") ||
        print "<H3>Err: Can't open phone book file<\H3>";
    while(<MYFILE>)  # Our Read loop {
        $in_line = $_;

        if ($search_type eq "and"){
            $found_flag = "Y";
        }
        else{
            $found_flag = "N";
        }
...
...
print "<P>";
print "Go to the ";
print "<A HREF=/~wizjd/cgi-bin/add_phone.cgi> Add a record
        </A>\n";
print " to the phone book, or see the  ";
print "<A HREF=/~wizjd/cgi-bin/phone.txt> Perl Source Code</
        A>\n";
print " for this page.";
print "<HR>";
print "<A HREF=/~wizjd/test.html>Back to Examples Page<A>\n";
print("</BODY>\n");
print("</HTML>\n");
```

I'd like to point out a couple of things because of the likelihood that you may
make use of a CGI script at some point in your Web-page-authoring career and
because understanding the basics is nice — even if you don't end up doing the
actual coding yourself.

The first thing I want to point out is that the line at the top of the listing, #!/
usr/local/bin/perl, *must* be the first line in the file in order for Perl to
recognize the fact that it is, in fact, Perl. No room for creativity is available here,
even though the hash mark denotes that the line is technically a comment line.

The second thing to notice is the system-wide environment variables that this
script accesses. Two in particular are worth noting, because they relate directly
to the HTML form attributes:

✔ STDIN If the value for this environment variable contains data, the CGI script knows that the calling HTML file contained the form attribute METHOD=POST and that the contents of this environment variable are the POSTed data.

✔ CONTENT_LENGTH This environment variable is related to STDIN; its value describes how much data STDIN holds. By the way, $save_string isn't an environment variable; it's a Perl variable that's being assigned the data (in the form of a stream of attribute-value pairs) that came over from the client. You have to put a dollar sign in front of a variable name in Perl if you want that variable to be a string.

Finally, take a look at all the print statements near the bottom of the listing. This area is the section of the CGI script that's putting together the return value (just like the return value of a function!) — in this case, the return value is an HTML file to be sent back to the client. This section of the CGI script is constructing the return file one line at a time, and together the HTML statements form the Web page that's redisplayed to the user back on the client.

Quick! Guard the Door!

Unlike Java applets or Netscape plug-ins, CGI programs are executed on the Web server where they reside. So as an HTML page builder, your interaction with CGI programs is limited to sending parameters and accepting return data. That limited interaction means your security exposure (at least, on the client) is no greater than it always is when you've got a working modem installed.

Of course, that fairly reasonable security exposure doesn't mean that you don't still have security issues to worry about! For one thing, you need to make sure that the Web server that hosts your CGI programs is secure. (Usually that means that a designated system administrator is keeping the machine physically locked up and password-protected to restrict unauthorized access).

You also need to make sure that your request is actually going to the Web server that you think that it's going to, and that the response that comes back has arrived unmolested from the Web server that was supposed to return it.

What You Need to Get Started Integrating CGI Programs

You've got two choices when it comes to using CGI programs: using someone else's programs (that's my favorite) or programming CGI programs yourself. The following sections explain what you need to do for both scenarios.

Executing CGI programs that already exist

Just because you find a CGI program on a server somewhere doesn't automatically mean that you can use that CGI program. If you run across a CGI program that you want to use, typically you need to contact the Web administrator (sometimes called a *Webmaster,* but only if the individual in question is in the habit of wearing a cape with a big *W* on it) of the hosting server to see if you can get access to the CGI program. After all, from the Web administrator's point of view, *you're* the security risk. Even if you have an honest face, you're basically asking permission to run a program on someone else's box (and potentially pass it all kinds of information that could radically affect how it behaves).

That's all there is to it! After you've gotten the appropriate permissions, you can reference the fully qualified name of the CGI program in your script. Here's how:

```
<FORM NAME="myForm" METHOD="POST"
ACTION="http://altavista.digital.com/cgi-bin/
          query?pg=q&what=web&fmt=.&q=JavaScript">
```

You set the form's `ACTION` attribute in order to specify the CGI program to which you want to submit the form's data. In the preceding statement, the `query` program located in the `http://altavista.digital.com/cgi-bin` directory is being sent four value-attribute pairs as input parameters:

```
pg=q
what=web
fmt=.
q=JavaScript
```

The ? between the name of the program and the first parameter enables the JavaScript interpreter to know that some parameters are coming; you use the & to separate each attribute-value pair. What could be simpler?

You don't have to specify attribute-value pairs explicitly in the definition of the `ACTION` attribute. If you don't specify them explicitly in the definition, every element name and value in your form is automatically sent in pairs to the CGI program.

Creating CGI programs

Two separate steps are involved in creating and installing a CGI program for use by the world at large. The first step is to choose an implementation language and code the program; the second step is to find a Web server that the CGI program can call home and have the CGI program installed there.

Coding in the coal mine, going down, down, down

Coding CGI programs is a little beyond the scope of this book. Fortunately, plenty of other good books (along with online documentation and examples) are available. A good one to check out is the *CGI Bible* by Ed Tittle, Mark Gaither, Sebastian Hassinger, and Mike Erwin.

Finding your CGI program a good home

Chances are that you won't be able to just up and copy your very own CGI program to a Web server. Even if you know what directory your CGI program needs to reside in on a given server, you'll probably find that you don't have the capability to write to that given server (those darn permissions issues). Giving people read-only access to servers is like keeping a front door locked — the process is easy, and it deters a good percentage (though not all) of the folks who may have mischief on their minds.

 CGI programs are grouped together in a special directory on a Web server for a couple of reasons. One reason is to make life easier for the administrator: When files are in one place, performing file operations (such as granting permissions and backing up data) on them all in one fell swoop is easier. Another reason is to signal to the calling programs that they need to *execute* the CGI programs, not just load up the CGI programs and display them in a browser session like a garden-variety HTML file.

What you need to do is to contact the Web administrator, or Webmaster, of the Web server you have in mind (probably a Web server that's geographically close, charges the least, and/or is administered by your cousin, Sheila) and respectfully request that your CGI program be installed.

Integrating with JavaScript

As you may have noticed in the example earlier in this chapter (reproduced below), JavaScript does not actually interact with CGI programs at all — HTML does. The <FORM>...</FORM> declaration specifies everything necessary to run a CGI program on form submission, with nary a JavaScript statement in sight.

```
<FORM NAME="myForm" METHOD="POST"
ACTION="http://altavista.digital.com/cgi-bin/
            query?pg=q&what=web&fmt=.&q=JavaScript">
```

In other words, the relationship between CGI and JavaScript is technically one of coexistence rather than integration: They both contribute their special talents to the Web application, but they don't do it by interacting directly with each other — instead, they do it by taking turns. This type of interaction enables you to use JavaScript for the client-side stuff (its *raison d'être*) and bring in the big guns — the CGI program — later, after you're satisfied that everything is as you (and the user of your form) want it to be.

Although the most common time to call a CGI program is when an HTML form is submitted, technically you can invoke one anywhere in your Web page that can legally accept an URL (for example, from a link). Following is an example that shows a CGI program being invoked on form submission, *after* the input data has been *scrubbed* (validated) by JavaScript statements.

All of the source code in this chapter is reproduced on the companion CD.

Listing 19-3: Source for HTML Invoking CGI Program after JavaScript Validation

```
<HTML>
<HEAD><TITLE>CGI and JavaScript Coexistence</TITLE></HEAD>
<SCRIPT LANGUAGE="JavaScript">
function validateInputData(inputForm) {
    if (inputForm.firstName.value.length) {
        alert("The form will be submitted.")
            return true
    }
    else {
        alert("Please enter a value for the name field.")
        return false
    }
}
</SCRIPT>
<BODY>
<FORM NAME="myForm"
onSubmit="return validateInputData(this)">
<P><B>Enter and sign in, please.  Then hit the return key:
            </B>
<INPUT TYPE="text" NAME="firstName" SIZE=25>
</FORM>
</BODY>
</HTML>
```

You may want to take note of a couple of things about the preceding example: First, the example has no submit element. That means that the user has no button to push to indicate that the form should be submitted. In the absence of such a button, the user must press the Return (Enter) key in order to submit the form. Remember that the submit element goes ahead and submits the form come hell or high water; after the user clicks the submit element, the submittal process cannot be stopped (Chapter 10 contains a section devoted to the submit element). If you want the flexibility of being able to decide at the last second whether or not to submit a form, you're left with two choices:

✔ Allow the user to press the Return or Enter key to submit the form (as shown in Listing 19-3)

✔ Create a regular push button with an associated `onClick` event handler that calls `validateInputData()`

Either approach works; the choice of approaches is up to you. Keep in mind that the example shown in the preceding listing is simple (just one input field to validate) in order to explain a point. In real life, your `validateInputData()` method can be as huge and as complicated as you need it to be.

You can look at the Location field in Figure 19-2 to verify that the form was actually submitted. See how the value that was input is appended to the end of the URL? But where did the input data go?

As a matter of fact, the input data went nowhere. In this example, no value for the `ACTION` attribute was ever defined, so the interpreter used the name of the HTML file as the default. (In this example, the source file called `list19-3.html` is located in the `c:\JavaScript` directory of the client machine.) Leaving the `ACTION` attribute undefined until you've gotten your logic hammered out is an excellent approach to debugging your scripts. This lack of definition enables you to concentrate on getting any bugs in the up-front function (your JavaScript validation statements) corrected before introducing CGI errors and complicating things.

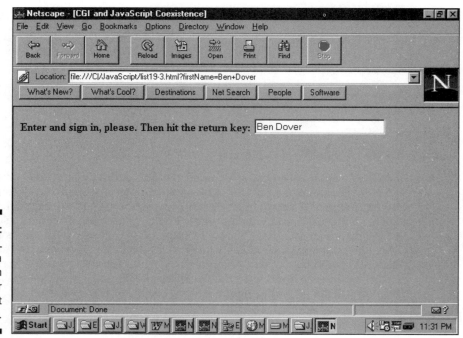

Figure 19-2:
HTML invoking a CGI program after JavaScript validation.

Part V
The Part of Tens

The 5th Wave   By Rich Tennant

WANDA HAD THE DISTINCT FEELING HER HUSBAND'S NEW SOFTWARE PROGRAM WAS ABOUT TO BECOME INTERACTIVE.

In this part . . .

Part V begins with a list of some great JavaScript-related Web Sites that you'll find to be full of useful information about all aspects of JavaScript. If you feel the need to communicate with real, live people about your JavaScript scripts, however, Chapter 21 provides you with a list of some user groups that enable you to do just that.

These online resources are followed closely by the most common mistakes that you're likely to run into when you implement your Web pages (along with tips on how to avoid them). And finally, no computer book worth its salt would be complete without at least a few handy debugging techniques. Chapter 23 provides you with lots of bug-related tips that make debugging — if not downright pleasant — at least entirely bearable!

Chapter 20

Top Ten JavaScript-Related Web Sites

*G*etting help learning how to do something has never been easier than it is right now. Why? The Internet, of course! Because of the Internet's roots in government and university installations, the Internet remained a closely knit, mostly academic community until as recently as a couple of years ago. Inevitably, of course, commercialism reared its ugly head, and this commercialism has had a tremendous impact on all things 'Net — and not all bad, either. (For example, the commercialism of the Internet is directly responsible for the proliferation of Web tools and languages like JavaScript.)

Although marketing and advertising have become quite common on the Internet, the spirit of sharing and intellectual collaboration hasn't been snuffed out by any matter of means. Helping other people (and maybe showing off a little in the process!) is a fundamental joy. And because access to the Internet is relatively cheap and easy, everybody and his dog indulges — as you see as you visit the URLs listed in this chapter.

Web Sites to Check Out

With no further ado, then, on to the good stuff: a list of JavaScript-related Web resources. You'll find tips, tricks, tutorials, examples, and up-to-the minute documentation. A description of the goodies each site offers is listed followed by the site's URL.

1. A JavaScript *jump page,* containing links to tons of useful JavaScript sites.

```
http://www.sapphire.co.uk/javascript/collections.html
```

2. From introductory to advanced topics, this tutorial covers JavaScript from a programmer's-eye-view and is updated frequently. The first, and still (arguably) the best.

```
http://rummelplatz.uni-mannheim.de/~skoch/js/index.htm
```

3. An "unofficial" repository of JavaScript *FAQs* (**f**requently **a**sked **q**uestions) — and, of course, the answers to those questions.

```
http://www.freqgrafx.com/411/atlas/jsfaq.html
```

4. A library of useful JavaScript code snippets, yours for the taking.

```
http://www.freqgrafx.com/411/library.html
```

5. Gamelan (pronounced "gamma-lahn") is famous in the software industry for its Java resources, but it also contains a heaping helping of JavaScript materials. Don't miss this one!

```
http://www-b.gamelan.com/pages/Gamelan.javascript.html
```

6. The "definitive" JavaScript resource on the Web, this site enables you to ask questions directly of a JavaScript pro.

```
http://www.inquiry.com/techtips/js_pro/
```

7. This site contains links to a collection of JavaScript demos from around the world.

```
http://www.tisny.com/noframes/js_demo.html
```

8. Visit the following URL for some simple JavaScript examples.

```
http://ls.ctc.edu/Exp/Technique/Java/lshtml.html
```

9. Check out this site for still more JavaScript examples.

```
http://planetx.bloomu.edu/~mpscho/jsarchive/
```

10. An HTML primer, this site contains links to every conceivable HTML topic.

```
http://www.ncsa.uiuc.edu/General/Internet/WWW/
        HTMLPrimer.html
```

Stop, Thief!

Perhaps you're saying to yourself, "This woman is *actually encouraging* me to steal other people's source code. Isn't that immoral or illegal or something? I bet she munches grapes in the grocery store when no one's looking, too!" Well, yes, I do enjoy the odd gratis grape from time to time. The thorny issue of code theft, though, is quite another matter.

The legal issues involved in using others' work in electronic form have yet to be defined. Lawyers all over the world are going crazy at this very minute, attempting to figure out who has rights to what in this brave new world (and how they can profit, of course!). The original copyright laws made sense when the means of reproducing materials was expensive and time-consuming, but that's all changed, hasn't it? If you put your source on the Web, millions of people worldwide could theoretically use and benefit from it almost instantly, without reimbursing you so much as a penny — and therein lies the rub. You want an audience? You got an audience. Now you want to protect your work from the audience and force them to pay? Well, *that* issue is still being hammered out.

And what about geographical boundaries? Whose copyright laws prevail when you're talking about a global distribution mechanism like the Internet? Can a citizen of another country be put in jail in Kenya if that citizen breaks Kenyan laws by illegally downloading source from a server located in Nairobi?

Until the legal beagles come up with something, all we have to go on is common sense. (I know. Bummer, isn't it?) Much of the source you run into contains comments that give you explicit permission to reuse it in any way that you see fit. If you run across source that says it's copyright protected, though, that's another story. If you still want to use it, contact the author and ask for permission. (It never hurts to ask!) If in doubt, don't copy a file line for line; instead, take a look at how the programmer solved the problem and base your solution on the overall approach.

Chapter 21

Top Ten JavaScript-Related Usenet User Groups

. . . .

In This Chapter

▶ Accessing user groups with Netscape News

▶ Taking advantage of the essential JavaScript-related news groups

. . . .

*T*he Web sites listed in Chapter 20 are a great source of information. Sometimes, though, you just have to send a message to a real, live person and ask a point-blank question. User groups (also known as *news groups*) can be a great time-saver, especially when it comes to researching specific how-to's and known bugs.

In order for you to access any of the user groups on the Usenet, you need to have a *news* server defined. Generally, you set up both a Web server and a news server as part of the browser installation and configuration process (see Chapter 2 for installation and configuration details), but you can always add news support later.

How Do I Access User Groups?

When you participate in a user group, either by viewing other peoples' messages or by posting your own, you need to go through a special protocol (the *news* protocol). Netscape Navigator has a news protocol built right in, so all you need to do to switch from surfing the Web to perusing the news is to select Window⇨Netscape News from the Navigator menu.

For more information on the ins and outs of Netscape News, visit the following URL:

```
http://www.home.netscape.com/eng/mozilla/3.0/handbook/docs/
       mnb.html#C6
```

Internet Explorer, on the other hand, doesn't have built-in user group access. There are a variety of products available for Windows 95, any one of which you can use to access user groups. One, Internet News and Mail, claims to be Internet Explorer-compatible. Take a look at the following URL for more information:

http://www.microsoft.com/ie/most/howto/mailnews.htm

Must-See User Groups

Although user groups come and go, a few have already established themselves as *the* place to be for JavaScript-related development. The entries in Table 21-1 are such groups.

Table 21-1	JavaScript-Related User Groups
Group Name	**Description**
comp.lang.javascript	If you only follow one user group, make it this one. This forum is the place to get answers for anything. This group is very well attended and is currently the premier JavaScript information group.
comp.infosystems.www.authoring.html	Get answers to HTML questions answered here.
comp.infosystems.www.authoring.cgi	Visit here for all your CGI needs.
comp.lang.java	If you can't solve a JavaScript/Java integration problem via comp.lang.javascript, try this group.
comp.lang.perl.misc	One of many Perl user groups, this is the one to visit first.
comp.lang.c	Interested in coding CGI programs in C? Check out this group.

Just the FAQs, Ma'am

Before you post a message to a user group, it's a good idea to get the *FAQs* – **f**requently **a**sked (and hopefully, **a**nswered!) **q**uestions, that is. The reason is that just about everyone asks the same questions when they're new to a group. Rather than bore old-timers with the same tired old questions, these questions (and answers), along with the stated purpose of the user group, are saved in files called FAQs. There are a few ways to get hold of the FAQs for a user group, one of which should do the trick:

✔ Check the user group you're interested in; perhaps the FAQs were recently requested.

✔ Check the user group news.answers.

✔ Search the Web using the keyword "FAQ."

✔ If you've got access to a file transfer protocol utility (ftp), you can use it to contact rtfm.mid.edu, the big FAQ archive in the sky. Login as "anonymous" and search the public directory /pub/usenet to find the FAQ for the user group you're interested in.

✔ Post a message to the user group you're interested in politely requesting the whereabouts of the FAQ.

Chapter 22

The Ten (Or So) Most Common JavaScript Mistakes (And How to Avoid Them)

*E*very JavaScript author makes mistakes. (Actually, I like to think of it in the reverse — it's the JavaScript *interpreter* that makes the mistakes by not figuring out what we humans mean by something. Yeah! That's it!) Most of the time, the errors that you make fall into one of the categories listed in this chapter. The good news is, the errors are all easy to fix. The better news is, JavaScript tells you quickly — and in no uncertain terms — when it encounters one.

Check out this book's companion CD to see the sample listings scattered throughout this chapter. They are named appropriately, so you can find them easily. For example, you can find Listing 22-1 in the file list2201.htm.

Missed steak? I don't even *like* steak!

Because JavaScript statements are embedded in HTML files, some of the mistakes you may find yourself making are actually HTML mistakes. For example, the following is an HTML error (the word **TYE**="button" should be **TYPE**="button"):

```
<INPUT TYE="button"
   NAME="testButton" VALUE="test"
onClick='test()'>
```

In this case, JavaScript won't display an error message, because the error doesn't concern it in the least. What *will* happen is that your button element won't display properly. If your page doesn't behave properly and JavaScript doesn't alert you, you're probably dealing with an HTML error. If this happens and you can't find the solution in this chapter, congratulations! You've made an uncommon mistake. Check out *HTML For Dummies,* 2nd Edition, by Ed Tittel and Steve James for some good, solid advice.

Punctuation Errors

Spelling and capitalization errors easily take first prize for being the most common mistakes to plague JavaScripters of all stripes, from the greenest beginner to the most highly seasoned veteran. The JavaScript interpreter gives you a great deal of leeway; for example, you don't have to know right off the bat what kind of value (string, number, pattern, Boolean, and the like) you want to poke into a variable when you declare it. (That's how you can get away with just saying var nameOfVariable.) However, after you *do* declare a variable, the way you spelled the variable when you declared it is the only way that you can legally refer to it again. For example, the following code snippet may look okay at first glance, but there's a problem on the sixth statement: A variable called aSting is used, and it hasn't been declared. Something *like* it has been declared (aString), but as the saying goes, close only counts in horseshoes.

```
<HTML>
<HEAD><TITLE>JavaScript Mistakes</TITLE>
<SCRIPT LANGUAGE="JavaScript">
function test() {
    var aString = "some text"
    alert("aString is " + aSting) // Oops!
}
```

Figure 22-1 shows the error message that JavaScript pops up when this code is run, and the example in this figure is typical of the error message you see when you make any spelling or capitalization error, whether the error concerns a variable, a custom function, a JavaScript keyword, or what have you.

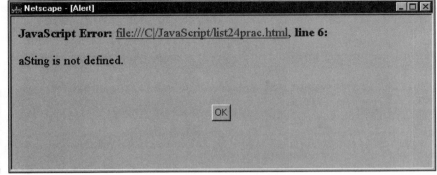

Figure 22-1:
JavaScript
error:
misspelling.

Unmatched Pairs

JavaScript scripts are typically rife with pairs: pairs of opening and closing tags (courtesy of HTML), pairs of parentheses, pairs of quotes and double quotes. The JavaScript interpreter treats the stuff between the pairs as one entity, and if one half of the pair is missing, it gets confused. Mighty confused, in some cases. (For the complete scoop on HTML and JavaScript syntax, take a glance at Chapter 3.)

Following are examples of the kind of error messages you can expect to be treated to if you make the mistake of leaving off the opening or closing half of a pair of something.

Lonely angle brackets

```
<FORM NAME="myForm">
<INPUT TYPE="button" NAME="testButton" VALUE="test"
onClick='test()'>
<P>
First name: <INPUT TYPE="text" NAME="firstName" LENGTH=15
Last name: <INPUT TYPE="text" NAME="lastName" LENGTH=30>
</FORM>
```

From looking at the preceding code, you'd think that the display would include two text elements, one to hold a first name, and one to hold a last name. It doesn't, though. Take a look at Figure 22-2 to see what this code actually produces.

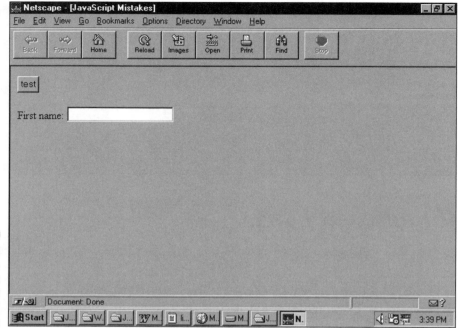

Figure 22-2:
Where's the
text input
field for Last
name?

Hmmm. Take a look at the fifth statement, the one that declares the first input field. Notice anything missing? Why, there's no closing angle bracket on the INPUT tag after LENGTH=15! Add that puppy and the second text field displays like a champ:

```
First name: <INPUT TYPE="text" NAME="firstName" LENGTH=15>
```

If a text element doesn't appear — no error message, no nothing, just blank space where the element should have appeared — immediately suspect a missing angle bracket on the line right before the invisible text element.

Lonely tags

Listing 22-1 depicts a tiny little script, perhaps the first attempt at a JavaScript-enabled Web page. At first blush, perhaps you don't see anything amiss. If you were to load this script, though, you'd see the page in Figure 22-3 — and I'm sure that you'll agree after you see Figure 22-3 that something is *definitely* amiss!

Listing 22-1: Source Containing a Missing Tag

```
<HTML>
<HEAD><TITLE>JavaScript Mistakes: Missing SCRIPT Tag</TITLE>
<SCRIPT LANGUAGE="JavaScript">
function test() {
    var aString = "some text"
    alert("aString is " + aString)
}
</HEAD>
<BODY>
<FORM NAME="myForm">
<INPUT TYPE="button" NAME="testButton" VALUE="test"
onClick='test()'>
<P>
First name: <INPUT TYPE="text" NAME="firstName" LENGTH=15>
Last name: <INPUT TYPE="text" NAME="lastName" LENGTH=30>
</FORM>
</BODY>
</HTML>
```

Once again, no JavaScript error popped up, so the first place to look is at the HTML statements. Because the first recognizable line appearing in Figure 22-3 contains `function test()`, which is the first line of the JavaScript section, that's a good place to start looking. Aha! No closing `</SCRIPT>` tag!

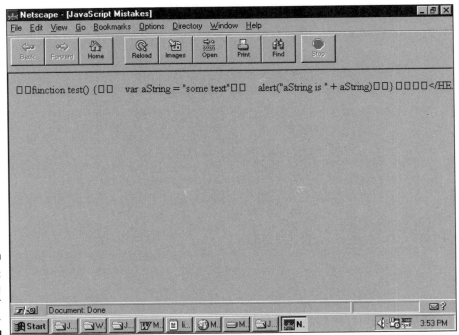

Figure 22-3:
Missing tag
error
message.

Whenever you see garbage displayed on your page (*garbage,* in computerese, refers to non-alphabetic characters like the squares you see in Figure 22-3), check all of your HTML statements to make sure that all of the two-part tags, such as `<TITLE>`...`</TITLE>`, `<SCRIPT>`...`</SCRIPT>`, `<BODY>`...`</BODY>`, and so on, aren't missing their closing halves.

Lonely parentheses

When you look closely at the body of the `test()` function in the following example, it's easy to see that the closing parenthesis is missing on line three. As your JavaScript skills increase, though, you may find yourself putting together whopping long statements that contain many pairs of parentheses, often nested a few layers deep — and that's when you're most likely to make this kind of mistake.

```
function test() {
    var aString = "some text"
    alert("aString is " + aString
}
```

Lonely quotes

Take a look at the example in Listing 22-2.

Listing 22-2: Source for Missing Quote Error

```
function test(inputValue) {
    var aString = "some text"
    alert("Wow, I sure do love JavaScript!" +
      "\nHere's what the public is saying about JavaScript: "
            +
      inputValue)
}
...
<INPUT TYPE="button" NAME="testButton" VALUE="test"
onClick='test("hello)'>
```

See the last line, the one that defines the `onClick` event handler? The mistake here is that no closing double quote appears after the word `hello`, which is even easier to figure out after you see the display that this code generates (shown in Figure 22-4). Here's how the corrected statement looks:

```
<INPUT TYPE="button" NAME="testButton" VALUE="test"
onClick='test("hello")'>
```

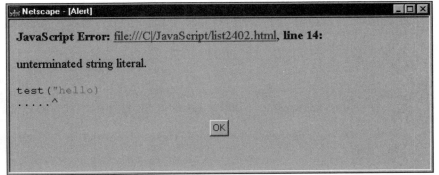

Figure 22-4: Missing quote error message.

Putting Scripting Statements Between HTML Tags

When you're new to JavaScript, remembering the order that things need to go in may be a little difficult. For example, JavaScript statements are valid only when they're placed between the `<SCRIPT>`...`</SCRIPT>` tags. If you forget and place them between some other HTML tags, you're bound to get an unexpected result.

The good news is, recognizing what you've done as soon as you load your page and taking a look at it is really easy! Check out the source shown in Listing 22-3 to see what I mean.

Listing 22-3: Source Containing Misplaced Scripting Statements

```
<HEAD><TITLE>JavaScript Mistakes: Misplaced SCRIPT
          Statements</TITLE>
<SCRIPT LANGUAGE="JavaScript">
function test(inputValue) {
    alert("Wow, I sure do love JavaScript!" +
      "\nHere's what the public is saying about JavaScript: "
          +
      inputValue)
}
</SCRIPT>
function addNumbers(numberOne, numberTwo) {
   return numberOne + numberTwo
}
</HEAD>
...
```

What a difference a line makes, huh? If the closing `</SCRIPT>` statement is moved down just below the `addNumbers()` function, this page works just fine. Again, no JavaScript error is generated, because as far as the JavaScript interpreter can tell, you *want* that text to display on your page.

Anytime that you see your well-crafted JavaScript statements displayed in living color on your page, you can be pretty sure that the problem is that your statements are outside the bounds of the `<SCRIPT>`...`</SCRIPT>` tags. Move the statements back to where they belong and they should behave. (Well, at least the statements won't display — they still may not be perfect!).

Nesting Quotes Incorrectly

Nesting single and double quotes together, like so, is perfectly legitimate:

```
onClick="alert('This is an example of nested quotes.')"
```

or

```
onClick='alert("This is another example of nested quotes.")'
```

Just make sure that you don't nest double quotes inside double quotes, or single quotes inside single quotes; doing so gives JavaScript a headache, as you can see in Listing 22-4.

Listing 22-4: Source Containing Incorrectly Nested Quotes

```
<INPUT TYPE="button" NAME="testButton" VALUE="Push Me"
onClick="alert("Here is an example of incorrectly nested
          quotes.")"
```

Treating Numbers as if They Were Strings

Humans tend not to make that big a fuss over the difference between text and numbers, at least not in most contexts. ("Number, word, sentence — what's the difference? They're all answers!")

Numbers and text strings are two very different things to most programming languages, though, including JavaScript. Take a look at Listing 22-5 and Figure 22-5, which show what happens when you try to treat a number as though it were a text string:

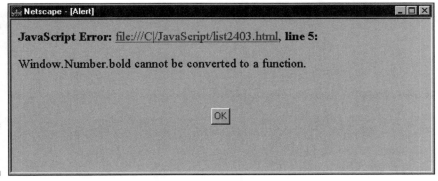

Figure 22-5:
Error
message
displayed
when a
number is
treated as if
it were a
string.

Listing 22-5: Source Containing Statement that Treats a Number Like a String

```
<HTML>
<HEAD><TITLE>JavaScript Mistakes: Treating a Number like a
           String</TITLE>
<SCRIPT LANGUAGE="JavaScript">
function testIt(inputValue) {
    document.write(inputValue.bold())
    document.close()
}
</SCRIPT>
</HEAD>
<BODY>
<FORM NAME="myForm">
<INPUT TYPE="button" NAME="testButton" VALUE="test"
onClick='testIt(2)'>
```

The problem occurs when the number 2 is passed from the definition of the onClick event handler to the testIt() function, which isn't set up to handle numbers. If you look at the testIt() function, you can see that it's taking whatever the input value is (in this case, the number 2) and trying to call the string object's bold() method on it. And that ain't flying. The only thing that you can call a string function on is a string, and 2 isn't a string! (If you'd like more information on what a string is, take a look at Chapter 10).

Sometimes you *are* going to want to send a number to a function and have that function deal with it. When that happens, all you need to do is add lines like the following to your function:

```
function testIt(inputValue) {
    // set up a temporary string variable
    var aString = ""

    // put input value into the temporary string variable
    aString += inputValue

    // call the bold() method on the string version of
    // the inputValue

    document.write(aString.bold())
    document.close()
}
```

Now, you can send whatever value you like to the `testIt()` function, and `testIt()` will behave nicely!

Treating Strings as if They Were Numbers

The preceding section shows what happens when you treat numbers as if they were strings. As you may guess, the reverse — treating strings as if they were numbers — also causes grief in JavaScript. Let me explain by way of the code snippet shown in Listing 22-6:

Listing 22-6: Source Containing Statement that Treats a String Like a Number

```
function calculateTax(inputNumber) {
    return inputNumber * .50
}
...
<INPUT TYPE="button" NAME="calculateTaxButton"
            VALUE="Calculate"
onClick='alert("The tax is " + calculateTax("boo"))'>
...
```

When the button labeled *Calculate* is clicked, the string *boo* is sent to the `calculateTax()` function, where it's immediately multiplied by .50. Now, if you can tell me what the result of *boo* times .50 is, you're a better mathematician than I'll ever be! JavaScript doesn't know, either, so it displays an error message.

Once again, in JavaScript as in life, a way to do what you want exists — if you know how to go about doing it! If you want to create a function that expects a number but that can deal gracefully (in programming circles, *gracefully* is a euphemism meaning "doesn't blow up in your face") with the situation if it encounters a string, all you need to do is add a few lines similar to the lines shown in Listing 22-7 to the very top of your function.

Listing 22-7: Source for a Function that Expects a Number but Deals with a String

```
function calculateTax(inputNumber) {
    var myNumber = parseFloat(inputNumber)
    if (myNumber) {
        return myNumber * .50
    }
    else {
        alert("A non-numeric value was passed to a function
            that expected a number")
        return inputNumber
    }
}

...
<INPUT TYPE="button" NAME="calculateTaxButton"
        VALUE="Calculate"
onClick='alert("The tax is " + calculateTax("boo"))'>
...
```

In this new, improved, better-tasting version, the first thing the
`calculateTax()` function does is see if it can convert whatever value it
received into a number. If it can (for example, if a number or a string, such as
1234.56, were passed to `calculateTax()` instead of the string *boo*), it converts
the value, if necessary, and then goes on to perform its calculations on the
converted value. If the `calculateTax()` function can't make a conversion
(what number does "boo" convert to?), it recognizes that it can't and doesn't
bother to perform any calculations at all.

Logic Errors

Logic errors are the most difficult errors to track down because they don't
generate one specific type of error message. (You never see the JavaScript
interpreter spit out a `That is not either how you calculate the interest
on a 20-year loan` message, for example.)

How could JavaScript possibly know what you're logically trying to do?
JavaScript doesn't read your code and analyze it and confer with other interpreters to figure out what you really meant by your code, as an art critic would;
JavaScript just skims your code for syntax errors. If you want to give your users
the option to submit a form, but then don't actually submit the form when they
indicate Yes — that's up to you. JavaScript is not your mother.

Only one way to track down logic errors exists: the old-fashioned way. And unfortunately, no shortcuts are available. (Take it from someone who has tried every shortcut in the book and then tried to invent some!)

To track down logic errors, use these hints:

✔ **Be very sure that you understand what it is you want to do.** As the old saying goes, "If you don't know where you're going, how will you know when you get there?".

✔ **Come up with at least three completely different scenarios and write down, on paper, the results you expect from each.** Try to pick cases that stretch the boundaries. For example, if you're writing a script that calculates order totals, your scenarios could include one where a customer orders nothing, one where a customer orders a billion dollars' worth of your products, and one where a customer orders two items.

✔ **Test each scenario to make sure that your Web page produces the results that you came up with in the second hint.**

Not Asking for Help

One of the biggest mistakes that beginning JavaScript authors make is not asking for help. Now, don't get me wrong; you have to at least crack open the documentation, otherwise people will tire of your questions easily.

Still, the online community exists to help you out. In most cases, contributors are genuinely eager to share their experiences and answer your questions. Why suffer when you don't have to? If you run into a question or a problem, give it your best shot, and then ask. I guarantee you that you can save yourself a great deal of time (and a great deal of hair-pulling, too).

Chapter 23

Ten (Or So) Tips for Debugging Your Scripts

*I*n Chapter 22, you see some of the most common mistakes (called *bugs*) JavaScript authors tend to make. This chapter expands on that theme by showing you the quickest, most direct ways to pinpoint and fix any bugs you happen to make. Most language compilers and interpreters come complete with tools for debugging; unfortunately, JavaScript is so new that no debugging tools exist for it just yet. That means that for now, you have to rely on your wits (and the advice in this chapter).

Debugging is kinda like doing dishes: Neither chore is exactly a ton of fun, but both are necessary — and you always feel better when they're finished! Debugging doesn't have to be a *dreaded* chore, though. You may find that, with a little help (like the tips presented in this chapter) and a little experience, the job gets easier and easier.

Do What I Mean, Not What I Say: Isolating the Desired Behavior

Strange as the following statement may sound, the first step to successful bug extermination involves determining whether or not you've actually encountered one. If your JavaScript script doesn't behave the way that you expect it to, you could be dealing with a bug. Or your script may be working as designed, and the problem is in your understanding of how the script is *supposed* to work.

That you need to understand exactly what you're trying to do before you begin the testing process should go without saying, but in my experience, folks who have this kind of understanding are pretty rare. Ever have one of those experiences where someone comes up and asks you if she can help, and you say, "No, it's just that I'm trying to flimflam the whibberdeejibbet . . . Oh! That's it! Thanks!" The act of explaining something, from square one, to someone else is just about the best debugging "tool" around, because it encourages you to articulate your logic step by step.

Isolating the Bug

Assuming that you've encountered a genuine bug, you need to try to hone in on it and identify precisely which lines of code are affected. Does the problem occur right after the page is loaded, before you've had a chance to interact with it? If so, the problem is probably either HTML-related or in the code that you set up to handle the onLoad event. Does it occur when you type text into an input field? Check the statements that handle the onChange and onBlur events. When you push a button? Check your onClick event-handling code. When you close the window? The culprit is probably lurking in your onUnload event handling statements.

If your page doesn't display properly when it's loaded and you don't have an onLoad event handler defined, the problem isn't with your JavaScript code at all; instead, look for the error in one or more of your HTML statements.

When you've decided on a place to begin your search — say, with the function that's called from one of your onClick event handlers (I'll call it buggyFunction()) — the next step is to dig a little deeper. Try setting up a test button that exercises that same function, as the following one does:

```
<INPUT TYPE="button" NAME="testButton" VALUE="Test"
onClick="buggyFunction("some", "parameters")
```

Then pass the offending function some hard-coded parameters (that is, strings or numbers, not previously defined variables, in order to rule out the possibility that the variables have been set incorrectly) and see what happens. If the function still fails, you know that the bug is in your function. If it behaves correctly, you need to check the parameters that the original onClick is sending to the function (see "Displaying Variable Values" later in this chapter).

Setting up a special function to test your code is a good idea, because that way you don't end up altering your real code. Until you find and correct the mistake (or "bag it and tag it," as a friend of mine used to say), your goal is to change as little source code as possible so that you don't introduce new bugs into your file at the same time that you're eliminating old ones.

Another strategy along these lines is to make a copy of your original HTML file before you make *any* changes. Few things are more frustrating than modifying a file beyond recognition, only to have it perform even worse than when you started — and then forgetting how the code originally looked!

If buggyFunction(), in turn, calls other functions, apply the same strategy: From the onClick event handler attached to your test button, call each of the other functions in turn and see if *they* perform as expected. Step by step, you can track that wily bug down.

Consulting the Documentation

The *JavaScript Authoring Guide* is the most definitive resource available regarding the JavaScript language. After you've got an inkling of what statement is in error, you can look this guide up quickly online by loading the following URL:

```
http://home.netscape.com/eng/mozilla/3.0/handbook/javascript/
                              index.html
```

Displaying Variable Values

One of the most useful debugging techniques around involves displaying the value of variables at various stages in their little lives. For example, say you have a function whose job is to calculate the total cost of an order. Based on your understanding of the way the total should be calculated, you've determined that this function always returns an incorrect value; you just don't know *why*.

Seeing what JavaScript *thinks* is going on at every stage in the process (from the very beginning of the function right down to the statement that calculates the return value) is very useful. Take Figure 23-1, for example. Clicking the Calculate button causes the error that you see displayed — $40 for 4 pigs at $25 each, indeed! You can tell from the message that there's an error, but the message isn't much help at telling you exactly where the error is; so some debugging statements are in order. A good place to put display statements is inside the function that's triggered by the Calculate button's onClick event handler, as shown in Listing 23-1.

Listing 23-1: Tracking Down a Bug with Alert Display Statements Is a Great Idea

```
function calculateTotalPrice(numberPigs) {
    var totalPrice
    var smallOrderCost = 10
    var bigOrderCost = 25

    if (numberPigs <= 100) {
        totalPrice = numberPigs * smallOrderCost
        alert("Setting total price for small order: $"
          + totalPrice +
            "\nnumberPigs is " + numberPigs +
          "\nand smallOrderCost is " + smallOrderCost)
    }
    else {
        totalPrice = numberPigs * bigOrderCost
        alert("Setting total price for big order: $"
          + totalPrice +
          "\numberPigs is " + numberPigs +
          "\nand bigOrderCost is " + bigOrderCost)
    }
    return totalPrice
}
```

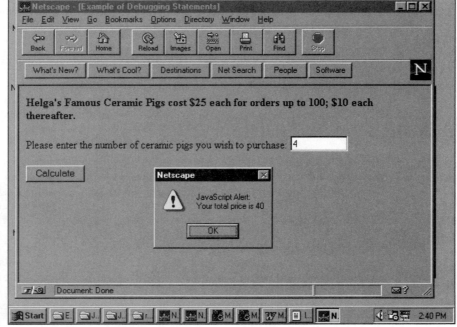

Figure 23-1: Incorrect result generated when the Calculate button is clicked.

As shown in Figure 23-2, the problem is that the values for bigOrderCost and smallOrderCost were mistakenly switched — and this switch is borne out when you look at the code. Lines 3 and 4 set the smallOrderCost to 10 (instead of 25) and the bigOrderCost to 25 (instead of 10). (After all, you want to reward people, not punish them, for ordering huge piles of your products!)

The more knotty and complex your logic is, the more this technique can help you pinpoint your bug.

Breaking Large Blocks of Statements into Smaller Functions

As I've stated before, limiting any functions that you create to about a screenful of text is good design practice. You don't have to take my word for it, though; a time or two debugging a monster-huge function should convince you! (For more on the subject of functions, flip to Chapter 4.)

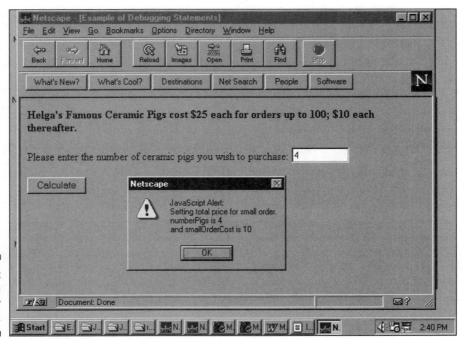

Figure 23-2:
Debug
display
statements.

Limiting function size is good for a couple of reasons. One reason is that experience (many peoples' experience, not just mine) has shown that functions that are too big to fit on the average monitor display tend to be poorly designed from a standpoint of reuse. That is, usually (and I say *usually* because this really is a rule of thumb) when a function gets that big, it's that big because you're trying to make it perform more than one conceptual task — and ideally, a function is an implementation of just *one* conceptual task. The long, ugly function in Listing 23-2, which performs two different tasks, demonstrates why this philosophy is a good one.

To increase your ability to reuse your code

Listing 23-2 shows some code that you may have a hard time reusing.

Listing 23-2: This Source Contains a Monster Function that Calculates Two Separate Things: Sales Tax and Total Price.

```
function calculateTotalPrice(numberPigs, purchasingState) {
    var price, totalPrice
    var smallOrderCost = 25
    var bigOrderCost = 0
    var stateTax = 0

    if (purchasingState == 'AZ' ||
        purchasingState == 'AL' ||
        purchasingState == 'HI' ||
        purchasingState == 'MT' ||
        purchasingState == 'TX' ||
        purchasingState == 'WY') {

        stateTax = 0.08
    }
    else if (purchasingState == 'CA' ||
          purchasingState == 'OR' ||
            purchasingState == 'ID'){

        stateTax = 0.10
    }

    if (numberPigs <= 100) {
        price = numberPigs * smallOrderCost
    }
    else {
        price = numberPigs * bigOrderCost
    }

    totalPrice = price + (price * stateTax)
    return totalPrice
}
```

The function in Listing 23-2 executes correctly, but it's pretty long because the function is trying to do two things: It's trying to calculate the state tax, and it's trying to calculate the total price of a customer's order. Breaking this function up into two, as shown in Listing 23-3, makes the code easier to understand, debug, and maintain by

✔ Creating a reusable function (Now you can call the `calculateTax()` function from anywhere else in your JavaScript script.)

✔ Isolating the conceptual goals you're trying to achieve, so that each function can be tested separately (and any bugs can be flushed out that much quicker)

Listing 23-3: Same Source As Listing 23-2 — But Now Organized into Two Compact Functions

```
function calculateTax(theState) {
    returnValue = 0
    if (theState == 'AZ' ||
        theState == 'AL' ||
        theState == 'HI' ||
        theState == 'MT' ||
        theState == 'TX' ||
        theState == 'WY') {

        returnValue = 0.08
    }
    else if (theState == 'CA' ||
        theState == 'OR' ||
            theState == 'ID'){

        returnValue = 0.10
    }
    return returnValue
}

function calculateTotalPrice(numberPigs, purchasingState) {
    var price, totalPrice
    var smallOrderCost = 25
    var bigOrderCost = 0
    var stateTax = 0

    stateTax = calculateTax(purchasingState)
    if (numberPigs <= 100) {
        price = numberPigs * smallOrderCost
    }
    else {
        price = numberPigs * bigOrderCost
    }

    totalPrice = price + (price * stateTax)
    return totalPrice
}
```

To decrease your frustration level

Debugging a huge function is *hard*. I don't know about you, but it's hard for me to remember anything at all about statements after I've scrolled them off the screen. Some folks even resort to printing out their functions, because they intuitively know that they can't grasp something that they can't see in its entirety at one fell swoop. You don't get extra brownie points for keeping your number of custom functions to a minimum, so go ahead and create as many as you need.

Honing the Process of Elimination

When bug-chasing, sometimes figuring out what *isn't* causing the problem is just as important as figuring out what *is*. For example, if you've got a bug in your HTML code, no amount of searching and testing your JavaScript code is going to help you fix the problem. By the same token, if the CGI program that you're invoking on submit is returning bogus information, no amount of time spent poking through HTML *or* JavaScript documentation is going to have much of an effect.

Although I can't tell you *exactly* how to pinpoint your errors, (if I could, I'd be rich!) I *can* tell you that good programmers have a general pattern that they follow when they're debugging.

For each test case (make sure that you have several), load the page and interact with it, note the reactions, and compare what happened to what you expected would happen for that test case. If a difference occurs, the first thing to do is to try to figure out whether the problem is related to your browser, JavaScript script, HTML statements, or CGI program.

Browser

A problem with your browser is unlikely to occur unless you've just downloaded and installed a new version or have been doing something in another application that may have altered the way that your browser works.

Symptoms

Your browser doesn't come up, or it does come up but it doesn't load any local files (as opposed to being able to load every file but the file that you're testing).

Hone-in strategy

If you've just re-installed your browser, try re-installing it again. If you still have problems, browse the technical help or contact the technical support line.

HTML

If you're new to JavaScript and HTML, you're likely to make quite a few HTML errors before you get the hang of it. Not to worry, though; HTML is one well-documented animal.

Check out the "About the CD" appendix for details on the HTML tools installed on the companion CD.

Symptoms

Your Web page displays only part of what you think it should display (buttons or other elements that you can see defined in your HTML source are missing). Or conversely, your Web page displays more than you expected (for example, some of your JavaScript statements are splashed on the screen).

Hone-in strategy

Note exactly what's displayed (or what's not displayed). If only the first two elements that you defined appear, check the source code that defines the second element — and every statement after that source code. If the second element is within a tag set (for example, between the <BODY>...</BODY> tags), check to see that the closing tag is placed and spelled correctly.

If JavaScript statements appear that shouldn't, note the very first word in the statement that's displayed and find that word in the .html source file; then check the line preceding the line that contains that word.

JavaScript

Most of your bugs are probably inside JavaScript statements because JavaScript is where all the fun is. So JavaScript is likely to account for the bulk of your code — and the more statements you have, the higher your chances of making a mistake.

Symptoms

Any bug that shows its face before a form is submitted, either in response to a user event (clicking a button, for example, or entering text) or in the course of calculating some numbers, is almost certainly a JavaScript bug.

Hone-in strategy

Here's where your skills at displaying variable values and breaking up functions really pay off. After you've traced a bug to an event or calculation, try to isolate that event or calculation. Create a test button that exercises the functions involved (*exercising* a function means calling it with a variety of parameters to see what happens in each case). If a function is long, break it up and exercise each resulting function separately.

CGI

Unless you're the author of your own CGI programs, you're a little limited in what you can do if they misbehave. At the very least, though, you should be able to recognize when one is malfunctioning so you can take steps to contact the appropriate person.

Symptoms

Your Web page displays errors when you try to submit a form, or the data that returns is not correct.

Hone-in strategy

The first step is to make sure that the CGI program exists and that you're able to call it. If you can't reach the CGI program, perhaps either your connection isn't working, the Web server is down, or the CGI program doesn't exist (or exists but isn't runnable for some reason). To test each of these scenarios separately, call the Web server directly from your browser (load just the first part of the URL and see what happens) and then call the CGI program directly (attempt to load the CGI program by itself and see what happens).

If the CGI program is being contacted, examine the data that's being sent to it (the data will appear in the Location field if you're running Navigator and in the Address field in Internet Explorer) to make sure it's reasonable. If it's not, the problem is somewhere on the client, in either your HTML statements or your JavaScript statements. If you *are* sending valid values to the CGI program, the problem is probably the CGI program itself, in which case you need to contact the CGI programmer directly for help.

Taking Advantage of Others' Experience

When you hit a hard-shelled bug, you really come to appreciate the Usenet user groups (sometimes called *news groups*) listed in Chapter 21. Not only can you browse the groups to see if someone else has already encountered the problem you're struggling with (which you should always do before posting, by the way), you can also post a message that contains a section of code and a description of the error. Many news-group contributors pride themselves on their ability to debug others' code, and technical support people (such as some of the folks at Netscape) often monitor the news groups as part of their jobs.

Exercising the Time-Honored Trial-and-Error Approach

When all else fails, just do something — anything. Make a change to your code, note the change, and then load the page and see what happens. The JavaScript interpreter makes testing things out both quick and easy for you. If the code change doesn't work, put the code back the way it was and try again. Whatever you do, don't be afraid to try something. The worst thing you can do is crash your browser (and believe me, browser crashes are not fatal — if they were, I sure wouldn't be alive to write this book!).

If you tend, like me, to be on the conservative side, make a habit of copying your HTML file to a safe place as soon as it begins to behave and at regular intervals thereafter. That way, if the unthinkable happens and you accidentally mangle the file while you're editing it, you can always drop back to your last good copy.

The best advice I can give you is to enjoy yourself! The following statement is trite, but in programming it's certainly true: The more mistakes you make, the more you can learn — and the easier creating your *next* Web page will be.

About the CD

. . . .

*T*his section explains what you find on the *JavaScript For Dummies CD-ROM,* as well as how to install the contents and run each of the examples. Here's a sneak-peek at the contents for those of you who just can't wait:

- ✔ Full working copies of each of the HTML/JavaScript listings that appear in the book
- ✔ A wealth of useful JavaScript utilities and examples
- ✔ Sound and image files used in the examples

What You'll Find

In addition to HTML files containing the JavaScript chapter listings, you also find the following tools and utilities on the companion CD. Many of the tools are shareware, which means that, if you like the product and use it regularly, the shareware's programmers ask that you send them a small payment for it. Here are the tools (listed in no particular order):

HTML Web Weaver Lite 3.0

HTML Web Weaver Lite 3.0 is a shareware Web page building tool from Miracle Software Inc. that runs on Macintosh. For details, visit `http://www.miracleinc.com/SharewareAndFreeware/WWLite/index.html`.

To install this tool to your hard drive, open the HTML Web Weaver Lite 3.0 folder on the CD, and then double-click the HTML Web Weaver 3.0 Installer icon.

JASC Inc.'s Paint Shop Pro

JASC Inc.'s Paint Shop Pro is a shareware graphics viewing and editing tool available for Windows. You can find a full description at `http://www.jasc.com/pspdl.html`.

To install Paint Shop Pro, do the following:

1. **Windows 3.1x: From the Program Manager, choose File⇨Run.**

   Windows 95: Click on the Start button, and then choose <u>R</u>un.

2. **Windows 3.1: In the dialog box, type** D:\PSP\WIN31\SETUP.EXE **(substitute your CD-ROM drive letter if different from D).**

Windows 95: In the dialog box, type D:\PSP\WIN95\SETUP.EXE **(substitute your CD-ROM drive letter if different from D).**

3. **Click on OK to begin installation.**

Ant Tools

The Ant Tools HTML conversion utilities, available for both Windows and Mac, work with Microsoft Word 6.0 to convert text into HTML and HTML into a real-life representation of Web page components (called *WYSIWYG,* which is short for *what you see is what you get*). You can find more information at http://mcia.com/ant/ or contact Jill Swift at jswift@freenet.fsu.edu. Ant Tools is shareware.

To install for Macintosh, just drag the Ant Tools folder from the CD to anywhere *except* inside your Microsoft Word folder. Next, start Microsoft Word and open the file ANT_INST.DOC in the Ant Tools folder.

To install Ant Tools for Windows 3.1, do the following:

1. **Open the File Manager.**

2. **Click on the toolbar's D drive button to show the contents of the CD.**

   If D is not your CD-ROM drive, click the appropriate button.

3. **Click once on the ANT TOOLS folder.**

4. **Choose File⇨Copy.**

5. **In the To: area of the Copy dialog box, type** C:\ **and then click on OK.**

6. **Open Microsoft Word, and then open the document ANT_INST.DOC in the C:\ANT_TOOLS directory.**

To install for Windows 95, do the following:

1. **Click on the Start button, and choose Programs⇨Windows Explorer.**

2. **On the right of the Explorer window, click on the CD-ROM icon.**

   The contents of the CD appear on the right half of the Explorer window.

3. **Click on the ANT_TOOLS folder on the right half of the window, drag the icon above the C drive icon on the left side of the window so that the C drive icon name is highlighted, and then release your mouse button.**

   This copies the ANT_TOOLS folder to your hard drive.

4. **Close the Explorer Window by choosing File⇨Close.**

5. **Open Microsoft Word, and then open the document ANT_INST.DOC in the C:\ANT_TOOLS directory.**

BBEdit Lite 3.5.1

From Bare Bones Software, Inc. BBEdit Lite 3.5.1 is a freeware text editor available for the Macintosh. Get the skinny on Bare Bones by visiting `http://www.barebones.com/`.

To install, open the BBEdit Lite folder on the CD, and double-click on the BBEdit Lite 3.5.1.SEA icon. In the dialog box that appears, choose a folder to install the program to your hard disk, and click the Save button.

WebTools Demo 1.4.1

From Artbeats Software Inc., WebTools Demo 1.4.1 is a collection of Web page design elements (buttons, patterns, icons, and so on) that can be used whether you're running Windows or Macintosh. For more information on this product, take a look at `http://www.artbeatswebtools.com/frdoor.html`.

This demo can be run directly from your CD. No installation is necessary.

To run the WebTools Demo, do the following:

Windows 3.1: From the Program Manager, click on File⇨Run. In the dialog box, type **D:\WEBTOOLS\DEMOSTRT.EXE** (substitute your CD-ROM drive letter for D if different).

Windows 95: Click the Start button, and choose Run. In the dialog box, type **D:\WEBTOOLS\DEMOSTRT.EXE** (substitute your CD-ROM drive letter for D if different).

Macintosh: Open the WebTools Demo 1.4.1 folder on the CD, and double-click on the Start Demo icon.

HTML Pro

HTML Pro is a shareware HTML editor for Macintosh explained in detail at the following site: `http://18.23.0.23/pub/WWW/Tools/htmlpro.html`.

To install, drag the HTML Pro folder from the CD to your hard drive icon.

Internet Assistant

Internet Assistant for Microsoft Word, from Microsoft, is an add-on program that works with Microsoft Word to create HTML documents. A version is available for Word 6.0 for Windows, Word for Windows 95, and Word 6.0 for

Macintosh. For details, see `http://www.microsoft.com/msword/Internet/IA/default.htm`.

To install the Word 6.0 updater patch, do the following:

If you use Microsoft Word 6.0 for Windows (not 6.0a or 6.0c, or the Mac version), you need to run a utility that updates your version of Word to 6.0a. Internet Assistant for Word 6.0 needs version 6.0a to operate. You don't need this patch if you are running Microsoft Word 6.0a, 6.0c, or Word for Windows 95 (a.k.a. Word version 7). To check your version of Word 6.0, start Word, and then select Help⇨About Microsoft Word. Your version number appears in that screen.

For information on installing this patch, check out the README.TXT file located in the directory INETASST\WORD6\60UPDPAT.

To install Internet Assistant for Word 6.0a and 6.0c for Windows, do the following:

Windows 3.1: From the Program Manager, click on File⇨Run. In the dialog box, type **D:\INETASST\WORD6\SETUP.EXE** (substitute your CD-ROM drive letter for D if different).

Windows 95: Click on the Start button, and choose Run. In the dialog box, type **D:\INETASST\WORD6\SETUP.EXE** (substitute your CD-ROM drive letter for D if different).

To install Internet Assistant for Word for Windows 95 (Word 7), do the following:

Click on the Start button and choose Run. In the dialog box, type **D:\INETASST\WORD95\WRDIA20Z.EXE**, and then click on OK (substitute your CD-ROM drive letter for D if different).

To install Internet Assistant for Word 6 for Macintosh, do the following:

Open the MacIA 2.0 Setup folder on the CD, and then double-click on the Internet Assistant Setup icon.

StuffIt Expander

StuffIt Expander, from Aladdin Systems, Inc., is a free file expansion utility for both Windows and Macintosh. The Windows version supports both Windows 3.1 and Windows 95, but will shrink Windows 95's long filenames to the 8-character DOS format. Product information can be found at `http://www.aladdinsys.com/products/products.html#FREEWARE`.

To install StuffIt Expander, do the following:

Windows 3.1: From the Program Manager, click on File⇨Run. In the dialog box, type **D:\STUFFIT\SITEX10.EXE** (substitute your CD-ROM drive letter for D if different).

Windows 95: Click on the Start button, and choose Run. In the dialog box, type **D:\STUFFIT\SITEX10.EXE** (substitute your CD-ROM drive letter for D if different).

Macintosh: Open the StuffIt Expander 4.01 folder, and double-click on the StuffIt Expander Installer icon.

Before You Begin

To best use the programs and files on this CD, be sure you have the following:

- A computer with a CD-ROM drive
- A sound card for PC users (okay, this is strictly optional, but it's a lot of fun!)
- Windows 3.1, Windows 95, Windows NT, or System 7.5 for Macintosh already installed, with the following:
    - If you're running Windows 3.1: a 386sx or faster processor, *at least* 8MB of RAM, and *at least* 3MB of free disk space
    - For those running Windows 95/NT: a 486 or faster processor, *at least* 8MB of RAM, and *at least* 9MB of free disk space
    - For Macintosh users: a 68020 processor, *at least* 9MB of RAM, and *at least* 6MB of free disk space
- A copy of either Netscape Navigator 3.0 or Microsoft Internet Explorer 3.0 (Chapter 2 tells you how to get a copy and install it, if you haven't already)
- A modem with a speed of *at least* 14,400 bps and an Internet connection (to connect to the World Wide Web)

The JavaScript For Dummies Chapter Files

Each of the chapter listings that appear in the book are contained on the companion CD in the directory C:\CHAPTERS. The naming convention used is list????.htm, where the question marks correspond to each specific chapter and listing number. For example, Listing 8-1 can be found in the file named list0801.htm.

In addition to the chapter listings, there are multimedia files and additional files for your review. To see a list and description of these items, please see the text file LISTINGS.TXT, located in the CHAPTERS directory/folder.

You may find it more convenient to copy the CHAPTERS directory/folder to your hard drive. To install the files on a Macintosh, just drag the Chapters folder from the CD to your hard drive icon.

To install the CHAPTERS directory with Windows 3.1, do the following:

1. **Open the File Manager.**
2. **Click on the toolbar's D drive button to show the contents of the CD.**

   If D is not your CD-ROM drive, click on the appropriate button.

3. **Click once on the CHAPTERS folder.**
4. **Choose File⇨Copy.**
5. **In the To: area of the Copy dialog box, type** C:\ **and then click on OK.**

To install the Chapters folder with Windows 95, do the following:

1. **Click on the Start button, and choose Programs⇨Windows Explorer.**
2. **On the right of the Explorer window, click on the CD-ROM icon.**

   The contents of the CD appear on the right half of the Explorer window.

3. **Click on the Chapters folder on the right half of the window, drag the icon above the C drive icon on the left side of the window so that the C drive icon name is highlighted, and then release your mouse button.**

   This copies the Chapters folder to your hard drive.

4. **Close the Explorer Window by choosing File⇨Close.**

Getting the Most Out of This CD

The best way to learn JavaScript is by doing JavaScript. If it's feasible for you, I suggest installing the CD's tools and chapter listings before you pick up the book (or at least before you're more than about a quarter of the way through). Then, when you come across a listing in the book, you can double-click on the corresponding HTML file you've already loaded and bingo! Interactive learning.

If you really want to make sure you understand a concept, be sure you take time to run the file and play around with it, too. Change something and see what happens. You can't go wrong, 'cause you can just reinstall from the CD.

The examples and utilities files are also referenced throughout the text. Some were designed to reinforce the concepts you're learning; others, to be real, live, workable utilities that you can incorporate into your own Web pages. Enjoy!

Index

● ●

Installing the *JavaScript For Dummies* CD-ROM Software

● ●

I've provided many tools you'll find useful for creating your own JavaScript scripts in your Web pages.

- ✔ HTML Web Weaver Lite 3.0, for Macintosh
- ✔ Paint Shop Pro, for Windows
- ✔ Ant Tools, HTML editing tools for Microsoft Word
- ✔ BBEdit Lite 3.5.1, a popular text editor for Macintosh
- ✔ WebTools Demo 1.4.1, a sample collection of buttons and art for Web pages
- ✔ HTML Pro, an HTML editor for Macintosh
- ✔ Internet Assistant for Microsoft Word for Windows and Macintosh
- ✔ StuffIt Expander, a free file decompression utility for Windows and Macintosh
- ✔ Listings of JavaScript examples as shown in the book and their corresponding multimedia files

For detailed descriptions and installation instructions for each program, please see the "About the CD" section, located after Chapter 23.